Pleasure and Quality
of Life

Pleasure and Quality of Life

Edited by
David M. Warburton and Neil Sherwood
Department of Psychology, University of Reading, UK

JOHN WILEY & SONS

Chichester · New York · Brisbane · Toronto · Singapore

Copyright © 1996 by John Wiley & Sons Ltd,
Baffins Lane, Chichester,
West Sussex PO19 1UD, England

Telephone   National   (01243) 779777
            International   (+44) 1243 779777

Other Wiley Editorial Offices

John Wiley & Sons, Inc., 605 Third Avenue,
New York, NY 10158-0012, USA

Jacaranda Wiley Ltd, 33 Park Road, Milton,
Queensland 4064, Australia

John Wiley & Sons (Canada) Ltd, 22 Worcester Road,
Rexdale, Ontario M9W 1L1, Canada

John Wiley & Sons (Asia) Pte Ltd, 2 Clementi Loop #02-01,
Jin Xing Distripark, Singapore 0512

Library of Congress Cataloging-in-Publication Data

Pleasure and quality of life / edited by David M. Warburton and Neil
   Sherwood
      p. cm.
   Includes bibliographical references and index
   ISBN 0 471 96511 1 (alk. paper)
   1. Pleasure. 2. Pleasure—Social aspects. 3. Quality of life.
I. Warburton, David M. II. Sherwood, Neil.
BF515.P45 1996
152.4—dc20   96-10653
                                                       CIP

British Library Cataloguing in Publication Data

A catalogue record for this book is available from the British Library

ISBN 0-471-96511-1

Typeset in 11/13 Palatino by Production Technology Department,
John Wiley & Sons Ltd
Printed and bound in Great Britain by Biddles Ltd, Guildford
This book is printed on acid-free paper responsibly manufactured from sustainable for-
estation, for which at least two trees are planted for each one used for paper production.

Contents

Contributors

Digby Anderson
Social Affairs Unit, 17 Hardwick Place, Woburn Sands,
Buckinghamshire MK17 8QQ, UK

Bill Bonnsetter
Target Training International, 7333 E. Helm Drive, Scottsdale
AZ 85260, USA

Keith Botsford
120 Cushing Avenue, Boston, MA 02125, USA

Christie Davies
Department of Sociology, University of Reading, Reading RG6
2AL, UK

Faith Fitzgerald
University of California, Davis Medical Center, Sacramento, CA
95817-2282, USA

Marianne Frankenhaeuser
Psychology Division, University of Stockholm, 1069 Stockholm,
Sweden

Chris Gratton
School of Leisure and Food Management, Sheffield Hallam
University, City Campus, Pond Street, Sheffield, S1 1WB, UK

Simon Holliday
School of Leisure and Food Management, Sheffield Hallam
University, City Campus, Pond Street, Sheffield, S1 1WB, UK

Claude Javeau
Department of Sociology, Université Libre de Bruxelles, Avenue Jeanne 44-CP124, 1050 Brussels, Belgium

K. Jung
Department of Sports Medicine, The Johannes Gutenberg University of Mainz, Albert-Schweitzer-Strasse, 55099 Mainz, Germany

Monicque M. Lorist
Faculty of Psychology, Department of Psychonomics, University of Amsterdam, Roetersstraat 15, 1018 WE Amsterdam, The Netherlands

Geoff Lowe
Department of Psychology, University of Hull, Hull HU6 7RX, UK

John C. Luik
Niagara Institute, Box 1041, 176 John Street East, Niagara-on-the-Lake, Ontario, LOS 1JO, Canada

Robert L. McBride
SensoMetrics Pty Ltd, 357 Military Road, Mosman, NSW 2088, Australia

James McCormick
Community Health Unit, Department of Community Health and General Practice, Trinity College, University of Dublin, 119 Pearse Street, Dublin, Ireland

Frank McKenna
Department of Psychology, Building 3, Earley Gate, Whiteknights Road, University of Reading, Reading RG6 2AL, UK

Petra Netter
Department of Psychology, Justus-Liebig University Otto-Behagel Strasse 10, D-6300 Giessen, Germany

Neil Sherwood
Department of Psychology, Building 3, Earley Gate,
Whiteknights Road, University of Reading, Reading RG6 2AL,
UK

Andrew Smith
Health Psychology Research Unit, University of Bristol, Bristol
BS8 1TN, UK

Jan Snel
Faculty of Psychology, Department of Psychonomics,
University of Amsterdam Roetersstraat 15, 1018 WE
Amsterdam, The Netherlands

Judy I. Suiter
Competitive Edge Inc., PO Box 2418, Peachtree City, GA 30269,
USA

Hera Tsimara-Papastamatiou
Department of Pathology, Athens University, 25 Ploutarchou
Str., Politeia GR-146, 71 N. Erythrea, Athens, Greece

Frank van Dun
University of Limburg, Faculty of Law, PO Box 616, MD 6299,
Maastricht, The Netherlands

David M. Warburton
Department of Psychology, Building 3, Earley Gate,
Whiteknights Road, University of Reading, Reading RG6 2AL,
UK

1

The Functions of Pleasure

David M. Warburton

Department of Psychology, University of Reading, Building 3, Earley Gate, Whiteknights Road, Reading RG6 2AL, UK

Pleasure has a central role in human life; it motivates people in numerous ways and serves many functions to the person and society. Individuals seek pleasure and create ways to obtain those pleasures. It is an idiosyncratic experience, because we all enjoy different things, but it is also a common experience and is part of the emotional vocabulary of all cultures.

On the other side, political constraints are devised to control what a person may enjoy and to what extent pleasure may be obtained. Certainly, it is clear that those in power, whether they be priests or politicians, have exercised their authority by their control of the pleasure of other individuals.

This introductory chapter will consider individual pleasure seeking, the positive contribution of pleasure to the quality of everyday life and the political control of pleasures.

PLEASURE: THE PERSONAL EMOTION

Despite the fact that pleasure is such a real feeling for most of us as individuals, it has proved very difficult to define. Aristotle described it as:

'Pleasure is the actions of the present, the hope of the future and the remembrance of things past.'

Pleasure and Quality of Life. Edited by D.M. Warburton and N. Sherwood
© 1996 John Wiley & Sons Ltd.

The definition of pleasure in terms of actions has some plausibility; it is true that people report pleasure in association with certain acts. However, the same behaviour does not always result in the same degree of pleasure, and so an alternative approach has been to define pleasure in terms of sensations.

Sensations arise from stimulation, and so stimuli can be classified as hedonically positive (pleasurable), hedonically neutral and hedonically negative (Bindra, 1978). This association has led to the idea that people act to maximize contact with pleasurable stimuli and so optimize the subjective experience of pleasure (see Young, 1966). This is an attractive theory of rational choice, because it proposes a single metric by which individuals choose among competing alternatives.

This idea has been encapsulated in the behaviourist concept of reinforcement (Skinner, 1938). A reinforcer is a stimulus which, when made contingent on a response, increases the probability of that response. It is clear that the primary reinforcers have great biological significance. Food and sexual contact are obviously connected with the survival of the individual and the population. It would seem of evolutionary importance that these biological experiences should be associated with a feeling of well-being (pleasure), which results in the repetition of the experience.

Certainly, one test of whether people are enjoying something is to see whether they go on doing what they are doing and whether they try to do it again. But if we define pleasure as a tendency to prolong or repeat, we should still not have succeeded in giving a complete account of it (Kenny, 1963). We can enjoy the first course of a meal, but we are not sorry that it is followed by the second. Thus, pleasure is more than the behaviour itself and the accompanying sensory experience, but is an emotional state.

A major problem in the psychology of pleasure has been that not all pleasurable acts are biologically important. Consequently, it has been argued that all pleasures do not reflect a single emotional state and that pleasures vary qualitatively and not quantitatively (see Peters, 1958). This question will be considered in the next section, on the neurochemistry of pleasure.

THE NEUROCHEMISTRY OF PLEASURE

Studies on the neurochemistry of pleasure suggest that *all* pleasurable experiences can be related to the same neurochemical system of the brain. Firstly, all pleasures can be lost in certain pathological conditions and following treatment with some types of drugs. One pathological condition during which pleasure is lost is depression. Depression occurs in all cultures and is defined by a standard set of symptoms (American Psychiatric Association, 1994). Not all of these symptoms occur in every individual who becomes depressed, but a person is considered to have a major depressive episode if he or she exhibits a loss of pleasure in all, or almost all, usual activities. The universality of the loss of pleasure by depressives in all activities (from sex to social interaction to intellectual pursuits) argues for mediation by a common brain system.

Secondly, the restoration of pleasure in these activities with drug treatment supports the notion of a common neurochemical system for all pleasures and the idea that the only difference between pleasurable acts is quantitative. Research has shown that those drugs that produce anhedonia (loss of pleasure) and those that can be used to treat depression act in opposite ways on the same neurochemical system in the brain, the dopamine system. The specific pathway believed to mediate pleasure passes from the brainstem to the nucleus accumbens and is known as the mesolimbic dopamine pathway. The pleasure from food or sexual activity also appears to depend on their ability to activate this mesolimbic dopaminergic system (Bozarth, 1991).

It is known that these drugs act very powerfully on this system, so it is believed that heroin and cocaine produce their pleasurable effects by an action on the mesolimbic dopaminergic system (Bozarth, 1991). As a consequence of this powerful action, the pleasures are so intense and so habit forming that they are difficult to resist, which often results in a condition known as motivational toxicity (Bozarth, 1994). Motivational toxicity is defined as the state in which drug taking completely dominates the user's life, to the exclusion of other activities. Motivational toxicity can be seen when the motivational priorities are altered so much that drug use disrupts normal behaviours, such as eating and sexual activity.

A crucial question is whether all pleasurable agents produce motivational toxicity. It is clear from everyday observation that most eating and sexual behaviour would not be described as constituting the degree of compulsiveness necessary to fulfil the definition of motivational toxicity. Similarly, tea drinking, coffee drinking, chocolate eating and tobacco smoking do not result in motivational toxicity and do not disrupt a person's normal eating or sex life. In fact, the use of these substances is completely compatible with normal living and is a natural accompaniment to these activities—the chocolate, cigarette and coffee taken after a meal, for example.

In the next section, I will consider the contribution of pleasure to the quality of everyday life.

QUALITY OF LIFE

Until recently, all indicators of quality of life reflected a 'disease' model, with typical indices of health status focusing on disease, illness and negative concepts like mortality rates, morbidity rates and degrees of disability. Health was taken as a baseline then deviations from this were measured, so quality of life was really measuring the amount of absence of ill health. However, survival rates are no longer enough for assessing quality of living; what matters is how the person feels, rather than how doctors think he or she ought to feel on the basis of clinical measurements of negative health. Research shows that there are wide discrepancies between a person's and his or her doctor's ratings of quality of life (McNeil, Weichselbaum and Pauker, 1978, 1981). For people, living is more than surviving.

Many definitions of quality of life fit this view, but, as one example, Czaikowski (1992) of the National Heart, Lung and Blood Institute in Bethesda, Maryland, wrote that:

> 'Health quality of life refers to an individual's life satisfaction and total well-being. The aspects of people's lives that are associated with health quality of life include, their perceived health; their ability to function normally in their life roles (e.g. work, leisure and family roles); cognitive abilities (e.g. memory and concentration).'

In this view, quality of life encompasses much more than physical well-being; it is a complex concept comprising diverse areas, all of which contribute to personal satisfaction and self-esteem. It is a concept of positive functioning in all spheres of life, emotional and cognitive. As Shin and Johnson (1978) phrased it, quality of life consists of having the resources necessary for the satisfaction of individual wants, needs and desires.

From these ideas, I will go on to argue that pleasurable activities can provide resources that can help to improve quality of life. The conceptual framework is that of the functional model.

THE GENERAL FUNCTIONAL MODEL

In this section, the characteristics of the functional model are described and illustrated. The functional model was first developed to account for smoking behaviour (Warburton, 1987a), but can be stated in a more generalized form. However, it is best illustrated by investigations of the use of pleasure products, since their effects on mood and cognition are amenable to laboratory investigation.

Firstly, the functional model is purposive; it views use as a means of satisfying everyday psychological needs, and thus as pleasurable. In these terms, product use can be seen as providing individuals with a means of controlling their psychological state. Use can be both a means of coping with problems and a way of enhancing psychological function. Alcohol and chocolate have mood elevating effects, and thus positive benefits for relaxing and unwinding. Caffeine (in moderate doses) and nicotine (in smoking doses) combine mood elevating, anti-anxiety and anti-anger and calming effects with cognitive enhancement, which would aid work achievement. In this way, it can be seen that these products would enhance quality of life, as defined above, and so their use can be seen as purposive. Refraining from such an activity will result in abstinence experiences, which are manifested as dysphoria and sometimes less efficient function in certain situations. Consequently, abstaining individuals may return to their preferred activity.

Secondly, the causes of use in the functional model can be due to both exogenous and endogenous causes. Given that use is an attempt by individuals to control their psychological state, then both internal and external factors will be determiners. Use will be the outcome of the interaction of the person and the situation. Depending on the situation, people will vary their consumption. For example, coffee drinkers will drink in the morning to give themselves an arousal boost at the beginning of the day and after lunch to counteract the post-lunch dip. Then, their use may taper off, if they find that caffeine keeps them awake, unless they want the caffeine to maintain electrocortical arousal for more efficient information processing in the evening.

Similarly, smokers will adjust their smoking behaviour in terms of the number of cigarettes smoked, smoke generation and amount of smoke inhaled to control the nicotine levels reaching the brain, and in this way they control their psychological state. Differences in smoking behaviour will be a function of the intensity or the individual–situation interaction, its duration and, more probably, its density (the product of intensity and duration). In other cases smoking may not even be initiated until the intensity, duration or density of the interaction is at a critical level.

Many smokers smoke in anticipation of a future need before the situation has occurred or the critical stress level has been reached and they are still coping. As smokers have learned to control their mood by smoking, enabling them to function more efficiently, then they will smoke to help them avoid the undesired consequences of other situations: consequently, anticipatory smoking can be seen as a rational coping strategy on the basis of their past experience. Here the smoking behaviour is very clearly a response to the individual's interpretation of the situation, his or her expectation about what may occur, rather than to the objective characteristics of the situation.

In the functional model, users are a heterogeneous group who use the products for different reasons. Thus, product use is a multidimensional behaviour, which must be conceptualized by a multifactorial model. In the previous examples, it can be seen that individuals can derive different benefits from the same product and so there can be several motives for use, such as mood changing and performance enhancement. However, a functional model does not require a single motive for all users: it only requires that a function of smoking can be identified by each user. Of course, an individual may have more than one motive, and use may have different functions for that person on different occasions.

In the functional model, the cause of product use can predate its initiation, and use is maintained because it satisfied these motives. There is now a considerable body of evidence that constitutional (genetic) factors underlie alcohol, caffeine and nicotine consumption. Consequently, use of products containing these chemicals can be seen as the outcome not only of the characteristics of the situation, but also of the personality of the individual. Personality characteristics will predispose the individual to select some activities over others. For example, a person with a low level of extroversion will lack self-confidence and not enjoy parties. However, consumption of alcohol will reduce the stressfulness of the occasion and enable the person to cope with the situation.

The functional model does not view use *per se* as a problem, although problems may arise from excessive use. The functional model does conceive of the possibility of non-problem use. An unanswered question is the extent to which excessive use can be seen as a function of the product or the characteristics of the user. Many things are done compulsively and there may be adverse effects on health and life functioning. At any one time, 1–2% of the population display obsessive–compulsive behaviour (American Psychiatric Association, 1994).

PLEASURE AND POWER

Another major function of pleasure is as a tool for the control of people. The control of the pleasures of others has been a major political issue in the past and still exists today. As Tiger (1992) pointed out, 'Powerful people enjoy it when they are able to define and restrict the pleasure of others'. Throughout the millennia, those in positions of power, whether they be religious leaders or politicians, have pronounced on which pleasurable things are permissible and which are not. Few people, certainly not politicians, lack opinions about the place of pleasure in society, the ways in which it should be pursued and the extent to which the pursuit should be governed. If they have sufficient influence, they want to impose their own viewpoint on pleasure on everyone else.

This ideology was satirized by George Orwell in his novel about the ultimate totalitarian society, *Ninety Eighty-Four*, where renunciation of pleasure was seen as the ideal:

> 'Big Brother added a few remarks on the purity and singlemindedness of Comrade Ogilvy's life. He was a total abstainer and a non-smoker, had no recreations except a daily hour in the gymnasium, and had taken a vow of celibacy, believing marriage and the care of a family to be incompatible with a twenty-four-hour-a-day devotion to duty.'

The Calvinist legacy in Europe and the Puritan tradition in the United States have had marked influence on attitudes to individual pleasure. In many sects that were based on Puritanism, individuals were not only exhorted to renounce personal pleasure, but were urged to exercise pastoral care over their neighbours. In other words, they should be responsible for controlling the pleasures of others. The invasion of authoritarianism into the domestic sphere is still a sinister fact of life. The power to control people in their home is the ultimate assertiveness of wielders of the power, and this is an aspiration of the health educators. Of course, we would like to believe that our society is the opposite of *Nineteen Eighty-Four*. We would like to suppose that our society is one in which a person's home is their castle, that the home is a place in which people can enjoy their pleasures in private and that their private activities are beyond society's control. However, this is a misconception.

In the United States, in particular, we can observe the war against pleasure being fought in the home. A company in Indiana with a 'no alcohol' policy dismissed an employee for drinking at home ('Down with Killjoys', *Sunday Telegraph*, 22 December 1991). Companies are insisting on urine testing employees for smoking away from work ('Accusations, Busybodies, New Puritans', *Time*, 12 August 1991).

The ultimate invasion is when educators ask children to report on the behaviour of their parents, as they did in Nazi Germany, in the Soviet Union and in *Nineteen Eighty-Four*. Many health education programmes urge children to put pressure on their parents not to smoke. In Connecticut, children were asked to report the alcohol consumption of their parents as part of the 'Here's Looking at You, 2000' health education programme, so that the 'over-indulgers' could be 'helped'. In addition, children were encouraged to exhort their parents 'to comb through the house, making it "safe". That meant inspecting the house for the presence of alcohol, nicotine and caffeine, as well as ammonia and muriatic (hydrochloric) acid' ('War on Drugs? War on Parents', *Wall Street Journal*, 18 June 1993). This infringement of privacy smacks of the witchcraft trials of the eighteenth century.

It is tempting to think of all, or at least the majority, of the forces behind the health promotion movement as altruistic. However, as Petr Skrabanek (1992) phrased it:

> 'With the approaching millennium, health promotion has become a rallying point for an assorted mixture of food promoters, smart entrepreneurs, tight-lipped moralists, semi-educated academics, green people, social reformers, international quacks, and power hungry nonentities.'

It seems that, in our society, health educators have become the new high priests of pleasure control with epidemiologists as their oracles. They exercise their influence via the media and legislation. If the health promoters capture the attention of the media, they can exercise their control by trying to influence us to adopt their own lifestyle. In this way they can put pressure on politicians, as well as by direct lobbying.

In the end, it is governments that decide which pleasures are criminal and, more often, which are permissible but taxable. An important reason for this taxation is that it enables politicians to be seen to be controlling and punishing pleasure takers, while hypocritically raising much needed revenue. It is a sad, but illuminating, fact that politicians only seem to get involved selectively in the promotion of pleasure. The pleasures that do get subsidized, e.g. opera and sport, are activities and so good, versus products, which must be bad and curbed by bans or by taxation. In Denmark, for example, excise duty is levied on all alcoholic beverages (beer, spirits and wine), chocolate, coffee, chewing gum, ice cream, soft drinks, sugar, tea and tobacco products, and twice on books, on both the paper and the finished product. Even in Belgium, duty is imposed on beer, spirits, chocolate, coffee, soft drinks, sugar and tobacco products.

CONCLUSION

Pleasure has a central role in human life and serves many functions to the person and society. Individuals seek pleasure and create ways to obtain pleasure. Many pleasures function as important guides, which direct us in our interaction with the world, moving us towards some stimuli and away from others. It is not surprising that the pleasure state is associated with biologically important behaviour, like eating and sexual activity.

Studies in the neurochemistry of behaviour have shown that all pleasures, even those not obviously of evolutionary importance, are mediated by the same brain system, including our enjoyment of alcoholic drinks, chocolate, coffee, food and tobacco products. It is in this way that these substances give us pleasure and enhance the quality of our lives.

However, there are obstacles to our enjoyment and enhancement of the quality of our lives. At the level of society, the control of the pleasures of others has been a major political issue in the past and still exists today. Those in positions of power, whether they be religious leaders or politicians, have pronounced on which pleasurable things are permissible and which are not. Ultimately, it is governments that decide which pleasures are criminal and, more often, which are permissible but taxable. Perhaps—but it seems unlikely—governments will recognize the positive contribution of pleasure to the lives of ordinary people and act accordingly.

Part I

Everyday Life and its Problems

2

The Costs of Job Dissatisfaction

*David M. Warburton and †Judy I. Suiter

*Department of Psychology, University of Reading, Building 3, Earley
Gate, Whiteknights Road, Reading RG6 2AL, UK and †Competitive
Edge Inc., PO Box 2418, Peachtree City, GA 30269, USA

INTRODUCTION

There is a vast literature on the impact of job stressors on an
individual's psychological and physical health with morbidity
and mortality outcomes. In this chapter, we consider the impact
of job dissatisfaction and lack of pleasure at work on health and
productivity, and give some estimates of costs to the person and
to the organization.

One of the enduring concepts in occupational psychology has
been the idea that optimal productivity and work satisfaction
are only achieved when there is a match between the characteristics of the person (ability, temperament, personality and
behavioural style) and the demands of the job. Work problems
arise when there is a personal characteristics–job demands disparity. Thus, the greater the fit between the individual's needs
and the work demands, the greater will be the potential for the
individual's satisfaction and work productivity (Furnham,
1992).

Pleasure and Quality of Life. Edited by D.M. Warburton and N. Sherwood
© 1996 John Wiley & Sons Ltd.

Caplan (1983) has distinguished between two types of person–environment match. The first type of fit is that seen from the perspective of the employer, the match of individual characteristics and the job demands. The second type of match is that between the specific needs of the person and what the individual perceives as being supplied by the work environment. A study of the importance of these two types of fit has been made possible by a global survey of office workers.

INTERNATIONAL STRESSOR SURVEY

Participants

The participants in the study were office workers from clerical grades to chief executive level. Loose quotas on age and sex were used so that samples were typical of all levels of an office population. Office workers were surveyed in Australia (182), Belgium (212), Canada (300), Denmark (301), France (306), French Switzerland (306), Germany (313), German Switzerland (319), Greece (308), Hong Kong (300), Italy (304), Luxembourg (102), The Netherlands (312), New Zealand (118), Spain (309), the United Kingdom (302) and the United States of America (1002). In total, 5296 office workers were interviewed, of whom 2705 were women and 2591 were men. In this chapter, the focus is on the global data and not on specific countries.

Interviews were conducted by native speakers in the person's own home; initial contact was by random digit dialling. This method was used in order to guarantee that the sample was 'random' and that the person could answer questions as truthfully as possible without feeling inhibited by being overheard at work or being under any time pressure.

Questionnaire

In this chapter, the focus is on the sources of pressure in the workplace resulting from mismatch. Additional evidence is derived from answers to questions about whether respondents felt relaxed or felt able to cope and whether stressors had caused them to take time off work.

THE STRESSFUL WORKPLACE

All of the office workers were asked whether they generally felt relaxed and able to cope or often felt 'under stress' when they were at work. Worldwide, nearly a third (32%) reported that they did not feel relaxed and able to cope. This value was marginally higher on average among women (34%) than men (31%), but was much higher among women in middle and senior management (38% and 37%, respectively). It was higher (36%) for office workers in larger companies (100 employees or more) than for workers in smaller companies (30% in companies with fewer than 25 employees).

Only 56% of stressed individuals would like to do the same job again, evidence of job dissatisfaction, whereas only 30% of relaxed individuals would not like to do the same job again. This statement indicates a high level of demotivation among employees.

In the following two sections, the reasons for feeling stressed and unable to cope are examined in terms of the match of individual characteristics and the job demands, and in terms of the match between the individual needs of the person and what the person feels the work environment is supplying.

MATCH OF INDIVIDUAL CHARACTERISTICS AND THE JOB DEMANDS

Evidence of a disparity between individual characteristics and job demands emerges from a subset of the survey questions. The dramatic indication is the global evidence of work overload: 60% of workers believed that they were too busy, had too much to do and that there were too few staff at work. Nearly eight out of ten office workers who felt stressed at work reported work overload (78%).

Further evidence of a mismatch between the demands of employers and the individual characteristics is that the additional work was perceived as unnecessary by 27% of the workers, as a group, and by 37% of those who felt stressed. One redeeming feature of the global office environment was that 86% did not find their work boring.

However, 46% of the workers believed that the situation had got worse over the past two years, with 66% of stressed workers believing that stressor levels had increased. Clearly, employers have unrealistic work expectations.

Part of the problem of overload could be reduced by better matching of individuals to their job. In our own research (Warburton and Suiter, 1994), we found that job disparity is a predictor of stress responses. An important aspect of job satisfaction is the match of the person to the demands of the job, with a poor match giving low levels of job satisfaction. Low levels of job satisfaction result in poorer physical and mental health, as well as higher levels of absenteeism.

In the study, we investigated the importance of a disparity between 'response to the environment' (what behaviour the person feels must be exhibited, in order to survive and succeed at the job) and 'basic style' (the core behavioural style of the individual) as a predictor of job dissatisfaction, poorer physical health, poorer mental health and absenteeism.

Profiling of 150 managers was conducted using the Managing for Success™ software. As well as the behavioural style information, we collected information on the managers' current state of mental and physical health. The mental health items tapped a range of different aspects, while the physical health items related to physical symptoms of the stress response.

The only variable that was examined was the primary behavioural style disparity. The DISC data from the Managing for Success™ software were transformed into percentages, and the percentage difference on the Primary Style was used as the independent variable. The dependent variables were job dissatisfaction and the amount of mental ill health.

The association between the independent and dependent variables was examined using simple bivariate regression analyses. The scatterplot showed that the assumption of linearity was invalid, so a logarithmic transformation was used. As well as determination of the correlation coefficient, Pearson r, a coefficient of determination, r^2, was calculated as a measure of the predictable variability, i.e. the percentage of overall variability in job dissatisfaction, mental health and absenteeism that is attributable to style disparity.

Job Satisfaction

The bivariate regression of job dissatisfaction on disparity gave a significant correlation (Pearson $r = 0.39$; $p<0.001$, $n = 150$) or a coefficient of determination of 0.152, i.e. 15.2% of the variability in job dissatisfaction is directly predictable from the variability in style disparity.

Mental Health

The bivariate regression of mental health on style disparity gave a significant correlation (Pearson $r = 0.38$; $p<0.001$, $n = 150$) or a coefficient of determination of 0.144, i.e. 14.4% of the variability in mental health is directly predictable from the variability in style disparity.

Physical Health

The bivariate regression of physical health on style disparity gave a significant correlation (Pearson $r = 0.23$; $p<0.01$, $n = 150$) or a coefficient of determination of 0.053, i.e. 5.3% of the variability in physical health is directly predictable from the variability in style disparity. It should be noted that the physical health scale is a psychosomatic scale with 'mental health' items, such as inability to get to sleep or stay asleep, decrease in sexual interest, tendency to sweat, feelings of the heart beating hard, etc.

Absenteeism

The bivariate regression of absenteeism on style disparity gave a significant correlation (Pearson $r = 0.27$; $p<0.05$, $n = 54$) or a coefficient of determination of 0.073, i.e. 7.3% of the variability in absenteeism is directly predictable from the variability in style disparity.

Alcohol Use

The bivariate regression of alcohol use on style disparity gave a significant correlation (Pearson $r = 0.31$; $p<0.001$, $n = 150$) or a coefficient of determination of 0.096, i.e. 9.6% of the variability in alcohol use is directly predictable from the variability in style disparity.

Cigarette Use

The bivariate regression of cigarette use on style disparity gave a weak association (Pearson $r = 0.29$; $p<0.1$, $n = 36$) or a coefficient of determination of 0.084, i.e. 8.4% of the variability in cigarette use is directly predictable from the variability in style disparity.

It has been argued that the use of alcohol and cigarettes as stress reducers is maladaptive, and so an inadvisable coping strategy. Consequently, it was of particular interest to make an analysis of the association between absenteeism and alcohol use and between absenteeism and cigarette use. This analysis revealed that in neither case was the correlation significant; for alcohol use the Pearson r value was 0.16 ($p >0.1$, $n = 150$) and for cigarette use the Pearson r value was 0.20 ($p >0.1$, $n = 36$). This controversial topic will be returned to in greater detail in a later section.

In summary, this analysis gives evidence for a mismatch between job demands and behavioural style (as measured by the DISC instrument) as a predictor of job dissatisfaction, mental health, physical health and absenteeism. In addition, it was a predictor of alcohol use and cigarette consumption. Although we examined style disparity on only one dimension, 15.2% of the variance for job dissatisfaction, 14.4% of the variance for mental health, 5.3% of the variance for physical health, 9.6% of the variance for alcohol use and 7.3% of the variance for absenteeism were attributable to variability in style disparity.

MATCH BETWEEN INDIVIDUAL NEEDS AND THE WORK ENVIRONMENT PROVISION

The survey also gives evidence of a mismatch between the individual needs of the person and perceived satisfaction of these needs by the work environment.

Personal Control

Over a third (37%) of the global work-force who were questioned believed that they were not consulted about decisions that affected their jobs. This proportion increased to nearly half (47%) among those who were feeling stressed at work. Eighteen per cent did not feel that they had much control over what they did at work and when they did their work. This lack of control over their work was reported by 24% of stressed workers. Not surprisingly, 15% (21% of those feeling stressed) believed that they were not treated like a person at work but more like 'a cog in a wheel'.

Personal control is extremely important for health. Animal studies have shown that a crucial factor in the response to change is not the situation *per se* but whether the individual can exert control over it, even if the situation is noxious (Warburton, 1991). Thus, Karasek (Karasek, 1979; Karasek *et al.*, 1981) has proposed that job strain in working environments is defined not only by the demands of the job (the amount of workload), but also by the amount of personal control over the job (job decision latitude). Problems arise when job demands are high and personal control is low. Of course, work stressors depend on how individuals perceive themselves and their jobs with respect to the organization (Warburton, 1979). As Fisher (1988) has argued, demand and control should not be seen as objective concepts, but as they are perceived by the individual.

Management

Perceived lack of control will be compounded when there is lack of confidence in the decision makers—the management. In the survey, 29% of the workers did not have confidence in the ability of their companies' management; the figures for those who said that they were not relaxed and were unable to cope with work was 38% (Table 2.1).

Part of this dissatisfaction may have been the result of a feeling that they were not properly appreciated at work. A total of 32% globally agreed with this statement, and this figure rose to 44% for the stressed workers. These workers feel that the benefits of their job, including pay, fringe benefits and prestige, are not commensurate with the hours worked, the amount of effort expended and the volume of work output.

The emotion most often aroused by lack of appreciation will be anger (Furnham, 1992). Some individuals will deal with the

Table 2.1.   *Match between individual needs and the work environment provision*

Relations with management	Global	Stressed
Number of office workers	5296	1736 (32%)
Not properly appreciated at work	32%	44%
Lack of confidence in management	29%	44%
Do not feel part of a team	23%	31%
Lack of team spirit not due to fellow workers: relationships with fellow workers good	85%	80%

perceived injustice by lowering their productivity or raising their fringe benefits by stealing goods and time by absenteeism. Studies have demonstrated that workers who felt underpaid reported greater job dissatisfaction and were less productive (Pritchard, Dunnette and Jorgensen, 1992).

In addition, 23% of all the workers surveyed did not feel that they were part of a team, in which everyone was pulling in the same direction. For workers who felt that they were not relaxed and not coping, the figure increased to 31%. This lack of team spirit is attributable to management rather than to fellow workers, because the vast majority of the work-force (85%) said that they found relationships with people at work rewarding, and the difference between the stressed workers and the global average was 5%.

Given that team building is considered an essential part of managerial behaviour, there has been very little research on the characteristics of teams and the individual difference reactions or role differences in teams (Furnham, 1992). Furnham has pointed out that team members perform best when their role is matched to their personal characteristics and abilities. For this purpose, measures of behavioural style (how the person acts) should be a stronger predictor than personality measures.

THE COSTS OF WORK STRESSORS FOR THE INDIVIDUAL

From the data outlined above, mismatch can lead to anger, anxiety and depression. All of these factors have been associated with a greater risk of illness and disease.

Anger

A meta-analysis of the relationship between anger and a number of illnesses found highly significant associations of anger with arthritis, asthma and coronary heart disease (Friedman and Booth-Kewley, 1987).

Anxiety

A meta-analysis of the relationship between anxiety and a number of illnesses found highly significant associations of anxiety with arthritis, asthma, coronary heart disease, headache and ulcers (Friedman and Booth-Kewley, 1987; Steptoe, 1981).

Anxiety disorders result in considerable use of medical care services and substantial costs to society in productivity losses. Recent research (Rice, 1994) has presented estimates of the costs of anxiety disorders in 1990. This study is the first to estimate the social and economic costs of anxiety disorders affecting around 27 million Americans, 11.3% of the population of the USA. Until this study was undertaken, no attempt had ever been made to estimate the economic impact of the major anxiety disorders collectively.

The study included the direct medical care expenditures, indirect morbidity costs (the value of productivity losses for people who are ill, disabled and unable to work), mortality costs (the present value of future losses for people who die prematurely because of these disorders), and other related costs (expenditures for crime, productivity losses for individuals confined in prisons as a result of a conviction for an anxiety disorder-related crime, the value of time spent to care for family members).

Anxiety disorders make up 32% of the costs of all mental illnesses. The mental health cost portion of the $666 billion total US health care budget is almost $148 billion, so the anxiety disorders portion of the mental health budget placed a burden of $46.6 billion on the US economy in 1990.

Anxiety disorders are unique among mental illnesses, because the indirect costs are substantially greater than the direct costs. Lost productivity, worker absenteeism, disability and other non-health-care related costs account for the large majority of the indirect costs.

Currently, public and private health insurance indemnity provides relatively little coverage for mental health costs, especially outpatient services.

Direct Costs

Direct costs for people suffering from anxiety disorders are estimated to be $10.7 billion in 1990, or 23% of the total mental health costs and almost 2% of total personal healthcare spending for all illnesses in that year. Almost one-fifth of the direct costs, $2 billion, are expenditures for medical services and charges for care in specialty institutions. In addition, this total included short-stay hospital care, physician and professional services, nursing homes and prescription drugs (estimated at $1.2 billion, or 11% of the direct costs), as well as the net cost of private health insurance (amounting to $747 million or 7% of direct costs).

Indirect Costs: Morbidity

Morbidity costs for anxiety disorders, the value of reduced or lost productivity, amounted to $34.2 billion, almost three-quarters of the total costs of anxiety disorders. In addition to morbidity costs for the non-hospital population, losses for the hospitalized populations were also estimated. People hospitalized because of anxiety disorders include those in mental hospitals and nursing homes; their morbidity costs amounted to $1.1 billion in 1990.

Other morbidity-related direct and indirect costs of anxiety disorders and, in particular, panic disorder are due to misdiagnosis by both patients and physicians (89% misdiagnosis rate). Panic disorder patients visit emergency wards with cardiac, respiratory, gastrointestinal or neurological symptoms, often with accompanying pain. The chest pain and racing or irregular heartbeat experienced by many panic disorder patients result in diagnostic procedural charges estimated at $7300 per patient.

When this figure is combined with the fact that these patients make several times more physician visits than the average patient, it is easy to see how the medical costs mount up. In addition, the presence of anxiety is associated with longer spells in hospital for medically ill patients. These other related direct and indirect costs were estimated at $367 million for 1990.

Indirect Costs: Mortality

Deaths due to affective disorders, including 10% of the total deaths due to suicide, result in a loss of $1.3 billion to the economy at a 6% discount rate.

In summary, the costs of work-force anxiety are high. As an approximation, the cost of anxiety is about $2000 per person. Any measures that an organization can take to reduce the incidence will pay dividends for the individual, the organization and the national economy.

Depression

Individuals with depression report substantially poorer intimate relationships and less satisfying social relationships than members of the general population and so will have a lower level of social support. Not surprisingly, people with depressive disorder have severe impairment in occupational functioning and take more time off work, as well as exhibiting impaired interpersonal relations.

Patients with depressive disorders have more physical illnesses than other primary care patients. Twenty-three per cent of patients in a study reported that their health had kept them in bed for all or part of one day, in comparison with 5% of the general population (USDHHS, 1993). This finding is supported by reports of the health status of individuals in the community, 48% of whom reported their health as only fair or poor, in comparison with 19% of the general population. Thus, healthcare use is increased in depressed people in comparison with other patients seen in general practice.

As with anxiety, a meta-analysis of the relationship of depression with a number of illnesses found highly significant associations of depression with arthritis, asthma, coronary heart disease, headache and ulcers (Friedman and Booth-Kewley, 1987). One note of caution is that anxiety and depression are not independent, and co-morbidity may be as high as 30% (USDHHS, 1993).

Depression is associated with higher mortality risk, independently of accidents and suicides. A recent report (USDHHS, 1993) indicated that patients with major depressive disorder had a 59% greater likelihood of death in the first year following admission to hospital with depression, and that patients aged 55 years or more had a mortality rate over four times greater than non-depressed, age-matched controls in the 15 months after diagnosis.

The cost of mood disorders has varied widely, depending on the variables included in the econometric models. For the UK, the cost of depression has been estimated as £3 billion ($4.5 billion) (Kind and Sorenson, 1993). For the USA, the cost has been estimated as around $40 billion, when the indirect cost of co-morbidity for alcohol and substance use problems was included.

In summary, the costs of depression are high. As an approximation, the cost of depression is about $4000 per patient, even higher than the cost of anxiety (about $2000 per person). Any measures that an organization can take to reduce the incidence of depression will pay handsome returns for the individual and the organization.

Product Use

The question of product use as a coping strategy was raised earlier, and we return to it here. As yet, we have not analysed the individual data for stressor indices and pleasure product use. However, as a very crude index, we examined the use of these products by the relaxed and stressed office workers. Coffee and tea breaks were found to be effective 'unwinders' by 70% of the relaxed, in comparison with 64% of the stressed, workers ($p<0.01$). Those workers who were stressed were marginally more likely to relax by snacking or smoking (both 29% versus 26%; $p<0.05$). No differences were seen for chocolate, ice cream or alcohol consumption during the working day.

THE COSTS OF NON-PERFORMANCE TO THE ORGANIZATION

The problem of forcing square pegs into round holes is that not only is it uncomfortable for the peg, but it is also costly to the organization. The costs of job dissatisfaction and lowered performance for the employees at work can be calculated from the costs of non-performance model.

The first stage of this model considers the new recruit to a job. On the first day, the newcomer is likely to be highly motivated, but relatively inexperienced in that organization. While the individual will have been selected for the job by the employer on the basis of his or her likelihood of fulfilling the job requirements, he or she will be unfamiliar with the procedures and practices of the organization. Thus, the following weeks and months of Stage One will be a learning time, with the costs of formal and informal training.

Within a short time, say three to six months, the employee will have moved to Stage Two, where he or she is now competent and still motivated. At this stage, the employee's output should be at its maximum.

Unfortunately, sometime later, Stage Three occurs for some employees. Depending on the person, the organization and the person–environment fit, a percentage of employees become demotivated, while still being competent at their jobs. The causes of demotivation will be those outlined earlier, of the person not being well matched to the job in terms of behavioural style or a mismatch between the individual needs of the employee and what the individual perceives as being supplied by the work environment. Additional sources of difficulty may be a person's inability to adapt to change or to interact with others and avoid interpersonal conflict.

During Stage Three, disenchanted employees may be spending time complaining—the 'ain't it awful' syndrome—and so demotivating others and recruiting them to Stage Three.

The final stage, Stage Four, is the period when the employee is demotivated and no longer performing competently. He or she may be job hunting and not concentrating on present tasks. If the employee does not quit the organization, employers typically need six months to build a file on non-performance in order to have grounds for dismissal.

The cost to the organization can be calculated from the percentage of employees at Stage Three, the total number of employees in the organization, their average monthly salary and the percentage of Stage Two performance at which they are operating.

Thus, if 20% of a 50-employee organization is demotivated, then there are 10 disaffected employees. If their average monthly salary is $2000 and they are working at 70% of capacity, then the $20 000 × 30% below capacity represents a loss of $6000 per month to the employer.

It is to be hoped that the 10 employees do not last the full six months in Stage Four. Ideally, management will recognize their demotivation, and the reasons for this demotivation in the organization, and takes steps to remedy the situation.

CONCLUSIONS

In this chapter, we have examined evidence for the idea that work satisfaction and optimal productivity are achieved when there is a match between the characteristics of the person and the demands of the job. Using the ARISE global survey of stressors in the work-place for office workers (ARISE/Harris Research, 1994), we examined the match of individual characteristics and job demands and the match between the needs of the person and what that individual perceives as being satisfied by the work environment.

Office workers throughout the world reported that they were too busy, had too much to do and that there were too few staff in the office (78% of those who felt stressed and unable to cope with the demands of work). Of the latter group, 37% felt that a lot of work was unnecessary and wasted time. In addition, the situation had got worse in the last two years (66% of stressed workers). Clearly, there are unreasonable work expectations on the part of employers, which are leading to high work demands (overload).

In addition, the stressfulness of working environments depends not only on the workload, but also on the amount of personal control the worker has over the job. Problems arise when job demands are high and personal control is low. Nearly half of workers who were feeling stressed at work believed that they were not consulted about decisions that affected their job, and a quarter felt that they did not have much control over what they did at work and when they did their work. This perceived lack of control was compounded by their lack of confidence in their management and the feeling that they were not appreciated.

The consequence of these factors was job dissatisfaction, demotivation and the production of anger, anxiety and depression. Numerous studies have documented the association of job dissatisfaction and these emotional states with absenteeism and physical ill health. Depression alone costs the UK £3 billion ($4.5 billion) and the USA $40 billion. Demotivation alone can cost $6000 a month for an employee working 30% below capacity.

Obviously, any measures that an organization can take to reduce the incidence of mismatch will pay handsome returns for the individual and the organization.

3

Stress without Distress in Tomorrow's Workplace

Marianne Frankenhaeuser

Psychology Division, University of Stockholm,
1069 Stockholm, Sweden

INTRODUCTION

It is our good fortune to live in a time when environments can be moulded to suit people. The demands and pressures facing people today are largely human-made, which means that they are not as unchangeable as were the demands confronting our ancestors. Although the human nervous system allows for considerable plasticity, there are limits beyond which people cannot be pushed without being harmed. New technology, however, seems infinitely flexible. Technology, depending upon how it is used, can make people grow, or it can make people shrink. A major task for biobehavioural and social scientists is helping to clarify when technological solutions can be relied upon to improve the quality of life, and when technical solutions may, in fact, deprive people of crucial sources of growth and development.

ADAPTING JOBS TO PEOPLE

The workplace is the site of dramatic transitions brought about by technological advances. The benefits of new technology in terms

Pleasure and Quality of Life. Edited by D.M. Warburton and N. Sherwood
© 1996 John Wiley & Sons Ltd.

of increased productivity and reduction of physically dangerous jobs are well recognized. Less attention has been given to negative side effects on both physical and mental health of automation and computerization. Some of the side effects can be eliminated if sufficient interest is paid to work organization and job content (Warburton and Suiter, this volume). However, we have hardly begun to exploit the enormous opportunities to adapt jobs to the worker's psychological and social needs.

In principle, work-induced stress levels and dissatisfaction can be dealt with in two ways: by changing people or by changing jobs. Corporate health promotion programmes generally focus on changing the employees' lifestyle by discouraging behaviours such as smoking and overeating and encouraging health behaviours, such as exercise, relaxation and adequate rest. Such interventions tie easily into traditional medical models.

However, the individual-orientated programmes need to be supplemented by organization-wide changes, which may involve altering the conditions under which people work, the tasks they perform and the rewards they obtain. Approaches involving changes at the structural level are even more controversial and complex than are changes at the level of the individual. It takes a broad scientific base to redesign jobs and modify work organization in harmony with human needs, abilities and constraints.

THE IMPACT OF PSYCHOLOGICAL RESEARCH

This is where behavioural science comes into the picture. In psychology, scientific achievements consist of knowledge about what drives people, what makes people feel happy or distressed, helpless or angry. Compare this to the products of the natural and medical sciences—the X-ray, the laser, the atomic bomb, the polio vaccine etc.—and you will understand how easily psychology is swept away.

Psychological research exerts probably its most powerful influence on human well-being by doing away with myths and prejudices about people, such as the myth that human beings are by nature lazy, that large groups prefer easy, repetitive tasks, and that a boring job can be compensated for by exciting leisure activities.

These prejudices have blocked the way for human-orientated changes in social structure and work organization. As knowledge about human nature grows, the prejudices are slowly withering away and being replaced by new attitudes, which pave the way for organizational changes.

This is a slow process, but the impact of psychosocial research can be speeded up considerably by adding a biological dimension to traditional research in organizational psychology. The task here is to combine methods and theory from different disciplines. This is the research strategy that my group in Stockholm has adopted in the study of stressors and coping at work. In addition to examining job stressors and job satisfaction in the conventional way by questionnaires and interviews, we have incorporated a set of physiological and hormonal measures (Frankenhaeuser, 1991a,b).

Before going further into this, I want to reflect on the fact that stressors have become such an important issue in our time, even in those parts of the world where living conditions, from a material point of view, are much less strenuous than in earlier times.

THE EVOLUTIONARY PERSPECTIVE

The inferior person–environment that we experience today can only be understood when put into an evolutionary perspective. There is a mismatch between the old human biology and the new sociotechnical environment. While today's demands are very different from those confronting our ancestors, they trigger the same bodily stress responses that served the ancient humans by making them fit for fight and flight. These bodily stress responses are totally inappropriate for coping with today's psychosocial pressures. There is nothing in the history of humankind to prepare us for the high-technology environment that we have so rapidly created for ourselves. Therefore, we pay a price in terms of psychological distress as well as psychosomatic disturbances, musculo-skeletal disorders, heart attacks and hypertension.

During the first decades of computerization there was altogether too much optimism about new technology automatically reducing stress and improving well-being. The truth is that modern technology is as hard on people as the old one, unless complemented by new organizational and leadership models that allow people to do three things: exercise control on the job, learn new things and relate to fellow workers (see Suiter and Bonnsetter, this volume).

TECHNOSTRESS

While stress levels do not seem to have diminished, stress has certainly changed its face. We now talk about technostress, meaning that technology is being applied in ways that frustrate basic human needs. A dominant feature of technostress is the accelerating rate of change. Demands on human adaptability and flexibility have increased drastically. Knowledge becomes obsolete almost overnight, leaving large groups in a state of uncertainty and bewilderment.

Another characteristic of technostress is the ever increasing demand on speed. The computer and other forms of electronic communication have set new norms for how long a time things should take, norms that are not adapted to human biology. This is why life today is coloured by time urgency, fear of lagging behind, fear of not keeping pace—much more so than in the old days, when the human brain and nervous system determined the pace and tempo of life.

It is a curious fact that the more timesaving machines we get, the more time pressure we experience. As an example, people today spend more time washing clothes than they did before laundry machines came into use. This is because we wash much more now than we used to do. In the same way we now use computers for complicated administrative routines that were not possible in earlier days. In other words, we now do many things that used to be impossible and hence, on balance, we gain no time.

MONITORING BODILY RESPONSES

The two main features of technostress, time pressure and rapid change, are reflected in bodily responses. By monitoring these one can get new insights into how work demands interact with mind and body. Thanks to advances in biomedical recording techniques, it is now possible to monitor bodily responses at the workplace, without interfering with the worker's activities. Using such monitoring techniques one can find out what makes the blood pressure rise, the heart beat faster, the muscles tense up. These are important pieces of information, which, together with stress-hormone assays and self-reports, help in identifying both stress-inducing and stress-reducing aspects of job content and work organization. This is one way in which the study of human stress and coping may contribute to intervention and prevention at the workplace.

The catecholamines adrenalin and noradrenalin, and the adrenal-cortical hormone cortisol are cornerstones in stress research. Generally speaking, these hormones facilitate both mental and physical adjustment to acute environmental demands. Hence, in the short term a rise in stress hormones is often beneficial and seldom a threat to health. But in the longer term, the picture may include damaging effects. Frequent or long-lasting elevations of stress hormone levels in the course of daily life may result in structural changes in the blood vessels, which, in turn, may lead to cardiovascular disease (Folkow, 1975). This means that consistently high levels of stress hormones should be regarded as warning signals, telling us that the person may be under too much pressure. Research can aid in identifying individuals and groups who are in the risk zone.

In a pioneering study of sawmill workers in Sweden in the 1970s, we were able to pinpoint aversive factors in assembly line work. Short repetitive work cycles, lack of control over work pace and inability to communicate with fellow workers were all reflected in increased stress hormone and blood pressure levels (Frankenhaeuser, 1971).

These physiological markers turned out to be powerful. They supported the workers' verbal reports, dissatisfaction and psychosomatic symptoms, and provided a novel input into the work reform programmes. It has been exciting to witness how much weight hard physiological data carry when presented, not only to corporate healthcare departments, but also to unions and management (Frankenhaeuser *et al.*, 1989). Their potential importance as an early warning of long-term health risks is so obvious.

This was an encouraging start, and over the years we have studied men and women in blue-collar jobs, as well as white-collar workers at different occupational levels, including executives and managers. We have identified specific characteristics of psychosocial factors that induce predictable changes in the worker's effort, physiological responses, mood and well-being.

PERSONAL CONTROL AS A 'BUFFER'

Data from both epidemiological and experimental studies support the notion that personal control and decision latitude are important 'buffering' factors, which help people, at the same time, to work hard, enjoy their job and remain healthy (Krantz, Lundberg and Frankenhaeuser, 1976). The chance of exercising control may buffer stress in two ways: firstly by increasing job satisfaction, thus reducing bodily stress responses, and secondly by helping people to develop an active, participatory work role. A job that allows the worker to use his or her skills to the full will increase self-esteem. Such jobs, while demanding and taxing, may help to develop competencies that aid in coping with problems and crises.

The pattern of stress hormones varies with the positive versus negative emotional responses evoked by the situation (Frankenhaeuser, 1971, 1975). When demands are experienced as controllable and manageable, the stress hormone output is generally lower than when negative feelings and uncertainty dominate. This means that the total load on the body, the 'cost of achievements', will be lower during demanding but enjoyable work than during less demanding but tedious work.

There is evidence that damage to the myocardium requires the simultaneous presence in the bloodstream of catecholamines and cortisol (Steptoe, 1981). Hence, the fact that cortisol has been shown to be low in controllable situations could account for the positive health effects of personal control. Such a neuroendocrine mechanism could explain the epidemiological data from national surveys in different countries, which show that high job demands and work overload have adverse health consequences mainly when combined with low control over job-related decisions (Karasek, 1979; Karasek and Theorell, 1990).

UNWINDING AFTER WORK

Another mechanism by which mental stressors might influence health outcomes has to do with the duration of the stress response. This takes us to the after effects of a day at work. While we are immersed in work, the body's 'stress machinery' tends to stay in full gear. This may be seen as the price we pay for good achievement. But when the work is over, how quickly do we unwind? Our studies show that this depends on the type of task and the type of person (see Frankenhaeuser, 1986).

Highly repetitive, machine-paced jobs tend to slow down unwinding. The pace and tempo of the machine 'clings on' and makes it hard to relax. As to individual differences, 'rapid unwinders' tend to be mentally better balanced, less anxious and more efficient in achievement situations. However, the speed of unwinding also varies in one and the same individual depending on the state of general well-being. For example, when rested and in good shape after a vacation period a group of Swedish workers were able to unwind more quickly than before the vacation (Frankenhaeuser and Johansson, 1986).

The issue of unwinding after a day's work is crucial for the wider issue of the work–leisure relationship. The prevailing view until a couple of decades ago was that one could compensate for a dull, boring job by rich and stimulating activities in the free time. We now know that this is not so. There is a 'spillover' from job experience to leisure (Kahn, 1981). In other words, those who hold boring and constricted jobs are not likely to engage in leisure activities requiring effort and planning. Those whose job is interesting are much more likely to be active in their leisure too. This is not due mainly to personality characteristics that lead active people to select exciting jobs. A longitudinal study of a Swedish national sample showed that workers whose job changed over a 6-year period to a richer job content and more autonomy and control also became more active outside working hours, participating in more educational activities and in union and cultural activities (Karasek and Theorell, 1990). There was no such increase in activity outside work in those whose job situation had not improved.

Since adequate time for recovery from work is a key concept in maintaining health, it is important to consider differences between groups in terms of opportunity to relax and unwind. This brings us to the issue of stress and gender.

STRESS RESPONSES AND GENDER

In the early days of stress research, knowledge about stress responses and coping was based almost entirely on the study of men. Men's stress responses were regarded as the norm for people, i.e. it was taken for granted that the results were valid for women, too. It came as a surprise when we found major differences between men and women in neuroendocrine responses to a variety of situations (Frankenhaeuser, 1991a; Frankenhaeuser, Parr and Ekvall, 1994). During rest and relaxation, there were no gender differences in the secretion of stress hormones. However, when exposed to achievement demands, men responded with a marked increase in adrenalin release, whereas women's adrenalin did not increase much. In one study after another we found that the old fight–flight response was much more readily elicited in men (Frankenhaeuser, 1993).

At the time of our first gender comparisons in the mid-1970s, gender roles in Sweden were much more rigid than they are today. As women have entered the labour market, differences between men and women in attitudes and values, as to what is important in life and worth fighting for, have gradually diminished. This increasing similarity between women and men in terms of how they assess and value different demands is reflected in their physiological and hormonal responses. In particular, women entering professional domains traditionally reserved for men now exhibit stress responses that used to be typical of men only. We have seen this in engineers, bus drivers and lawyers. Most of the women have adopted what used to be the male fight–flight response patterns. And today, we find that women in managerial positions have taken one step further, responding to achievement demands even more strongly than their male counterparts (Frankenhaeuser, Parr and Ekvall, 1994; Frankenhaeuser *et al.*, 1989).

This is the new trend. We interpret women's new stress response patterns as reflecting not only adaptation, but actually over-adaptation to the organizational structures and value systems shaped by men. In all large organizations, where we have studied managers, women aspiring to top positions report that they have to do better than their male colleagues in order to get the same recognition and the same chance for promotion. In fact, this is one of the strongest stressors for women managers.

A series of recent studies shows that women in managerial positions are more competitive and drive themselves harder than men. As leaders, the women are ambitious, determined and distinct. For this they pay a price in terms of higher stress levels than men. Moreover, women managers unwind particularly slowly in the evening after a day at work. The major obstacle for unwinding is the 'second job' that women take up when they return home, i.e. demands related to the family, children and household chores (Lundberg, Mårdberg and Frankenhaeuser, 1994). The main responsibility for most home management duties still rests with the woman of the family. Old traditions are stronger in the home than at the workplace. While this makes women's everyday life rich and rewarding, it is not conducive to intellectual work requiring sustained concentration.

CONCLUDING REMARKS

The main message of this chapter is that knowledge about human motives, abilities and constraints provides guidelines for shaping the psychosocial work environment to suit people. However, to make effective use of research-based knowledge, we need to increase the dialogue between the scientific community and the world of work.

This is a challenge to biobehavioural and social scientists to present their research in such a way that results can be translated into practical measures. The dialogue between the world of science and the world of work takes time to develop. There are no shortcuts to a productive exchange of ideas and competencies between researchers and their speaking partners in the workplace.

However, it is my experience that the opportunities for constructive dialogue are particularly good in the area of psychosocial factors at work and quality of life.

4

Stressors and Cancer

Hera Tsimara-Papastamatiou

Department of Pathology, Athens University, 25 Ploutarchou Str., Politeia GR-146, 71 N. Erythrea, Athens, Greece

INTRODUCTION

The possible link between stressors and cancer is a challenging topic to be investigated and very difficult to establish scientifically, because it represents a complicated field, embracing psychosomatic research, psycho-endocrinology and immunity as well as carcinogenesis.

Many scientists have noted the connection between the onset of cancer in relatives or friends after bereavement or divorce, or with problems in the occupational or family environment. These descriptive studies have led to the conclusion that the occurrence of severe emotional factors preceding the diagnosis of different kinds of malignancy must be 'something more than a coincidence'.

The difficulty of answering the question of whether or not there exists some causal link between stressors and the development and progress of cancer is demonstrated by the limited number of published papers on the topic, with objective criteria and controlled variables. Part of the problem was summarized in a perceptive editorial published in the *Lancet* (Anonymous, 1985), which said that 'Psychosomatic research finds itself uncomfortably placed between the purely organic and the purely psychological', and

Pleasure and Quality of Life. Edited by D.M. Warburton and N. Sherwood
© 1996 John Wiley & Sons Ltd.

that 'psychologists and immunologists do not meet much, and when they do meet, they speak different languages'.

In my view, we must be aware of the relation between immunity and cancer initiation and progress, and that cancer development is a multifactorial process with a long lag time with the logical danger of inferring causality from correlation.

Despite these problems, I will evaluate the evidence from four points of view:

1. The existing data on the association with basic principles referring to tumorigenesis.
2. The relationship of stressors to immunity.
3. The possibility that the relationship is reversed, so that in fact it is cancer that acts as a stressor.
4. Some personal views on the importance of pleasure and positive attitudes to life for health.

EVALUATION OF THE LITERATURE

The idea of a possible connection between psychological status and cancer is very old; Galen observed that, 'Cancer occurs more commonly in melancholic women than in those of sanguine temperament' (Mettler and Mettler, 1947). Although I am not sure what Galen meant by the term 'cancer', the medical literature of the nineteenth century contained various reports noting that emotional distress preceded the diagnosis of cancer. In these reports, deep anxiety, reduced hope and disappointment were followed by the growth and progress of cancer (Paget, 1870). In addition, 'the number of instances in which malignant disease of the breast and uterus follows immediately the antecedent emotion of depressing character is too large to be set down to chance' (Snow, 1893).

Since then, the idea that psychological factors play a role in the onset and progress of cancer continues to excite considerable interest and debate. The pertinence of what has come to be called 'psychoimmunology' has been discussed repeatedly by investigators in their search for a psychobiological model of carcinogenesis and cancer development. Studies suggesting that a susceptibility to cancer is often linked to emotional states such as anger or anxiety, to authoritarian attitudes and to behaviour characterized by passiveness or helplessness have appeared in the literature (Bahnson 1980, 1981; Rosch, 1979). On the other hand, studies rejecting such evidence have also been reported (Horne and Picard, 1979). A middle position suggests that, even in the presence of severe stressful factors, nothing would have happened if an underlying disease had not been present (Riley, 1981) .

There are also reports examining the relation between psychological factors and survival or relapses after the diagnosis of life-threatening diseases. It has been found that long-term survivors with Hodgkin's lymphomas, malignant melanomas, or cancer of the breast, the lung and the colon have been found to be less emotionally distressed, to complain less and to be better at solving their illness-related problems than short-term survivors, who are passive, stoical and denying (Greer and Morris, 1975; Weisman and Wordem, 1977).

A number of studies report significantly higher than expected death rates in male cancer patients with depressive illness (Watson and Ramirez, 1991; Whitlock and Siskind, 1979). In 1983, Greer reported a prospective epidemiological study using the Minnesota Multiphasic Personality Inventory (MMPI), of a randomly selected sample of 2020 middle aged men, who were followed for 17 years. A significant association was demonstrated between death from cancers and previous depression scores, even after adjustment for age, cigarette smoking, use of alcohol, family history of cancer and occupational status (Greer, 1983). However, not all studies have found an increase in mortality among depressed patients (Niemi and Jaakelainen, 1980).

One of the problems with these studies is the fact that the way in which the cancer patient reacted could be influenced by the physiological consequences of the malignant disease (hormonal or immune changes, neurotropic events) and might not, therefore, reflect the pre-morbid status. It is true that not only does the diagnosis of a life-threatening illness act as a potent stressor for the majority of the people, but also that some types of cancer, called neuroendocrine tumours, result in the over-production of hormone-like substances, which can act as stressors.

Theoretically, cancer and stress responses could be reciprocally related through both biological and psychological interactions. So, this question needs to be investigated from three main directions:

1. The possible aetiological connection, in the sense of influences of stress in the initiation and promotion of carcinogenesis, from both research and clinical perspectives.
2. The possible connection of stressors with the prognosis of cancer patients.
3. The possible connection of cancer with the development of stress conditions, as psychological sequelae of the tumour.

On the first point of a possible aetiological connection, some experimental studies in animals have confirmed that viral stressors and chemically-induced stressogens can both initiate or promote carcinogenesis *and* inhibit the neoplastic process (Goldman and Vogel, 1984; Justice, 1985; Kiecolt-Glaser *et al.*, 1985). It is obvious that stressful factors, like those mentioned above, cannot be employed with humans. Consequently, relationships are less well defined and not so clearly proven on a research basis.

There still remain contradictory results; some suggest a significant correlation between cancer diagnosis and stressful events within the preceding five years (Horne and Picard, 1979), whereas others show no association between cancer development and previous stressful events (Greer and Morris, 1975; Schonfield, 1975). It must be pointed out, however, that the majority of these results do not fulfil basic scientifically acceptable research criteria. Most of the results are based upon uncontrolled or inadequately controlled studies, without standardized psychological tests and without considering other predisposing factors for cancer development, such as biological and environmental factors, and factors related to personal habits.

However, there do exist:

- Predictive studies with the pre-diagnostic characteristics of individuals compared with post-diagnostic outcome (Temoshok, 1985).

- Prospective studies associating pre-morbid psychosocial characteristics, stress factors and health habits with the development of disease in the following 10 years (Cohen, Tyrrell and Smith, 1993).

- Studies relating stressors and/or psychosocial factors to disease progression and survival time, and others relating psychosocial factors to immunological variables, which could be associated with the onset of diseases in general (Herbert and Cohen, 1993).

- Cross-sectional studies, comparing the psychosocial characteristics of patients with those of matched controls (Greer, 1983).

Finally, there are some controversial hypotheses linking cancer proneness with certain personality types (Eysenck, 1991a; Solomon, 1987; Solvasan, Ghauta and Hiramoto, 1988). Some of these are based on retrospective, albeit controlled, studies (Greer, 1983). However, the results of prospective studies do not permit any firm conclusions about the cancer-prone personality (Johnston, 1991; Pohler, 1989). Clearly, there is a need to clarify the area in terms of biological and psychological characterization.

In an attempt to investigate the onset of cancer under stressful conditions, using objective criteria, the role of the immune system has been extensively considered. It is well known that:

1. Among factors influencing the growth of neoplasms, the place of host-defence related to immunological and hormonal mechanisms is of great importance.
2. Lymphocytes act as immunoregulators.
3. Stress stimuli have a broad activation of the body, via the hypothalamus (see Frankenhaeuser, this volume).

The stress response is activated by different stressful emotions, including anger, anxiety, depression and excitement. The raised level of cortisol in the blood, especially when it is chronic, leads to a weakening of the immune system by causing reduction of mitogen-antigen driven lymphocytic proliferation, resulting in lymphopenia, with consequent loss of the immunoregulatory role of these cells

(Fitzmaurice, 1988; Forni *et al.*, 1983; Gross, 1989). This leaves the body more susceptible to the action of different pathogenic factors.

Although such a pathway could have some relation to tumorigenesis, it cannot be considered as a sufficient mechanism for cancer initiation by stressors, since many other factors are required, such as viral, genetic and environmental agents.

Another immunological relationship of carcinogenesis with stressors could be discussed on the basis of the hypothesis that the immune system acts as a protector of the body against tumorigenesis, by activating the cell and humoral immunity against specific tumour antigens. Such an effect could occur through the activation of the cytotoxic T lymphocytes, via cells with specific receptors acting as cytolytics (lymphocyte–macrophages), via activation by lymphokines released by the lymphocytes, and via cells with specific action against tumour cells.

This hypothesis could explain tumorigenesis in the presence of lymphopenia caused by stress conditions, and it is has received some acceptance, because of the known higher incidence of some tumours in immunosuppressed people. Against the hypothesis are the facts that:

1. Tumours that develop via this mechanism are mainly lymphomas, which are neoplasms derived from the cells of the diseased (immune) system.
2. Not all neoplasms produce tumour specific antigens, thus escaping immunological surveillance.

In people, evidence of a reduced lymphocytic response due to stressors has been reported after recent bereavement (Bartrop *et al.*, 1977; Schleifer *et al.*, 1983). According to Jemmott *et al.* (1983) such lymphocytic responses, known as cell-mediated immunity, are related to the salivary secretory immunoglobulin A, which, in the presence of stressogens, is found in lowered rates in plasma in association with elevated serum cortisol levels (Baker *et al.*, 1985).

Even given this information, the direct correlation of stressful experiences and cancer development cannot be accepted for two reasons: firstly, because the onset of cancer is only determined from the onset of the clinical manifestations caused by the tumour, and secondly, because death from cancer results from a multitude of biological steps over a period of time, which depend on the considerable heterogeneity of tumours and variations in their growth rates. Consequently, the actual date of onset of cancer, in the sense of the pathological cellular changes leading to the initiation and then the promotion of carcinogenesis, cannot be identified even approximately. If the time cannot be identified even approximately, then it cannot be related to the presence of stressful conditions.

From this brief evaluation, it seems that we cannot have a certain answer to the question of whether stressors cause the onset of cancer, although there is a plausible direct mechanism. However, in my view, it would be a great mistake to dismiss the possibility of some aetiological relationship at this point in time.

The relationship of stressors to tumour progression is more plausible, with some recent experimental data pointing in this direction. I have mentioned the influence of attitudes to the diagnosis as a predictor of survival. Recent experimental data show that proteins protecting against the over-proliferation and migration of the cancer are found in lower levels in stressed patients, facilitating the progression and metastatic spread of the tumour.

Furthermore, there are cancer patients—unfortunately only a few—whose condition has been considered inoperable but who have lived for unexpectedly long periods of time as a result of their positive attitude to life. In addition, a minority of them, who have believed in their survival, have lost not only clinical manifestations of cancer but also radiographic and other clinical evidence. This suggests the importance of hope and not easily giving up for immunocompetence and for the protection of the body, even in the presence of cancer.

At the end of this chapter, I want to emphasize the positive contribution of attitude and behaviour to health. I believe that the pleasures and internal satisfaction offered by activities enjoyed in moderation are major contributors to psychological balance, immunocompetence and consequently physical health. I am convinced that people must search for ways to escape or protect themselves from the consequences of excess stressors, and this includes, within the confines of their illness, cancer patients.

Coming from the country which gave the expression 'all things in moderation' (*pan metron ariston*) to the world and speaking as a scientist who studies all possible cellular alterations related to risk factors for different kinds of diseases, I think that the only danger related to the use of pleasurable substances is to overstep the 'golden mean', and that both prohibition and uncontrolled indulgence are likely to be detrimental to the individual.

CONCLUSIONS

The possible connection between stressors and cancer has been investigated on the basis of the existing literature on the topic, and evaluated as a causal factor in the initiation and as a factor in tumour progression and survival. The results of this complex evaluation have led to the following conclusions:

1. No scientifically-accepted aetiological data have proven a direct link between stressors and the initiation of cancer.
2. There appears to be some relationship between stressors and the prognosis and survival rates of patients with an already developed tumour.
3. Both the fear of being diagnosed as having a life-threatening disease and the biological changes related to some histological types of cancer (such as neuroendocrine tumours) are stressors.
4. A positive attitude towards life and pleasurable experiences contributes to stress reduction and the possibility of increased longevity in all people, including those with existing pathology.

5

Individual Coping Strategies and Behavioural Style

*Judy I. Suiter and †Bill Bonnsetter

*Competitive Edge Inc., PO Box 2418, Peachtree City, GA 30269, USA
and †Target Training International, 7333 E. Helm Drive, Scottsdale,
AZ 85260, USA

'He who knows others is learned, but he who knows himself is wise.'
(Laotse — The Character of Tao)

INTRODUCTION

In order to discuss individual coping strategies and behavioural style, we must first examine why an individual might feel a need to develop such strategies. The common explanation is that people need coping strategies to deal with stress. Stressors have often been referred to as a twentieth-century problem, when in reality they have always been present, even in earliest mankind. However, the word 'stress' (stressors and the stress response) has come to be seen throughout the world as representing an undesired condition. This condition is more accurately described as 'distress'.

Distress occurs when the resources available to an individual are perceived to be less than what is required to achieve a desired outcome. Distress is usually associated with emotions such as anxiety, frustration and anger, and the person feeling de-energized. On the other hand, if the resources available are

Pleasure and Quality of Life. Edited by D.M. Warburton and N. Sherwood
© 1996 John Wiley & Sons Ltd.

significantly greater than those required to achieve a particular outcome, then boredom may be the result. Both of these conditions can lead to a person being less than productive.

It has been shown that when the demands of a situation and the resources available are perceived to be approximately equal, then the individual feels energized. Therefore, for the purposes of distinguishing the differences between these two states, we use the term 'distress' or 'de-energized' to refer to an undesirable state that can have negative consequences for the individual and 'energized' to refer to a desired state that can have positive consequences for the individual, including pleasure.

One other factor needs to be pointed out at this time: a person's perception is his or her reality, and two people can perceive the same event or situation very differently (see Warburton, 1979). What is a distressful situation to one person may be perceived as energizing by another. Therefore, answers to several questions will need to be explored in this chapter. They are:

1. What are the three basic types of distress and their primary causes?
2. How can mental and emotional distress be reduced?
3. What role does a person's behavioural style play in that process?
4. Will certain coping strategies work better for certain behavioural styles?
5. Why should individuals learn effective coping strategies?

THE THREE BASIC TYPES OF DISTRESS AND THEIR PRIMARY CAUSES

Distress has been subdivided into physical, mental and emotional, although the differentiation of mental and emotional is by no means clear.

Physical distress is caused by physical activity and is easiest to understand. As individuals engage in physical activity, they deplete their energy resources, and eventually their productivity (ability to continue to engage in this activity) will be reduced or depleted. All human beings require a certain amount of water, food and rest in order to optimize their physical output.

Mental distress is most often caused by a person being placed in a situation where he or she has to make an important decision. The process of making a choice and the fear of making the wrong choice can lead to mental distress. In addition, mental distress can be caused by certain work activities that tax the mind. If an individual is forced to engage in that activity over an extended period of time, a feeling of being de-energized will result. A good example of this type of distress is the mental distress that accompanies the preparation of personal or corporate tax returns.

Emotional distress refers to situations like the death of a loved one, divorce or a problem in the family. Positive events can also cause these same types of feelings; for example, the distress sometimes experienced by a bride or groom the night before a wedding.

All types of distress consume energy; however, emotional distress consumes the most, followed by mental distress. Physical distress consumes the least. Physical distress is the easiest to counteract; food, water and rest will usually bring about a fast recovery. Mental and emotional distress are more difficult to recover from and require a different approach. For the purposes of this chapter, we will be focusing most of our discussion on behavioural coping strategies that individuals can use when they are experiencing mental or emotional distress.

However, it is important to recognize that certain pleasurable activities such as drinking coffee, tea or alcohol, smoking or eating chocolate have also been shown by Associates for Research into the Science of Enjoyment (ARISE) research to have positive effects on reducing distress (see Warburton and Suiter, this volume).

CAN MENTAL AND EMOTIONAL DISTRESS BE REDUCED?

In order to reduce distress and decrease 'energy burn', one must examine the three basic options that most people have available to them. These are (i) to change the situation, (ii) to change their perception of the situation and (iii) to engage in distress reducing activities (Lazarus, 1966).

If one believes that the price for changing the situation is too high, then one will need to learn coping strategies in order to use options (ii) or (iii). For example, suppose you have a job that pays a very high salary, but you dread going to work each day and, in addition, the job market is saturated with people who have been laid off. Under those conditions, you decide that you are unwilling to quit or try to find a different job. Using option (ii), you need to realize that *you* made that decision and that it is not that 'you can't do anything about the situation', but that *you* have chosen not to. Recent research by Marianne Frankenhaeuser (this volume) has shown that having a sense of control over a situation can reduce distress, even if one remains in the same situation.

Hans Selye (1974) identifies four ways in which people respond to a situation that they find de-energizing: some people fight it, others choose flight, others tolerate it and, lastly, some ignore it. To be able to predict one's own reaction and those of others, it is necessary to examine the different behavioural styles people tend to use.

THE FOUR BEHAVIOURAL STYLES

The first researcher to look at behavioural differences in people was Hippocrates (400 BC), who identified four temperaments: sanguine, melancholic, choleric and phlegmatic. In the book *The Emotions of Normal People* (Marston, 1928) four behavioural tendencies were identified: dominance, inducement, steadiness and compliance. Marston argued that all people possess some of all four tendencies to one degree or another. He also related each behaviour to activity or passivity and to either a favourable or an unfavourable environment. His conclusions were as follows:

- Dominance produces activity in an antagonistic environment.
- Inducement produces activity in a favourable environment.
- Steadiness produces passivity in a favourable environment.
- Compliance produces passivity in an antagonistic environment.

Marston's model has been further refined through the creation of a self-assessment learning instrument that measures the amounts of each of these tendencies in any given person at a particular point in time (see Bonnsetter, Suiter and Widrick, 1994). Our current research indicates that approximately 4% of any population will exhibit behaviour primarily motivated by one of these factors, 50% by two of these factors and 46% combining three of these factors. In addition, we have explored the underlying focus of what each dimension is measuring:

- Dominance (D) measures how a person responds to problems or challenges. A person who exhibits high D behaviour on a frequent basis will usually be described as decisive, direct, task-orientated, a risk-taker and impatient.
- Influence or inducement (I) assesses how a person influences others to their point of view. A person who possesses a tendency toward high I behaviours will be seen by others as enthusiastic, trusting, talkative, convincing and sometimes disorganized.
- Steadiness (S) refers to how a person responds to the pace of the environment. An individual who displays high S behavioural tendencies will be described as amiable, systematic, a good listener, predictable and possessive.
- Compliance (C) refers to how a person responds to rules and procedures set by others. People who exhibit high C behaviours will be seen as precise, accurate, analytical, reserved and perfectionist.

Furthermore, research has shown that general orientation towards positive outcome expectation is synonymous with optimism, and the dimension of optimism versus pessimism is influential on coping responses (Scheier and Carver, 1987). Warburton and Suiter (1994) have further researched the tendency toward optimism and control optimism as it relates to these four behavioural tendencies, and have found that individuals with high D or high I tendencies are the most optimistic and those with high S or high C tendencies the most pessimistic. In addition, control optimism positively correlated with a high D behavioural style.

BEHAVIOURAL STYLE AND WORK ENVIRONMENTS

On the basis of the DISC model of human behaviour, we can now examine what types of situations might be de-energizing and which activities or situations would be energizing for each behavioural tendency, as well as their natural reaction to distressful situations or events.

Individuals with high dominance tendencies like a work environment that is fast-paced, competitive, future-orientated, free from controls and that focuses on results, not methods. Organizations that are very bureaucratic, where managers have to go through many layers of approval to make changes, are de-energizing to people with a high D style. Committee meetings where few or no decisions are made and working without support staff to handle the details are other ways in which these individuals become distressed. Their natural reaction is to exhibit a fight response.

People with high I tendencies like work environments that have a high degree of interaction, public recognition of their contributions, little conflict and where humour is appreciated. Work assignments that would require long periods of concentration on one task, little personal contact and small recognition for their efforts would have a negative effect on the high I energy level. Their natural reaction is to exhibit a flight response.

Individuals with a high S style need work environments that give them time to adjust to change, identification with a team, procedures to be followed and appreciation (especially for their loyalty). The high S behavioural style becomes frustrated and less productive in environments that have a lot of conflicts between people or departments, when their security is threatened, and when frequent changes in their role or functional responsibilities are made. Their natural reaction is to tolerate the situation.

People with a high C (cautious) tendency require a work environment that provides them time to think, accurate and timely information, an environment free from abrupt changes, standard operating procedures in writing and few surprises. When they are not given the proper (as they see it) amount of time to do an assignment the 'right' way, or are required to interact with other employees or managers for a high percentage of each day, and where change seems to be the task of the day, people with high C tendencies become unproductive and irritable. Withdrawal or avoidance is their natural reaction to a distressful situation.

CONFLICTS AND DISTRESS

Most people experience distress in their life from conflicts that fall into three main categories: intrapersonal (me–me), interpersonal (me–you) and personal–functional (me–job). Any one of these types of conflicts can cause energy drain.

Intrapersonal (me–me) conflicts are usually caused by suppressing natural behavioural tendencies or having coexisting tendencies that pull the individual in two very different directions. For example, a person who is challenge-orientated and wants immediate results may also have a perfectionist tendency and will therefore also want the task done correctly. This is like having one foot on the accelerator pedal and the other foot on the brake. Anyone who has ever driven a car knows how much energy that can burn! People who experience me–me conflicts on a daily basis may also be difficult to live or work with because if they do not recognize this contradiction in themselves, they may give mixed messages to others regarding their expectations.

Interpersonal (me–you) conflicts may be the result of two people who have very different behavioural styles trying to interact or communicate with each other. These types of conflicts are more prevalent when individuals do not understand their own style and/or do not have the knowledge or understanding to recognize the differences between their style and that of others with whom they are trying to communicate. For example, a person who has a high I behavioral style may try to convince a person with a high C behavioural style by using an emotionally-based rationale, and the person with the high C style keeps asking for facts to support the rationale being given. Another example of interpersonal conflict can occur between one person with a strong behavioural tendency in one dimension and another person who has a very low tendency in that same dimension.

When a person's natural behaviour is not matched to the behavioural demands of his or her job, distress will occur as a result of personal–functional (me–job) conflicts. The amount of distress or de-energy will be directly related to the length of time that the person is required to adapt or modify his or her behaviour. Adapting one's behaviour to a short-term situation will not result in a big energy drain; however, when a person is significantly mismatched to the job, he or she will usually start having some health problems that are distress related. The cost of distress in American business has been estimated at $200 billion annually because of premature death and health-related problems (Kind and Sorenson, 1993). In addition, as high as 70% of all accidents and illnesses can be traced to distress and how a person manages (copes with) it.

Research has indicated that 50–80% of all people in the Western world are not in their ideal job (*Atlanta Journal*, June 28th 1993). No one wants to admit after studying for a career that they made the wrong decisions. Also, those who hire people do not want to admit that they may have made a bad decision in their selection process. Me–job conflicts are the most serious for the individuals and their organizations because most people spend a high percentage of their day either at work or getting to and from work. In addition, me–job conflicts often lead to me–you conflicts, either at work or at home.

COPING STRATEGIES

When people with different behavioural styles become de-energized, they exhibit different distressed-induced behaviours and need to engage in different activities to counteract distress. These activities can be seen as coping strategies: 'Coping strategies can be defined as a set of responses mobilized in an effort to manage a situation; not all of which may be successful' (Steptoe, 1981). Individuals use coping strategies that fall into one of two forms—cognitive or behavioural—with the primary solution having either a problem or emotion focus that will result in effective or ineffective actions.

High D behavioural tendency people, when distressed, exhibit anger and need physical activity, preferably of a competitive nature, to recharge their batteries. In fact, in the ARISE survey (see Warburton and Suiter, this volume), 54% of individuals said that they rated physical exercise as a way of unwinding after a hard day.

Individuals with high I behavioural tendencies will become sarcastic and disorganized when de-energized. They need 'social time' interacting with others, preferably in a playful sort of way. For the high I style person, a little laughter goes a long way. In the ARISE survey, 82% of the respondents said that entertaining friends was a most pleasurable activity.

High S style individuals become distressed and depressed when they experience one or more of the types of conflicts mentioned earlier in this chapter. To recharge their energy level, these types of people require 'nothing time', such as taking a hot bath, watching television, reading or taking a walk. These types of activities were also rated very highly in the survey as coping strategies that people use to unwind.

People with a high C behavioural style become overly critical of themselves and others when they are in a state of distress. The coping prescription for the high C in this state is to be left alone, preferably where they can be outdoors, feeling a sense of oneness with nature, or at the very least being able to look outside. Individuals with a high C tendency have the highest aesthetic needs of all the behavioural styles and are often the individuals who have the longest journeys to work. Meditation and yoga were also listed as coping strategies 14% of the time.

What seems to be apparent from the ARISE survey and other research is that many people know what they do to unwind or cope when feeling distressed. However, they may not realize why certain activities work better than others and may not recognize the positive health implications of engaging in those activities. In a rapidly changing world, where new technology is redefining how people work and what work they do, organizations are increasingly going to need to understand and teach people about themselves and effective coping strategies, if the organizations are ever going to be able to reduce their healthcare costs.

THE COST OF ENERGY DRAINS

Current research by ARISE and many others indicates that distress is one of the most overlooked and misunderstood parts of what is causing healthcare costs throughout the world to escalate at an alarming rate (see Warburton and Suiter, this volume). In fact, research by Robert Golembiewski at the University of Georgia has found that 20% of 23 666 North American workers were experiencing alarmingly high levels of distress. He maintains that 'the death rate in the US goes up every time the unemployment rate goes up, which translates to 50 000 extra deaths for every 1 percent rise'. According to Golembiewski, the key to survival for de-energized people is 'learning what you can and can't control and what your main stressors are' (Golembiewski, 1995).

Other research statistics have shown that in 1991, job-related injuries and illnesses hit 6.8 million in the USA, which amounted to an increase of 200 000 claims from the previous year and the highest since tracking began in 1972. Nearly 9 out of every 100 workers became ill or suffered injury because of their job (US Bureau of Labor Statistics, 1992).

A study of 1569 Boeing Company employees revealed that workers who do not enjoy their job are 2.5 times more likely to file back injury claims as compared to those who like their work. Workers with high emotional stress were more than twice as likely to file a claim. Back injury claims resulted from lack of job satisfaction, not from work involving heavy lifting, strength or flexibility. Back injury is the most common and expensive muscle or bone problem and costs an estimated $30 billion annually in the USA (*Business Week*, April 1st 1991). Golembiewski (1995) also reported that:

> 'Dr Robert S. Eliot, a cardiologist who heads the Institute of Stress Medicine in Scottsdale, Arizona, (USA) estimates that as many as 500 000 Americans die each year from stress-related heart conditions alone. Of all the people who drop dead, 86 percent—nearly half a million a year—have lesions in their heart muscles that are produced by excess adrenaline due to too much stress.'

The health risks of hating one's job have been known to medical researchers in the USA since 1972, when a Massachusetts study showed that the surest predicator of heart disease was not smoking, cholesterol or lack of exercise, but job dissatisfaction (*Fortune*, November 12th, 1992).

The United Nation's International Labour Organization, in a 1993 World Labour Report, said that job stress had become a global phenomenon (*Atlanta Journal*, March 23rd 1993):

> 'Employers who act on causes of stress—organizational or environmental—can eliminate these roots... Such organizational stress-busters

involve giving employees more control over their job lives, such as intro-ducing flexitime or job sharing to give workers more leeway in their work hours and adopting a less confrontational style of management.'

CONCLUSIONS

As time pressures increase and the rate of change continues to escalate, the ability of human beings to cope will be a critical skill for survival for all people throughout the world. Hopefully, the information presented in this chapter is a significant first step in people being able to recognize the value of finding their own pleasures in life.

6

Effective Strategies for Stress Management in Everyday Life

K. Jung

Department of Sports Medicine, The Johannes Gutenberg University
of Mainz, Albert-Schweitzer Strasse, 55099 Mainz, Germany

It is well documented scientifically that all cells in the human body
are connected to one another via the nervous system. In the
hypothalamus, both pleasant and unpleasant events activate the
hypothalamus and trigger the release of the so-called stress hormones adrenalin and noradrenalin from the adrenal glands directly and cortisol, via the pituitary. Far less recognized among
scientists, and largely unknown among the general population,
are possible strategies to manage stressors in daily life. Or, more
important, what measures are appropriate to increase the body's
resistance to stressors?

In this chapter, I would like to concentrate mainly on effective
short-term stress management mechanisms in daily life and to
focus on semi-luxury items, such as alcohol, chocolate, coffee
and nicotine. On the one hand, they are popular in daily life for
stress management. On the other hand, their effects are heavily
disputed by the scientific community as to their effectiveness as
antidotes to stressors, despite their clearly determined effects
on pleasure.

Pleasure and Quality of Life. Edited by D.M. Warburton and N. Sherwood
© 1996 John Wiley & Sons Ltd.

ALCOHOL

There have been increasing positive scientific findings in recent years on the subject of wine and health (Jung, 1995). The positive effects of wine were recognized early in the history of humankind (see the Bible, e.g. 1 Timothy 5:23, 'use a little wine for thy stomach's sake and thine often infirmities'). As oral and written accounts from the widest range of cultures testify, its consumption acquired importance, above all in relation to religion and health. It was not until the development of scientific medicine and the discovery of chemotherapy that the medical use of wine was forgotten, as scientific interest turned instead to the negative effects on the liver and the brain. Not until recent years did positive reports begin to surface once more in relation to its beneficial effects in protecting the cardiovascular system, in fat metabolism and in modulating the immune system (Friedmann and Kimball, 1986; Klatsky, Armstrong and Friedmann, 1992).

Alcohol affects all organ systems positively or negatively depending on the quality and quantity and, above all, on the health of the person in question. As regards stress management, the significant effects are those on the cardiovascular system, the metabolism, the hormonal system, the nervous system and the immune system, via the mind. The most thoroughly researched effects are those on the heart (see also Netter, this volume), especially since the fundamental work of French oenologists (Renaud and de Lorgeril, 1992). However, it is generally acknowledged that the emphasis must be on regular, but moderate, consumption. The duration of drinking and the observance of latency periods have a further important role to play.

In the field of ventricle function of the myocardium, overuse of alcohol is an important contributory factor to the development of cardiomyopathy, but this connection is not proven in any way for moderate consumption. On the contrary, the favourable effects of alcohol are a decrease in coronary vessel resistance, an increase in the coronary blood flow, a reduction in the work of the heart and an oxygen saving. In the case of less serious coronary deficiencies, moderate volumes of alcohol are also favourable. Although frequent and copious intake of alcohol seems to be connected with a clear increase in blood pressure, lower and more moderate alcohol consumption (up to a maximum of 30 g per day) instead has the reverse effect of a systolic and diastolic reduction in blood pressure, if the values were previously high (Ireland *et al.*, 1984; Saunders, Beevers and Paton, 1981).

The basic mechanism is attributed on the one hand to vasodilatation and on the other hand to an altered calcium metabolism and a reduced sympathetic drive. As regards cerebral results, moderate wine consumption, as a consequence of its wide range of cardio-protective characteristics, is considered overall to have a preventative function. A similar finding is obtained in haemostasis, where moderate wine consumption leads to a reduction in the fibrinogen level and an increase in fibrinolytic and anti-thrombotic activity, which, combined with the high density lipoprotein increase, causes a reduction in the rate of coronary heart disease by around 30–60% (Yano, Rhoads and Kagan, 1977).

Three important effects of stressors on the cardiovascular system can be reversed by means of moderate regular wine consumption. Stressor-induced tachycardia can be reduced or eliminated by consuming alcohol, probably by means of a reduction in the production of stress-induced catecholamine (Ireland *et al.*, 1984). Possibly, there is also a direct and general inhibitory effect of wine on the autonomic nervous system, as well as the indirect effect via the reduction of plasma adrenalin.

Stressors lead to a change in the plasma-lipoprotein composition, with an increase in probability of the development of coronary heart disease; moderate alcohol consumption has the opposite effect. A stressor-induced change in the calcium level in the blood leads to high blood pressure, a development that is prevented by a regular, moderate alcohol intake.

While alcohol seems to affect the overall cholesterol level less, the effects on the high density lipoprotein increase and low density lipoprotein reduction are clear (Belfrage *et al.*, 1977). Factors that are generally recognized and observed are wine-induced inhibition of platelet aggregation and tendency to thrombosis, reduction in fibrinogen level and an increase in fibrinolytic activity. These, above all, are jointly responsible for the cardio-protective features of alcohol.

Two contradictory effects of alcohol on the oxygen metabolism work equally favourably against the development of coronary heart disease, namely the increase in the coronary blood flow and the reduced oxygen requirement of the myocardial cells.

As regards protection against coronary heart disease, it should be noted that, as with overall mortality, so too the mortality from heart disease for moderate, regular drinkers is found to be the lowest in contrast to strict abstainers and heavy drinkers/alcoholics. This pattern is best demonstrated by a U-shaped curve. Moderate drinkers have the longest life expectancy and the lowest rate of cardiovascular mortality.

While the negative influence of high wine consumption must be emphasized in terms of mental function, loss of coordination, loss of judgement, increased clumsiness, reduction in control functions, liver diseases, cancer of the throat, cardiomyopathy, irregular heartbeat and the risk of stroke, moderate wine consumption generally triggers positive effects: vasodilatation, reduction in vessel muscle tension, high density lipoprotein increase and reduction in thrombocytic aggregability. Overall, there is a 20–40% reduction in the risk of myocardial infarction, while overall mortality is reduced by 10–20%.

In the case of nervous disorders, wine has proved its worth for many years, with an extraordinary breadth of indications from anxiety, depression, agitation and frustration to sleep disturbance, anger and loss of concentration, loss of appetite and unprovoked sweating. Wine releases psychological tension and soothes existing anxieties (see Warburton and Suiter, this volume). The quantity of alcohol consumed has an important influence, however, as does the pattern of drinking. Other factors worthy of mention are age, sex, eating habits, ethnic origin, socio-economic status, cultural preferences and the taking of any other medication at the same time.

As regards the effects of moderate, regular wine drinking on the nervous system and the psyche, it is generally recognized that an age-determined decrease in brain function can thereby be prevented. Moderate drinkers retain their mental freshness in old age longer than abstainers. Quarter of a litre of wine per day seems to slow down the ageing process of individual tissues by up to a third. Alcohol, enjoyed in moderation, stimulates the appetite, promotes zest for life, increases creativity, provides a feeling of relaxation and well-being and eases away physical and mental discord—important indications also exist in daily life that may contribute considerably to the heightening of both subjective and objective well-being.

COFFEE

A similar fact applies to coffee as to other stimulant treats, in that the importance of moderation is unfortunately not taken into consideration by most doctors. They should not issue blanket condemnation, without considering the needs, taste and habits of the individual.

Particularly in the case of coffee drinking, there are frequent exaggerations with regard to its dangers (James, 1991). Apart from the fact that coffee is the greatest elixir of life to many people, the caffeine contained in it not only has the potential importance of a more or less harmful stimulant but, moreover, frequently has the effect of a genuine and desirable medicine.

The main constituent of coffee, caffeine, possesses the psychotonic effects of all xanthine derivatives occurring in plants. It belongs to the subgroup of psychopharmaceuticals, the psychostimulants. They increase mental activity, are intended to alleviate feelings of sleepiness and tiredness and enhance concentration and performance (Hindmarch, Sherwood and Kerr, 1994; Warburton, 1995). In addition, coffee has the effect of dampening, calming, balancing and harmonizing (Warburton, 1995).

CHOCOLATE AND OTHER SWEETS

Hyperphagic reactions in stressor situations are not unknown among psychologists (Booth, 1989). Frequent or increased food intake as a spontaneous reaction by some people to emotional tension, such as conflict, annoyance, stress, anxiety, sadness, strain, overloading and also boredom, is reported repeatedly by people, between 13–74% of those interviewed, depending on the author and sample. Certainly, it is proven that the hyperphagic reaction to stressors is by no means confined to obese people.

Furthermore, there are noteworthy nutritional physiological links. An important constituent of chocolate is short-warp refined sugar in the form, primarily, of glucose. Its consumption causes rapid absorption, with an immediate increase in the blood sugar level, whereby short-term effects of enhanced performance, increased concentration, euphoria and heightened activity set in. In particular, the euphoria is seen as a glucose-initiated increase of the production and release of endorphins into the peripheral blood supply. This effect is generally only relatively short-term, however, for up to 30 minutes, after which there follows an insulin-determined blood sugar reduction and an increasingly depressive mood, and, subjectively, the repeated consumption of sweets seems very desirable. This experience is described by Rogers (1994).

NICOTINE

The most heavily criticized stimulant treat from a health perspective is undoubtedly smoking. Without a doubt, smoke is at least hazardous to health, if not actually harmful, but opponents of smoking do not seem to realize that they are increasing stress levels and harming health through their behaviour more than tobacco consumption ever could.

It is not clear whether, similarly to wine consumption, there is a J-shaped curve with regard to the amount of smoking and mortality risk. This would mean that consuming a little tobacco does not lead to an increased risk to health compared to non-smokers, but that, at a threshold level, there is an accelerating risk as a function of the amount smoked.

For non-smokers, undoubtedly, nicotine and other smoke constituents are unpleasant, but for people accustomed to smoking, this is certainly to be assessed differently; they talk of distinct relaxation, well-being, feelings of pleasure, harmony and stress management.

These short-term changes have to be balanced against the potential risks to health. However, it has been shown repeatedly, most recently at the 12th World Cardiology Congress in Berlin (1994), that smokers are most likely to develop certain diseases because they do not eat enough fruit and vegetables and therefore do not receive sufficient vitamin A, vitamin E, vitamin C, magnesium and selenium, so that when they smoke, the free radicals cannot be neutralized and detoxified. These free radicals are responsible for what are known as the 'smoking diseases', which can be avoided to a great extent through appropriate nutrition or specific supplements of particular vitamins and mineral substances to the standard conventional diet.

Moreover, moderate consumption of nicotine is claimed by advocates not to be a risk factor in the development of certain diseases. For an accurate assessment of the overall risk, however, the following must be taken into consideration: all existing risk factors, including increased cholesterol level, hypertension, lack of movement, diabetic metabolism, hyperuricaemia, stressors, sex, age, previous illnesses, personality structure, diet and social environment.

COMPARISON OF STRATEGIES FOR STRESS MANAGEMENT

Without doubt, long-term effective everyday stress-management mechanisms are the most effective and preferable to continuing with medium- and short-term mechanisms over the longer term, because they alone are capable of preventing stressful situations, rather than merely countering stressors. These long-term methods are behavioural therapies, which use psychological learning theory and eventually lead to changes in behaviour. Latent stressed individuals who master these techniques, demonstrate to an increasingly impressive extent how, despite a certain disposition, they can handle stressors. The techniques must be learnt, a process requiring experienced psychologists and doctors. They are of less relevance to the minor upsets of daily life; they are used predominantly in the treatment of serious health disorders. Additional measures such as changing job, sports and other relaxation activities are also of importance.

The group of medium-term effective stress management strategies in daily life includes breathing exercises, hydrotherapy, physical training, good diet, relaxation techniques such as yoga, tai chi and chi gung, relaxation through self-hypnosis, focused self-relaxation and progressive relaxation using the Jacobsen technique, proper use of leisure time, adequate sleep and a harmonious life from a time and psychosocial perspective. They demand active participation by those concerned but guarantee subjective and objective improvement of symptoms of the chronic stress syndrome.

The semi-luxury articles discussed in this chapter are rarely suitable as a long-term strategy for stress management in individual cases. Stimulant treats remain in the long term what they are in the true sense of the word: purveyors of happiness, enjoyment and culture. However, this is only the case when they are used sensibly and in moderation. Their effects on inner harmony and physical as well as mental well-being are desirable, and it is these objectives that should be the prerequisites to their consumption.

7

Pleasure, Relaxation and Unwinding

Geoff Lowe

Department of Psychology, University of Hull, Hull HU6 7RX, UK

INTRODUCTION

In a previous publication, I highlighted the apparent conflict between society's (health-related) message decrying pleasurable substances and the individual's 'sensible' use of enjoyable substances (Lowe, 1994). I noted that most people believe that '...whilst some pleasurable substances may, in excess, be bad for us, it is even more likely that enjoyable pleasures really are good for us' (Lowe, 1994, p. 108). This chapter takes this issue on board and considers the extent to which people appreciate the pleasures of socially enjoyed substances—tea, coffee, chocolate, cigarettes and alcohol—in terms of their contribution to quality of life.

Most recent research that assesses the quality of life dimension is primarily health or medically related. Attempts are being made to measure, in objective terms, a person's 'quality of life' as a sufferer from various illnesses or after recovery from medical intervention or treatment regimes. I shall not be going along that path. Rather, I shall be considering quality of life from the point of view of the ordinary (healthy) person, who engages in certain pursuits that add a bit of pleasure, enjoyment, satisfaction and contentment to life and thereby enhance its (subjective) quality.

Pleasure and Quality of Life. Edited by D.M. Warburton and N. Sherwood
© 1996 John Wiley & Sons Ltd.

THE MASS-OBSERVATION ARCHIVE

'I am sitting outside a cottage/farmhouse somewhere in France (or maybe anywhere else in southern Europe) on a warm evening. It's a rural area—there is no traffic noise, no dogs barking, nobody asking me to do things for them. I have a good novel and a glass of red wine. In the background the crickets are chirping. Perhaps I am sitting with my wife, who is reading a book as well, or perhaps I am with a group of six male friends who I go cycling with every other year and we have been for a meal and some drinks in the local bar. This for me is probably the ultimate pleasure!' (male manager, mid 40s, Devon)

The above is a quotation from a response to a recent Mass-Observation directive (1993), which asked respondents to write about pleasure(s) and good times/moments. One of the interesting aspects from an initial sampling of those reports was the amazing variety of 'pleasures' that people reported. Typically expected features involving places, scenery, art, music, sex, books, food and drink, films/concerts, memories, children, etc. were fairly common. But there were also many individualistic, 'simple' or unusual pleasures.

'When rotters get their comeuppance, I get a surge of pleasure' (housewife, aged 53, Norwich); another lady talks of 'droplets of pleasure' such as 'watching birds queuing up at a bird-bath' or 'the enormous pleasure from the first mouthful of a serving of lovingly cooked early new potatoes freshly dug from the garden's first crop'. The pleasures of socially enjoyed substances have to be viewed alongside such a wide range of other droplets of pleasure of everyday lifestyles, which enhance the ordinary person's quality of life.

A 43-year-old woman from Birmingham likes 'long summer evenings, sitting outside drinking wine', and 'the feeling you get when communicating well with others'. She also likes Radio 4, 'especially the quite unexpected little aural treat when driving along'. This respondent made an interesting point about food. She likes 'all different sorts for all sorts of different occasions and moods. Breakfast cereals for comfort, bread to nibble and chew for texture and taste, authentic curries for a treat, black olives, cooked breakfasts in hotels, coffee at least once an hour'.

Situations that involve a combination of physical comfort or intellectual and cognitive aspects induce high levels of pleasure:

'Last hour before going to sleep at night, a warm bed, the weather shut out, a hot drink, an absorbing novel and the knowledge that I don't have to get up at the crack of dawn to go to work in the morning' (retired schoolteacher, female, single, Morpeth).

Some respondents take their pleasures very seriously: 'Chekhov's *The Cherry Orchard*, Strauss' *Der Rosenkavalier*, a fine claret and grand marque champagne' (male, retired, National Health Service supplies officer, north-east England). Others enjoy them vicariously: 'The achievements of my family. I get kicks in sharing vicariously in these. Sex—even vicariously' (clergyman, mid-60s). This respondent did, however, report one direct source of enjoyment: 'I get pleasure from smoking my pipe. So there!'

Another respondent who widened the range somewhat was a male lecturer, mid-40s, from Bristol: 'Going to the toilet. I shan't elaborate, but I find this greatly satisfying. Few things are more underrated'. He goes on to mention 'unhappiness. I've come to realize that I've derived considerable pleasure from wallowing in my own quite mild and tolerable unhappiness. The introvert suspects happiness as banal or boring, or an illusion, and finds far more to exercise his mind in medium-grade misery'.

Many respondents seem convinced of, or want to believe in, the truth of the adage that a little of what you fancy does you good: 'I find that I start fancying things like chocolate or sweets. Once I have satisfied my craving I am all right, but I can go in the kitchen and hunt for food three or four times in an evening. I have tried losing weight, but I have given up trying' (35-year-old housewife); 'Even people who are generally cutting down (a bit) enjoy little treats that keep life interesting' (68-year-old female). Some of the rationalizations offered for consuming 'nice' things are intriguing: 'Recently I have been very unhappy as I have been picking up high frequency from the roof of the new Co-op shop. This makes me very restless and I keep eating chocolate and sweets and fancy cakes—anything I can afford to make me happy' (62-year-old female).

CULTURAL BACKGROUND/CONTEXT

Many insights about everyday pleasures and enjoyment can be gained from such reports and other observations from 'ordinary' people. But researchers working with such data need to report inferences about people's implicit cultural knowledge—ingrained beliefs and perspectives that are so customary that they typically cannot be readily articulated by informants. Moreover, we need to be reminded that all such activities take place within a cultural background or context that itself contributes to the pleasure and enjoyment.

Psychologists (and especially psychopharmacologists) typically initiate their substance-use studies with the assumption they apply in studying almost all aspects of human behaviour. This assumption is that there are universal forces that cause people to do the things they do. The task for psychologists studying substance use, therefore, is to uncover these universal forces. Such an assumption, then, enables psychologists to ignore the vast array of particular substance-use patterns and practices that occur around the world, because these variations are supposedly generated by the same universal forces or primary cause. Unfortunately, the assumption also prevents them from recognizing that, since substance use and related activities derive meaning and significance from the specific culture in which they occur, cultural differences in such behaviours are not simple variations on some cosmic consumption chord. They are instead distinctive behavioural patterns that possess different meanings and significance because of the different cultural worlds in which they were socialized and in which they now occur. In other words, such activities differ from culture to culture precisely because of their diverse origins and because of the distinct meanings that different cultures have given to these acts.

Our Mass-Observation respondents provided ample evidence in support of this point. For instance, when asked about the most important cups of tea during the day, one female respondent (aged 45) wrote: 'The first cup of tea in the morning is very important and so is the one I have when I come home at night. It is a sign of being home and a signal to my mind that I can now relax. For this reason, I don't drink much tea at work, as tea is associated with home. I don't think I realized this before!'

ETHNOGRAPHIC STUDIES

When trying to make sense and draw inferences from such qualitative data, I have, in the main, used grounded theory and ethnographic approaches. Using grounded theory, we seek to discover generalized relations among various categories of material and their properties. Ethnographic content analysis is used to document and understand the communication of meaning, as well as to verify theoretical relationships (Tesch, 1990).

Experience with ethnographic studies has influenced my research on substance use. On a somewhat superficial level, it is exciting to read so many fascinating accounts of differing, and sometimes unusual, consumption practices and of the people who engage in them. But this excitement arises not just from the delightful practices being described, but also—and especially—from the immediacy of the descriptions, the detail of which often provides us with clearer insights into the specific behaviours and motives, as well as their meaning and significance within the larger sociocultural context in which they took place. Such insights and immediacy are rarely found in traditional psychological or large-scale sociological studies of drinking, smoking and related substance-use behaviours.

The ethnographic literature typically possesses a more balanced perspective on substance use. Psychologists and health professionals are generally preoccupied with pathology and, as a consequence, focus primarily on substance 'abuse'. Many ethnographic studies present a welcome antidote to this pathological bias by simply describing the socialization of substance use and its various manifestations within a society. What we need are systematic investigations of what constitutes normal consumption patterns (for example, in the case of alcohol, see Lowe, Foxcroft and Sibley, 1993). Psychologists and substance-use researchers in general could learn much from this more balanced perspective. We need to develop baselines of substance use behaviour within different cultures, and different subgroups within cultures, first, in order to understand which users among these various subgroups are devious in problematic ways. As I mentioned in a previous report (Lowe, 1994), many people are irritated by seemingly disproportionate concerns with 'abnormal' ingestive behaviour. In the case of alcohol, even very moderate drinking patterns are sometimes frowned upon. Such messages were perceived and rejected by many respondents: 'It is said one should never drink alone. Rubbish. It [sherry] is a pleasant start to the meal, and wonderful for the morale' (62-year-old female).

DIFFERENT SUBSTANCE-USE PLEASURES

Warburton (1990) argues that all substance-use pleasures are not the same, especially smoking: 'I am more likely to smoke more when drinking or relaxing with a book and certainly the one after meals gives a lot of pleasure. However, as I am truly addicted, in moments of stress or when the brain seems unable to function, then a cigarette is definitely called for. Incidentally, I have already had two cigarettes since I started this [writing this report]' (54-year-old female). Warburton refers to a 'functional smoking' model, in which different smokers can smoke for different reasons and the same smoker may smoke for different effects on different occasions. This model, clearly, can be extended to other substance-use patterns.

Reward

Many people use substances, especially 'nice' foodstuffs, as a pleasurable reward: 'Later [after 24 hours without chocolate], well, I didn't have a chocolate last night and I'm very pleased with my self-control. It seems I have it both ways: if I have a chocolate I enjoy that; if I resist the temptation I enjoy the feeling of self-esteem that gives. I used to eat a chocolate everyday at bed-time but now I go up there when I'm depressed and have one then. But I'm actually trying to keep chocolate eating as a reward for getting down to 10st 6lbs' (59-year-old housewife).

Positive Expectancies

Many surveys (e.g. Alvarez *et al.*, 1991; Bauman and Bryan, 1980; Eiser, Morgan and Gammage, 1987; Foxcroft and Lowe, 1993;

Johnston and O'Malley 1986; McCarthy, 1959) continue to show that substance users, both young and old, ingest primarily for positive reasons (e.g. they like the taste, the 'buzz', to feel relaxed, 'high', and to 'feel good'). Mass-Observation reports, however, highlight important 'ritualistic' aspects of substance use: 'I think the drinking of tea and coffee is as much a social thing today: you sit down for five minutes, have a chat, relax, and then you feel refreshed to get on with whatever you are doing' (female, aged 60); 'I have given up coffee and smoking recently for 36 hours. Life seems a bit flat without them' (female, aged 67). Another lady (aged 36) tried giving up tea-drinking for a day: 'The afternoon seemed long, with no well-earned tea-break to divide it up. I'd never considered the importance of those little landmarks in the day. Something friendly and familiar had been missing from my day.' 'My favourite cups are Monday to Friday breakfast. I usually have it when I get back from taking Freddie to school. I have broken the back of the housework and I settle down to my two oatcakes and cheese, some rough porridge, raisins and lots of milk left soaking since I got up and two hot cups of coffee—all taken with Radio 3 and the *Guardian*. Half an hour of near heaven' (47-year-old female teacher). Most of these substances, when used for pleasure, have a common temporal pattern. Sinnett and Morris (1977) observed that the temporal patterns of drug use are highly correlated with the nationwide temporal pattern of TV watching, suggesting a pleasure-orientated, recreational use.

Older Respondents

Most of these respondents from Mass-Observation surveys are middle-aged or older. Recent trends indicate increasing proportions of the population in these age groups. Moreover, for such individuals, particularly those with restricted opportunities for the pursuit of pleasure, substance use can offer lifestyle benefits. Kastenbaum (1988) suggests guidelines for the moderate use of alcohol by older individuals and reports on studies of positive responses to the availability of small amounts of alcoholic beverages in nursing homes. Moderate amounts of alcohol, he says, can improve the quality of life for institutionalized elders and enhance their social milieu. Community studies also show that the moderate and regular use of wine is linked with favourable changes in the lives of older community residents (e.g. better sleep quality, improved mood, increased concentration and increased self-confidence).

Drug-Seeking Behaviour

Ronald Siegel, in his book *Intoxication: Life in Pursuit of Artificial Paradise* (1989), addresses the ageless question of why we seek drugs. He argues that the desire for intoxication is actually a fourth drive, as unstoppable as hunger, thirst and sex:

> 'The pursuit of drugs—whether caffeine, nicotine, alcohol, opium, mari-juana, or cocaine—is universal and inescapable. It is to be found across time and species, and in the private lives of presidents and citizens alike. The struggle between this natural drive and society law has become a deadly war that can never be won. But there is an answer: the lessons gleaned from animals show that we can make peace with the fourth drive, understand that drugs are a kind of medication needed to change how we feel, and use the technology and education that is our human distinction to design safe intoxicants.'

WIDESPREAD NORMAL SUBSTANCE USE

Given that people have always been consumers of substances (alcohol, and related mood-altering agents), it seems highly likely that they will continue these pursuits (cf. Siegel); while, unfortunately, a small proportion misuse such substances so that they become problem users, the vast majority of people use substances sensibly or indeed minimally. Prohibition (banishing or 'illegaliz-ing' substances) does not work. We cannot prevent people using substances. So what is it about sensible drinkers/users that makes them sensible/skilled users? It may be worth while to focus on this group rather than on the abusers. One approach might be to analyse these people for skill aspects and incorporate this infor-mation in the development of alcohol/substance-use education strategies. One might further use such information to persuade drink/substance industries to focus on quality and drinking/sub-stance-use as a skilled behaviour.

Recently, Dr John Rae of the Portman Group, at the 9th International Conference on Alcohol (1993), argued strongly that attention should be directed towards normal/sensible drinkers, who make up the vast majority of drinkers in the UK, rather than the disproportionate focus on problem drinkers. In other words, although we still need to understand more about contributory influences on problem drinking in order to develop intervention and prevention measures, it may be more helpful and advantageous to find out what it is that makes drinkers sensible drinkers.

Drinking and Substance Use as Skilled Behaviour

'Sensible' drinking and other substance use can be regarded as a skilled behaviour, and the greater the skill, the more/better the pleasure and enjoyment. For instance, bon viveurs and wine connoisseurs add fine grain to the quality of life dimension. Psychologists have long recognized that drinking is a learned behaviour (as are, presumably, other acts of consumption), but few have gone so far as to view substance use as a skill. To do it well is to achieve the desired effects without damage to oneself or others. That is the skill, and some people manage it better than others:

> 'I feel I can really enjoy a pint of Guinness or a glass of wine just to relax and be sociable. I do find a drink can remove tension and I can even be more quick-witted with a drink; it's knowing how much, and yourself, very well.' (female, aged 48)

Skill involves practical knowledge, like how to ingest and the names of specific beverages and substances, and what quantities or doses are appropriate to which. Other knowledge regarding customs, rituals, rules and meanings we pick up via the usual processes of socialization. This is the process by which we learn when, where and what kinds of consumption are appropriate to which contexts. We learn that not all consumption is the same. We learn a repertoire of drinking and ingestion styles so that we use different styles on different occasions for different purposes in different contexts. Most of us, when away from home, enjoy pleasures by the 'away rules', which will generally be different from the 'home rules'. It is also the way we learn that we celebrate special occasions with alcohol and related substances, and that the more special the occasion, the more special the drinks and substances have to be.

So the real skill in drinking and in consuming other substances is in balancing three aspects: dose, purpose and context. To have good experience of drinking and substance consumption, it is necessary to get all three aspects correct or in harmony. This approach appears to have certain similarities with the 'driving as a skill' approach. Although there used to be awards for the 'Pipeman of the Year', one must beware of taking the analogy too far. We are not necessarily advocating the 'Institute of Advanced Drinkers', or being able to achieve a 'Grade 8 in Ecstasy'.

McKechnie (1993) asked people to say what stages of 'drunkenness' they liked most and the one that they usually reached when drinking. More than half (56% of men and 59% of women) usually reach the stage they most enjoy. However, 25% of men and 23% of women overshoot, reaching a higher stage of drunkenness than the one they most enjoy. A great degree of skill is required to monitor the effects of alcohol and other substances on ourselves, especially as the effects are delayed in time and we have to anticipate from previous experience what is likely to happen.

Coping versus Leisure/Relaxation

One particular concern that McKechnie (1993) raises is that many people seem to believe that using alcohol and related substances as medication for anxiety, depression, stress and pain is fine. However, this type of consumption could well be quite dangerous. We need to emphasize the use of alcohol and other 'pleasurable' substances as part of our leisure and relaxation, and get away from the general reliance on substances to cope with life's problems.

Context and 'Third' Places

Furthermore, these substances are frequently consumed in particular places, and society needs to ensure that appropriate substance-orientated places (e.g. pubs, cafes and other good 'third' places) are readily available to relevant groups of people, and to acknowledge that everyone needs opportunities to relax and unwind, frequently in the context of socially enjoyed substances:

'The warmth of the little pub and their no-delay service stand in pleasant contrast to the waiting, formality, boredom, and frustration evoked by city offices, museums, churches, concert halls, airline terminals, and retail stores. Not far from the likes of these may usually be found a pub into which one, given the interlude of freedom, may "bolt" and therein soothe the irritations of urban chafing with an interval of pure felicity.' (Oldenburg, 1989, p. 126)

Skilful pleasure orientation in the right context enhances the quality of life, both individually and culturally.

CONCLUSIONS

In this chapter I have considered the extent to which people appreciate the pleasures of socially enjoyed substances such as tea, coffee, chocolate, cigarettes and alcohol in terms of their contribution to quality of life. Such pleasures have to be viewed alongside a wide range of other 'droplets of pleasure' of everyday lifestyles. The ethnographic approach was emphasized, whereby such positive experiences are considered within a particular cultural background or context. Special insights into substance use and enjoyment (alongside other 'pleasures') are gained from the immediacy of these subjective descriptions, over and above observations derived from surveys and laboratory studies. While many surveys continue to show that substance users, both young and old, ingest primarily for positive reasons, Mass-Observation reports highlight important 'ritualistic' aspects of substance use. Most of these substances, when used for pleasure, have a common temporal pattern. Moreover, 'sensible' drinking and other substance use can be regarded as a skilled behaviour, and the greater the skill, the more/better the pleasure and enjoyment. Furthermore, these substances are frequently consumed in particular places, and society needs to ensure that appropriate places are readily available, and to acknowledge that everyone needs opportunities to relax and unwind, frequently in the context of socially enjoyed substances. Skilful pleasure orientation in the right context enhances the quality of life, both individually and culturally.

Part II

The Positive Contribution of Pleasure to Everyday Life

8

Health and Pleasure

Petra Netter

Department of Psychology, Justus-Liebig University, Otto-Behagel
Strasse 10, D-6300 Giessen, Germany

MODELS, MEASURES AND MEDIATORS

The concepts of pleasure and health are rarely dealt with in the same paper, since health researchers seem convinced that health is something threatened rather than obtained by pleasure. A few preliminary considerations have to precede an analysis of the relationship between the two concepts.

Definitions and measurement of health are frequently based on the World Health Organization definition that health is 'a state of complete somatic, psychic and social well-being', which replaces previous negative definitions of health as the lack of disease (WHO, 1958). Unfortunately, the incorporation of psychological variables, such as 'psychic and social well-being', 'effective coping', etc. generates problems for epidemiological research, because such variables can rarely be traced back to identifiable external conditions of the person. Therefore, definitions of a more medical nature are usually applied, morbidity and mortality versus number of activities and interests and emotional well-being.

Definitions and measurements of pleasure are also complex: immediate target variables of pleasure are usually those of subjective well-being based on positive emotions, motivational aspects (like preparing for activities associated with happy emotions) and

Pleasure and Quality of Life. Edited by D.M. Warburton and N. Sherwood
© 1996 John Wiley & Sons Ltd.

positive effects on cognitive functions (like improved attention, memory and decision making). There is the enjoyment derived from products such as alcohol, coffee, food, tobacco, chocolate and other sweet things, and there are the cognitive experiences such as achievement of life goals, aesthetic experiences, mental or physical activities and, finally, achievement of will-power in health behaviours, like jogging or losing weight, or even abstaining from pleasures like smoking and drinking. So, when investigating the relationships between pleasure, health and product use, one has to consider the following conditions:

1. The direct relaxing or stimulating influence of the product.
2. The effect of reduction of potentially hazardous health-related behaviours, like overeating and lack of exercise, associated with the pleasure derived from exercising self-control.
3. The possibly greater effect of the same behaviours in point 2, when they are done for the sake of pleasure and not for health reasons.

This chapter concentrates only on examples of the direct effects (point 1), since for the other sources of pleasure very little systematic research is available.

With respect to outcome, several models can be created. The first model would test if health is restored or diseases are ameliorated. A second model would assume prevention of illness (i.e. to maintain health). The third model would investigate whether health can be improved above ordinary levels immediately or whether morbidity and mortality can be reduced in the future. In health research, many experiments and studies have been conducted on the basis of the first two of these models, but few attempts have been made to identify those beneficial conditions that can improve health beyond the average level.

Cause–effect relationships between pleasure and long-term effects, like survival time or prevention of diseases, have to consider internal mediators such as neurochemical, endocrinological and physiological responses, as well as acute psychological effects such as positive emotions. The methodological approaches that have been used to relate product use to either the short-term psychological states of pleasure or the long-term effects on health may either be epidemiological (correlational or interventional) or experimental studies. Usually in experimental approaches short-term effects of conditions on biological and emotional mediators are the major targets of research, whereas epidemiological studies aim at long-term effects, such as survival time, prevention of diseases or quality of life.

Both types of studies have their disadvantages: epidemiological studies suffer from confounding factors, such as the correlates of the motivation for selecting certain methods of obtaining pleasure, which may be related to health outcome, such as personality type. An example of this is the evidence linking extroversion with cancer and behaviours like smoking (Grossarth-Maticek, Eysenck and Vetter, 1988). Similarly, in intervention studies, the motivation to take part in the intervention programme may be a common denominator for its influence and the health measure. The experimental approach, on the other hand, has the disadvantage that it can only investigate short-term indicators of pleasure, which may not be valid predictors of health outcome.

BIOLOGICAL MEDIATORS AND THEIR INTERRELATIONSHIPS

Before analysing the effects of biological systems, therefore, we have to define positive emotions. They may be described by their position on the axes of hedonic tone on the one hand and arousal on the other. The sensation of pleasure may be achieved by relaxation as well as by excitement, i.e. equal levels of hedonic tone may be based on different levels of arousal. Consequently, similar levels of arousal may be represented by highly positive affects, like excitement, or negative affects, like anger or anxiety.

Neurotransmitters

When information about pleasure is processed in the frontal cortex and the limbic system, neurotransmitters like dopamine, serotonin and noradrenalin are released. In particular, dopaminergic receptors have been shown to respond to conditions of reward, elicited, for instance, by alcohol or nicotine (Di Chiara, Acquas and

Carboni, 1991), but also by food intake and sex (Phillips, Pfaus and Blaha, 1991). Experiments have shown that chemical or surgical interruptions of dopamine release in the nucleus accumbens in the limbic system deprive the animal or human of the experience of reward derived from the product ingested (Phillips, Pfaus and Blaha, 1991).

Serotonin has been shown to be released in states of relaxing conditions, therefore it reduces the drive to be active, sexually aroused, attentive and hungry. Therefore, some of the relaxing pleasures are certainly associated with release of serotonin. According to Wurtman's theory (see Wurtman and Wurtman, 1979), serotonin levels in the brain may be increased by a diet rich in tryptophan, the precursor of serotonin, and deficiencies of this transmitter have been found to be associated with reduced impulse control (Coccaro and Siever, 1995). Consequently, people with low serotonin levels will have more problems in giving up pleasures, even when these pleasures are health threatening.

Noradrenalin is also involved in reward (Cools *et al.*, 1991); it is the neurotransmitter particularly released in situations of arousal (joy as well as anxiety and anger). It has also been found to be increased by alcohol (see Warburton, 1975). Thus, it must be kept in mind that most neurotransmitters are not specific for certain emotions, and may therefore indicate negative as well as positive arousal, depending on the situation and the individual.

The neurotransmitter beta-endorphin has been advanced as a typical product of reward. In addition to its role in protecting the organism from actual or threatened pain, it is certainly involved in mediating reward from products of pleasure, as shown by animal experiments on self-administration (Bozarth, 1991).

Catecholamines and Cortisol

Briefly, the catecholamines (adrenalin and noradrenalin), which are observed as transmitters in the brain, are also involved in behavioural and emotional changes when produced in the periphery by the adrenal medulla and from sympathetic nerve endings. Apart from increases associated with any kind of stressor that requires 'fight or flight' responses, the catecholamines have been found to be elevated during positive emotions such as watching happy movies and may be markers of a well-functioning healthy personality. This can be concluded from the fact that high adrenalin releasers in a stressful task tend to perform better and have higher ego strength than low releasers (Frankenhaeuser, 1980). But, again, the non-specificity of these hormones may be seen in the fact that they have also been found to be increased by physical exercise, pain, anger and fear.

Cortisol, on the other hand, has almost always been associated with distress, in particular with uncontrollable stress and helplessness (Frankenhaeuser, 1986). Joyful or satisfying events that are effortful but under control lead to a decrease of cortisol levels (Frankenhaeuser, 1986), yet extreme excitement as derived from dangerous experiences (e.g. parachuting) leads to a rise in cortisol levels (Levine and Ursin, 1980).

The Immune System

Cellular as well as hormonal parameters of immunocompetence have been shown to be decreased with acute and chronic stressors, leading to increased rates of viral infections and increases in the incidence and growth rates of cancer (Fisher, 1988; Jemmott and Magloire, 1988; Kiecolt-Glaser and Glaser, 1991). Conversely, an increase in immunocompetence by positive affect derived from social support and relaxation can also be demonstrated (Baron *et al.*, 1990; Thomas, Goodwin and Goodwin, 1985).

Personality

There are hints that personality may be a confounding factor relating pleasure to health outcome, by its influence on perception of events as sources of pleasure or distress (see Eysenck, 1991b). A major factor in this respect is optimism (Scheier and Carver, 1987), which is not only related to extroversion and emotional stability in personality psychology (Eysenck, 1991b) but also influences self-assertiveness.

These personality factors interrelate with elements of health belief models, in which perceived threat is the result of perceived vulnerability in combination with perceived severity of impending diseases. Perceived severity of impending diseases is influenced by knowledge about the effect of a product on the organism and its risk to health. A perceived threat itself will determine health behaviour, influenced by expectations about costs and benefits as well as competence to change one's behaviour. These components will certainly influence the choice, amount and enjoyment of products liable to induce pleasure and detrimental effects upon health when used in excess.

EVIDENCE FOR POSITIVE EFFECTS OF 'PLEASURE PRODUCTS' ON INDICATORS OF HEALTH

Ethanol

Among the products that give pleasure, it is easiest to find evidence for positive effects of ethanol on health. The protective effect of ethanol against heart disease has been demonstrated (see Jung, this volume). A protective effect of ethanol against myocardial infarction is suggested by data comparing the rates of abstainers to people who consume either two drinks or three or more drinks per day in myocardial infarction and different control groups. The teetotallers had higher coronary risks than alcohol drinking groups (Friedmann and Kimball, 1986; Klatsky, Armstrong and Friedmann, 1992). This effect is possibly mediated by the reduction of stress-induced increase in heart rate (Netter and Vogel, 1990). This fits with the general tension reduction hypothesis of ethanol (Cappell, 1975).

Of special interest is the study by Grossarth-Maticek and Eysenck (see Eysenck, 1991b), which addresses the question raised earlier as to whether the motive for product use is reflected in health outcome. Grossarth-Maticek and Eysenck classified drinkers as S-drinkers (drinking to drown their sorrows) or P-drinkers (pleasure drinkers). They found that the death rates of P-drinkers over a 13-year period were lower than those of non-drinkers, while those of S-drinkers were higher than those of non-drinkers.

Caffeine

The general outcome of caffeine research has been that caffeine cannot be accused of increasing coronary diseases, especially when controlling for the stressful lifestyle leading to myocardial infarction. In addition, coffee appears to have a protective effect on individuals prone to coronary heart disease (Grossarth-Maticek and Eysenck, 1990). This would link with the evidence that caffeine can enhance alertness and induce a positive mood (Warburton, 1995; see also Snel and Lorist, this volume; Warburton, this volume).

Nicotine

The pleasure from nicotine at smoking doses may be attributed partly to the release of mesolimbic dopamine, and also to the release of catecholamines (Di Chiara, Acquas and Carboni, 1991). Positive mood effects have been reported (see Warburton and Suiter, this volume). Positive factors include stimulation as well as relaxation in combination with social aspects like facilitation of social interaction and reduction of body weight together with abolition of negative affects (frustration, nervousness, impatience, boredom). In addition, nicotine acts on the cholinergic pathways and mediates cognitive enhancement as a source of pleasure (see Warburton and Suiter, this volume).

However, these positive psychological consequences need to be set against the potential dangers to physical health derived from the inhalation of smoke with its tar, smoke acids and benzpyrines, although the magnitude of these effects has been disputed (see Eysenck, 1991b).

CONCLUSIONS

One salient fact when reviewing the positive effects of pleasure-inducing products on health is that there seems to be an inverted U-shaped relationship for the relation between dose and the positive or negative consequences for health.

A second important observation is the non-specificity of most biological indicators, most of which may signify feelings of pleasure as well as negative affects. As a consequence, more studies should be conducted investigating the relation of affect to long-term health outcome and attempts should be made to elucidate the role of elevated physiological or hormonal mediators.

9

Stressors, Product Use and Everyday Skills

Neil Sherwood

Department of Psychology, University of Reading, Building 3,
Earley Gate, Whiteknights Road, Reading RG6 2AL, UK

INTRODUCTION

The desire to transform mundane activities such as washing and dressing into enjoyable events like bathing and fashion, the explosion of leisure activities in affluent societies and the pan-cultural use of social products such as alcohol, chocolate and tobacco would seem to indicate that pleasure has a central role in people's lives. However, we have only just begun to identify and quantify the subjective and objective benefits that may accrue from the pursuit and realization of pleasure. One strong hypothesis is that pleasure may act to counter the negative effects of stressors.

A recent survey undertaken for ARISE (ARISE/Harris Research, 1994) has shown that social products such as coffee, chocolate, tobacco and alcohol play an important role in the way that people deal with stressors in their lives. When needing to combat stressors at work, 68% of respondents said that they would drink a cup of tea or coffee, 50% said that they would have a soft drink, 27% said that they would smoke a cigarette and 27% said that they would have a snack—responses related to the use of pleasure

Pleasure and Quality of Life. Edited by D.M. Warburton and N. Sherwood
© 1996 John Wiley & Sons Ltd.

products that were only exceeded by the 81% who indicated that they would talk and joke with their colleagues.

A similar pattern emerges later in the day, when respondents were asked how they dealt with unwinding after a stressful day. Among a greater number of pleasure choices afforded by leisure time (sex, music, television etc.), coffee (37%), tea (30%), smoking (28%), alcohol (25%) and chocolate (24%) still rated highly, suggesting that such 'treats' are not merely associated with relief from immediate stressors but may also operate to assist relaxation later in the day. But can the reported positive effects of such products be objectively identified and measured?

THE MEASUREMENT OF EVERYDAY SKILLS

Much of our understanding of the effects of product use come from studies of reward and punishment conducted in rodents, and effects in human subjects remain poorly understood. Questionnaire studies have consistently identified changes to cognition and affect as primary outcomes (Bättig, 1985; Russell, Peto and Patel, 1974). However, the conditions under which these effects appear are still not well understood. Similarly, while electrophysiological and neuro-imaging techniques have shown that compounds such as caffeine or alcohol may alter the functional activity of the human brain (de Wit *et al.*, 1990; Lorist, Snel and Kok, 1994) they cannot tell us how these effects may be expressed in everyday human behaviour and whether these effects are significant for the successful resolution of the problems of everyday life.

A more obvious method to measure the impact of product use in humans exists through the techniques of experimental cognitive psychology (Broadbent, 1971). This argues that any effects on the central nervous system can be judged ultimately by the changes they produce in human behaviour (i.e. changes to sensory thresholds, cognitive function, mood, sleep patterns), as assessed by empirical rating and measurement systems. In addition to being an objective means of assessing the operation of the central nervous system, the investigation of human behaviour is important because a breakdown in the integrity of the psychological processes underlying integrated normal functioning can have serious consequences through a general impairment of life skills and an increased risk of accident. Conversely, any facilitation of these processes may have therapeutic value and improve quality of life.

STRESSOR AND PERFORMANCE

High stress levels are known to disrupt the efficiency of information processing in the central nervous system, and this is reflected in poorer scores on a variety of indices of human performance (Hancock and Caird, 1993; Rose and Fogg, 1993). However, low stress levels have also been associated with poor performance (Matthews, Davies and Holley, 1993), suggesting that the relationship is most easily described by an inverted U-shaped function, with optimum performance at intermediate stress levels. Consequently, the use of pleasure products may impact on the stress response in two ways. In low stress levels, such products may increase arousal in subjects, and in high stress levels they may reduce arousal, both leading to the same result of improved performance. However, it is not certain that all pleasure products have the capacity for such a homeostatic effect.

Two mechanisms may account for these actions. Firstly, product use may divert attention from the problems in hand and allow the user to focus on the factors associated with the social and contextual use of the product. In this model, displacement serves to counter stressors and would explain the highly ritualistic behaviours associated with processes as simple as drinking alcohol or eating food. Secondly, many of these products possess a mild pharmacological profile, which may act directly on the central nervous system (CNS) to induce or reduce CNS arousal, either through a direct action on pleasure pathways or indirectly through improvements to cognitive and psychomotor performance. This may improve performance over that seen at resting levels, to mitigate the effects of fatigue seen after a prolonged period of work or to counter mental overload by focusing attention on the task in hand.

NICOTINE AND PERFORMANCE

Looking solely at the performance effects of nicotine, two recent experiments will serve to show how skilled performance may be affected by the use of social products. In the first, 15 non-abstinent volunteer smoker subjects were asked to operate a simple driving simulator on three occasions, once while smoking their own cigarettes freely, once while chewing a single piece of 2 mg nicotine gum and once without any treatment. From a standardized five-minute baseline measure, both active treatments were found to have facilitated brake reaction times ($p<0.04$) and car steering accuracy ($p<0.01$) compared to the no-treatment condition, but these effects were strongest where subjects had smoked during the trial (Figure 9.1). While the enhancement of performance in the gum condition suggests that nicotine was responsible to a large degree for these effects, the superior performance after smoking suggest that, in addition to the presence of nicotine, the control of delivery offered by the cigarette or sensory qualities such as taste and aroma may be of importance in the effects of smoking on skilled performance.

In a second experiment (Sherwood, 1995), an attempt was made to hold these taste and aroma characteristics constant by asking volunteer smoker subjects to operate the driving simulator on four occasions while smoking single cigarettes which varied by machine weighted nicotine yield but yielded similar levels of tar. Twelve non-abstinent volunteer smoker subjects were asked to operate the simulator on four occasions while smoking single cigarettes yielding <0.1, 0.6, 1.0 or 2.1 mg of nicotine but similar levels (8–10 mg) of tar. Data were again transformed with regard to baseline performance and showed brake reaction times to be improved after all active treatments ($p<0.01$) but tracking accuracy to be improved after the two cigarettes of middle strength alone ($p<0.05$) (Figure 9.2). These results suggest that there may be an optimal dose range for the psychomotor effects of nicotine as delivered from cigarettes over which smokers can operate a degree of personal control. The lack of effect of the 2.1 mg cigarette on steering accuracy suggests a nicotine boost above preferred levels with a consequent loss of performance. This would seem likely in that sub-

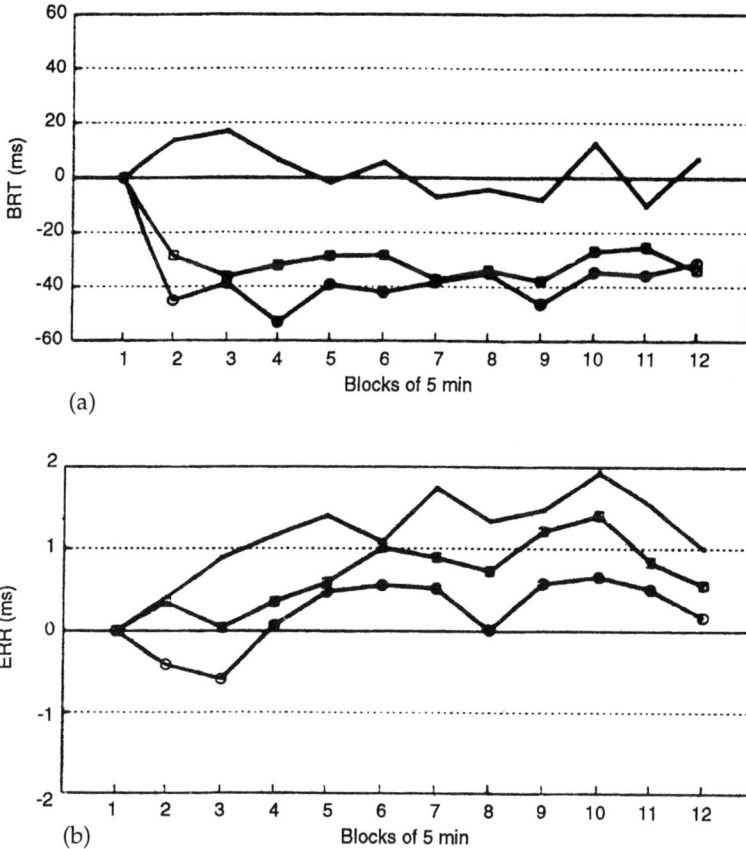

Figure 9.1.   *(a) Mean brake reaction times and (b) tracking error scores after (———) no smoking, (○) free smoking and (□) 2 mg nicotine gum.* p<0.05 *for free smoking and gum, compared to no smoking*

jects were non-abstinent at the start of the session and would already have raised systemic levels of nicotine.

These studies suggest that the mild pharmacological properties of nicotine may, combined with the opportunity of personal control offered by cigarette smoking, assist smokers to deal with the negative impact of stressors. As a practical example of this, Dye, Sherwood and Kerr (1990) found that the variability in CNS arousal across the menstrual cycle, as measured by the critical

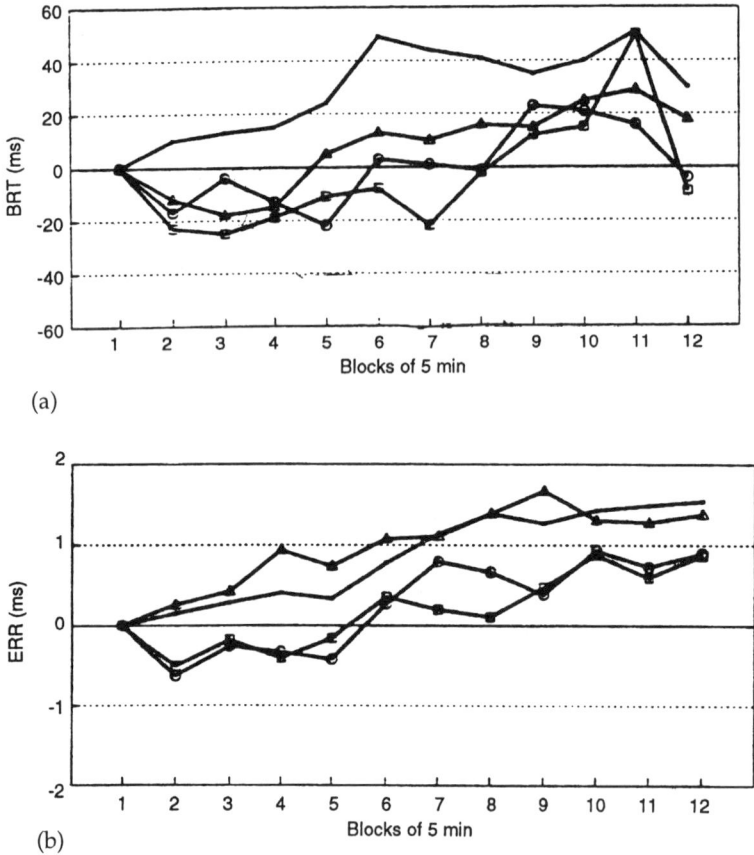

Figure 9.2.   *(a) Mean brake reaction times and (b) tracking error scores after cigarettes yielding (——) <0.1, (O) 0.6, (□) 1 and (Δ) 2.1 mg nicotine. p<0.05 for 0.6, 1.0 and 2.1 mg nicotine, compared to 0.1 mg*

flicker fusion (CFF) threshold, accurately correlated with reported psychological symptoms of activation and distress. However, these effects were not found among those women who smoked more than 15 cigarettes a day, who showed lower overall thresholds and no pre- or post-menstrual rise in CFF scores.

Taken together, the results of these experiments suggest that in addition to the total load of nicotine, the sensory qualities of smoking and the control of nicotine delivery are important factors in mediating the psychomotor effects of nicotine. Smoking allows the smoker to vary puff frequency, depth of inhalation and degree of smoke dilation (Henningfield, 1984). Increases in venous blood nicotine levels after one cigarette may range from 5 to 30 ng ml^{-1} (Armitage *et al.*, 1975). The end result is that smokers can achieve the desired psychopharmacological effect through some alterations to their smoking pattern. In this respect, personal control in tobacco smoking is one route to pleasure and psychological satisfaction. Curiously, it has often been exactly this aspect of product use that scientific investigations have chosen to avoid in their strenuous efforts to standardize treatment parameters to meet the requirement of experimental control. Future studies of all social products need to examine individual preferences, which may be core factors in their use.

CONCLUSIONS

One important aspect of quality of life is the ability to cope, to function normally with full integration of the psychological processes underlying skilled behaviour. In this respect, coffee, tea, chocolate and tobacco are fully compatible with the demands of everyday life in that these psychological processes are not compromised. Further to this, the evidence presented here suggests that some aspects of psychomotor performance may even be enhanced by these products, allowing the individual to benefit from improved behavioural functioning and to counter the negative effects of stressors. This is particularly the case when people have been allowed personal control over the administration of these products.

In the examples shown, it appears that smokers may be able to manipulate nicotine intake and other parameters of smoking to control and optimize their performance. If this hypothesis is supported, it could follow that the use of social products has a role in modulating mood and assisting in the amelioration of acute psychological illness (anxiety, depression, menstrual distress), protecting against chronic psychological illness among the elderly, such as Parkinson's disease and dementia, reducing the use of drugs with known negative consequences such as cocaine or the opiates, and helping to regulate the sleep/wake cycle. For the individual this may mean better psychological function and improved quality of life; for society, the amount of treatment for, and consequences of, disturbed psychological health may be substantially reduced.

To construct a model of how personal control of such products may operate in the real world, one need only consider the lorry driver who eats a chocolate bar to offset the effects of fatigue in motorway driving, or the student who drinks coffee to enable studying late into the night or the stressed office worker who smokes to focus attention on the task in hand and then again afterwards to relax from the pressures of work. Products that improve psychological functions such as vigilance and memory also have an added benefit in that for society productivity is increased and the risk of accident is reduced. Experimental strategies to investigate these hypotheses are required to further our understanding of product use as an important aspect of human behaviour, and pleasure as an essential response to the problems of everyday life.

10

Caffeine and Information Processing

Jan Snel and Monicque M. Lorist

Faculty of Psychology, Department of Psychonomics, University of
Amsterdam, Roetersstraat 15, 1018 WB Amsterdam, The Netherlands

INTRODUCTION

Coffee drinking is a worldwide, socially accepted custom. However, the reasons why people drink coffee are, surprisingly, not
exactly known. One reason may be that caffeine is stimulating,
especially during sub-optimal conditions such as fatigue, monot-
ony, and diminished alertness or concentration. A recent review
(Van der Stelt and Snel, 1993) concluded that coffee seems to have
its most stimulating effect during conditions of under-arousal. The
findings that formed the basis of this conclusion focus, in particular, on studies that have measured task performance, reaction time
and subjects' reports of their mood and perceived exertion. Although it appears from such studies that caffeine improves task
performance, it is impossible to determine from test scores alone
which specific element of the information processing chain underlying the improved task performance is influenced by caffeine. In
other words, it would be interesting to know on which specific
aspects of cognitive function caffeine exerts its effect.

Aspects or stages of information processes involved in performing tasks concern stimulus encoding, stimulus evaluation, central
processes (such as memory search and focusing of attention) and
those processes that deal with generating responses (like taking

Pleasure and Quality of Life. Edited by D.M. Warburton and N. Sherwood
© 1996 John Wiley & Sons Ltd.

the decision whether or not to respond, response selection and preparation, response related motor processes and performing the actual motor response itself). To answer the question as to whether caffeine has non-specific or specific effects on stages of information processing, we conducted a series of studies using the additive factors method (Sanders, 1983; Sternberg, 1969). With this method, specific task variables are manipulated systematically in such a way that it becomes possible to ascertain whether a substance, such as caffeine, has its efficacy on specific stages of information processing.

CAFFEINE AND VISUAL PERCEPTION

Our studies had two objectives: firstly, to investigate whether caffeine affects specific and/or non-specific cognitive functions and, secondly, to determine whether these effects are dependent on the state of the subject. The general experimental procedure involved a cross-over design in which an amount of caffeine equal to the caffeine content of about two cups of strong coffee was taken by moderate, non-smoking regular coffee drinkers (students) who drank between two and seven cups of coffee a day and were around 23 years of age. Task variables such as stimulus quality (intact versus degraded stimuli), stimulus–response (in)compatibility and time-(un)certainty were manipulated in a systematic way in order to discern their specific role in effects of caffeine. The male and female subjects received 3 mg anhydrous caffeine per kilogram of body weight or placebo mixed into a cup of decaffeinated coffee. Administration of the caffeine was double-blind.

The experiments took place in a dimly lit room, in which visual stimuli were presented on a screen. After a practice session, in the experimental sessions, after a 12-hour period of abstinence from caffeine-containing beverages, the task of the subjects was to react as quickly and as accurately as possible to the stimuli in a specific way. During task performance electroencephalographic (EEG) recordings were made from Fz (frontal), Cz (central), Pz (parietal) and Oz (occipital) scalp locations. The experimental procedure is outlined in Figure 10.1.

```
Arrival of subjects                      —|  0   min
Sleep quality, anxiety                   —|  5
    saliva, blood pressure
                                         —|  20  3 mg kg⁻¹ caffeine
Electrodes on
    Saliva, mood, blood pressure         —|  50 - 60
pause
                                            70
    Tasks
                                            150
Pause
                          Mood           —|  155
                    EEG at rest
                                            160
    Tasks
                                            190
Electrodes off
Saliva, blood pressure                   —|  210
        anxiety, mood, symbol            —|  225
```

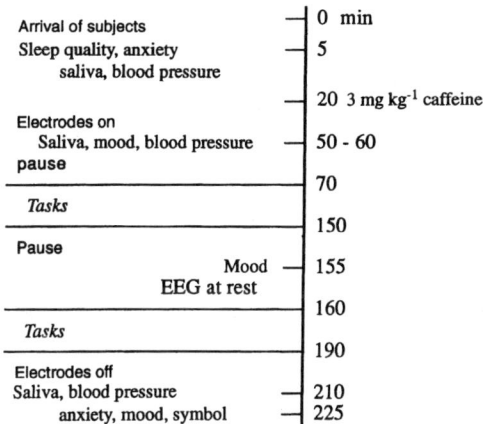

Figure 10.1   *Outline of experimental procedure*

The additive factors method suggests that sub-optimal conditions, i.e. lack of sleep or stimulus degradation, have effects on arousal and activation and therefore on the corresponding stages of information processing. This was tested in a study by Lorist, Snel and Kok (1994), in which the task variable 'stimulus quality' was manipulated. Subjects were asked to react to intact or degraded stimuli (digits) that were presented randomly on the left or the right of the computer screen. The instruction for the compatible stimulus–response condition was to respond with the hand ipsilaterally to the location of the stimulus, whereas in the incompatible condition the response had to be given with the hand contralaterally to the stimulus location. In the time-(un)certainty condition the inter-stimulus intervals were either fixed or variable. Their relationship to the additive factors method is shown in Figure 10.2.

The results showed that caffeine shortened reaction time and decreased the number of errors. The quicker responding was interactive with stimulus-degradation and variable inter-stimulus intervals. In the event-related potentials (ERPs) of the EEG the stimulating effects of caffeine were revealed as an amplitude-increase of the early N_1 component and the P_3, which are said to represent perceptual processing of the physical characteristics of

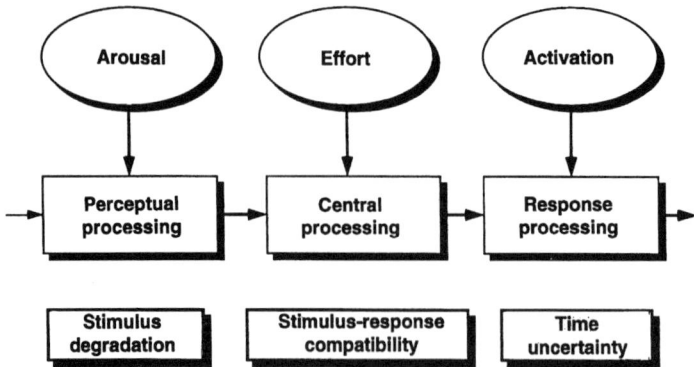

Figure 10.2   *Simplified version of Sanders' cognitive–energetical model*

stimuli and stimulus evaluation, respectively. The main conclusion was that caffeine affects perceptual and response stages of information processing, but not the central processing of information. Of interest, even if the subjects were kept awake until three o'clock in the morning, it was discovered that the beneficial effects of caffeine were found in both well-rested and fatigued subjects, suggesting that caffeine can do more than compensate performance impairment due to fatigue.

More recently, the question as to whether effects of caffeine can be related to specific cognitive functions was answered by using a selective attention task (Lorist *et al.*, 1994). The subjects' task was to react to a target by pushing a button, and to ignore other stimuli. A target was a stimulus that belonged to a memory set of two or four letters and that appeared on the correct diagonal of the screen. Again, ERPs were used to provide information on the time course of specific information processing functions and/or the extent to which these functions are activated or 'utilized'.

With caffeine, the subjects were faster and more accurate, whereas the ERP data showed larger early N_1 components and a larger negative difference wave (Nd) at first at the central parietal site of the scalp. The difference wave (Nd) of irrelevant and relevant non-targets is called selection negativity. The interpretation of the findings was that selection of relevant information is more adequate with caffeine, but also that caffeine had a striking effect on the ERPs of the irrelevant stimuli, independently of memory load, stimulus category or state. This effect prevailed over the centro-posterior area. Caffeine counteracted fatigue-induced effects, especially at the central and parietal sites.

In summary, we found two consistent, positive effects of caffeine on the input side of information processing. Firstly, caffeine exerts its effect on the processing of the physical features of stimuli, in particular. Secondly, caffeine improves selective attention by facilitation of perceptual processing of relevant information, while at the same time it promotes better disregarding of irrelevant information. In other words, caffeine appeared to improve the signal-to-noise ratio.

CAFFEINE AND OTHER SENSORY MODALITIES

An interesting question is whether the beneficial effect of caffeine on visual information processing is reflected in other sensory modalities. This question can be addressed by several experimental paradigms. The usual way is to let subjects consume caffeine and study the effects of the systemic presence of caffeine on sensory systems. Another way is to administer caffeine directly on a specific sense organ and to study whether information processing in this sensory system is changed, directly or indirectly. A third way concerns the possibility of conditioning to the social context in which coffee is consumed. To study conditioned responses to caffeine, it is necessary to see whether the presence of coffee alone might induce changes in information processing. Investigations into the sensory effects of caffeine have employed all three approaches.

Vision: Luminance

In the 1970s, Diamond and Cole (1979) showed that taking a 90 mg or 180 mg dose of caffeine lowered (improved) the visual luminance threshold (measured as the amount of light emitted from a surface in a given direction) by 20% or 38%, respectively. In a follow-up study using 380 mg caffeine, Diamond and Smith (1974) confirmed this result. The drop in detection threshold was maintained for the whole 80-minute test session. Caffeine also counteracted the decrement in sensitivity that was found during the latter part of the placebo session.

Vision: Colour Discrimination

In 1974, Lyle observed that an excess of caffeine caused flashing lights, flickering scintillating obscurations of parts of the visual field (scotomas). Caffeine improved colour recognition of blue and red, stimulated the perception of long wavelengths (red, 670 nm) but depressed the perception of shorter wavelengths (violet, 420 nm). Böhme and Böhme (1985) studied colour discrimination in young men and women with the Farnsworth–Munsell 100-hue test (FMT). In this test, the subject's task is to place 22 disordered hues in consecutive colour order. The two doses of 100 mg and 200 mg caffeine induced a higher colour discrimination ability in both men and women in the red (670 nm) to yellow hues (550 nm) and, for women only, an improved colour discrimination of blue–green (530 nm) to blue (490 nm) hues. Fine and McCord (1991) studied 43 female students who were low caffeine users (0–7 caffeinated beverages a week) or high caffeine users (>7 caffeinated beverages a week). They found that the high caffeine group had 57% fewer errors in all sectors of the colour discrimination test than the low caffeine group. In a study by Kohen, Zrenner and Schneider (1986) six male subjects (18–39 years) received 7.5 mg caffeine per kilogram of body weight (a rather high dose), followed by a maintenance dose of 3.75 mg per kilogram of body weight 2–3 hours after the initial dose. Although caffeine did not influence significantly the colour discrimination ability, the mean error score decreased by 23% from 35 to 27.

Touch or Tactual Mode

The effects of caffeine on the sense of touch were studied by Gupta and co-workers (see Gupta and Gupta, 1990) in high and low impulsive male students with placebo or caffeine doses of 1, 2, 3 or 4 mg per kilogram of body weight. After blindfolding, the subjects were presented a 4.0 cm wide test block in one hand and an adjustable comparison block in the other hand. The comparison

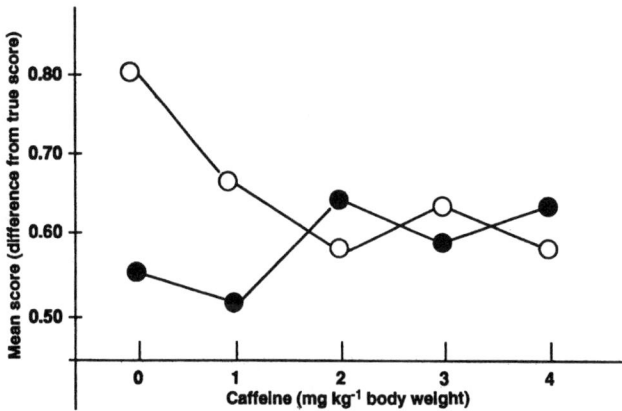

Figure 10.3 *The effects of caffeine on the sense of touch in (○) high impulsives and (●) low impulsives. Source: Gupta and Gupta (1990)*

block could be adjusted by the experimenter in units of 1 mm. The task was to report whether the adjustable block had the same felt size as the test block, while feeling with the thumb and index finger. Scores, among others, included the absolute difference between post- and pre-induction judgements (Figure 10.3).

As expected, caffeine substantially reduced this so-called kinaesthetic after effect (KAE) in high impulsive subjects. In low impulsive subjects, the larger the dose of caffeine, the more the KAE was enhanced. Caffeine led to different dose–response trends in high and low impulsives. In view of the finding that smaller doses of 75–150 mg caffeine did not influence the performance of low impulsives, it was concluded that low impulsives probably work near their optimal level. The considerable increase in the level of arousal of low impulsives produced by higher doses of caffeine (225–300 mg) affected their performance in an inverted U fashion, leading to poor width judgements and thus to an increase in KAE. The performance of low impulsives, however, was much less affected by the drug conditions than that of high impulsive subjects. The simple dose effects indicated that 76.1% variation in the main effect of treatment and the interaction was due to the effects of caffeine on high impulsives, whereas only 23.9% explained variance was due to drug effect in low impulsives.

A greater stability of performance was predicted in introverts by Eysenck (1982). Introverts probably possess a stronger tendency to use the CNS more extensively and in this way attempt to compensate for the adverse effects of supra-optimal or sub-optimal arousal. In general, the results obtained on KAE suggest that low impulsive subjects (who may be introverts) are more stable to psychopharmacological variations caused by caffeine, which is consistent with findings on studies related to cognitive performance. In their replication study, Gupta, Dubey and Gupta (1994) found that in high and low impulsive students (aged 19–24), a caffeine dose of 1, 2, 3 and 4 mg per kilogram of body weight decreased the error in perceptual judgement among high impulsives. Caffeine explained 70.4% of variance for the high impulsive subjects, but had no main effect in low impulsives (29.6% explained variance).

Described in terms of the well-known inverted U-shaped relationship between arousal and performance, less impulsive (presumably highly aroused) persons may be considered to be closer to the optimal level of performance, but are relatively more resistant to the effects of caffeine on their physiological state than high impulsives. Eysenck and Eysenck (1985) proposed a pair of inverted U functions. Introverts experience a positive hedonic tone to stimulation at lower intensities than extroverts; correspondingly, a negative hedonic tone (e.g. pain) appears at a correspondingly lower intensity. If caffeine enhances arousal, then it would shift these curves to the right so that lower levels of stimulation might be perceived as unpleasant. Extroverts experience a positive hedonic tone to stimulation at higher intensities (inverted U shifted to the right), and negative hedonic tone appears at a correspondingly higher level.

Nociception or Pain Perception

Whether caffeine affects the sensitivity to touch was checked by Haier and co-workers using the perception of pain (Haier *et al.*, 1991). Thirty healthy men (18–45 years) received the analgesic drug flurbiprofen (50 mg) with or without 100 mg of caffeine. The subjects had to report their reaction to electric shocks as pain stimuli on four categories after four periods of half an hour. The shocks were a 1–31 mA biphasic pulse lasting for 1 ms on the dorsal side of the left arm, 15 cm above the wrist. The statistical analyses showed, as expected, an analgesic effect of flurbiprofen, but no greater or faster effect for this drug combined with caffeine when all subjects as a group were taken. However, of relevance to the aims of the study, the importance of arousal on pain perception was illustrated by the finding that caffeine increased the analgesic effect of the drug in introverts for the lower intensities of felt pain, while in extroverts drug analgesia increased only with higher intensities of felt pain. These findings suggest that introverts who take analgesics in combination with caffeine may even experience potentiation of pain stimulation. In other words, the higher arousal induced by caffeine may cause in introverts greater sensitivity to negative stimuli.

It also suggests that subjects who are seen as more introverted are less likely to seek sensation, are more pain sensitive and will attempt to reduce incoming stimulation.

There are relatively few studies concerning the effects of caffeine alone on pain behaviour in humans. Of interest, however, are those studies in which caffeine is used as an analgesic adjuvant in humans. From a thorough and detailed review by Sawynok and Yaksh (1993) of postpartum pain, post-surgical pain (dental extraction) and headache, it appeared that caffeine potentiated the pain relief by anti-pain drugs from odds ratios 1.29 to 1.92 for acetaminophen, from 1.55 to 1.58 for acetaminophen and aspirin combinations and from 1.0 to 2.9 for ibuprofen (Figure 10.4).

In a study on pain resulting from dental extraction (Forbes *et al.*, 1990), 64 mg of caffeine could not alleviate the pain. However, Ward *et al.* (1991) observed that 130 mg of caffeine, but not 65 mg of caffeine, could alleviate non-migraine headaches compared to placebo. In a meta-analytical study, Laska *et al.* (1984) reviewed 30 studies on pain. Based on these independent investigations, potency estimates in postpartum, headache and dental pain states indicated that the addition of caffeine, in particular in the range from 65 to 200 mg, resulted in a clear increase in the activity of anti-nociceptive or anti-pain drugs (NSAIDs; non-steroidal anti-inflammatory drugs). Anti-pain drugs/caffeine combinations have been widely examined in a wide variety of pain states. The

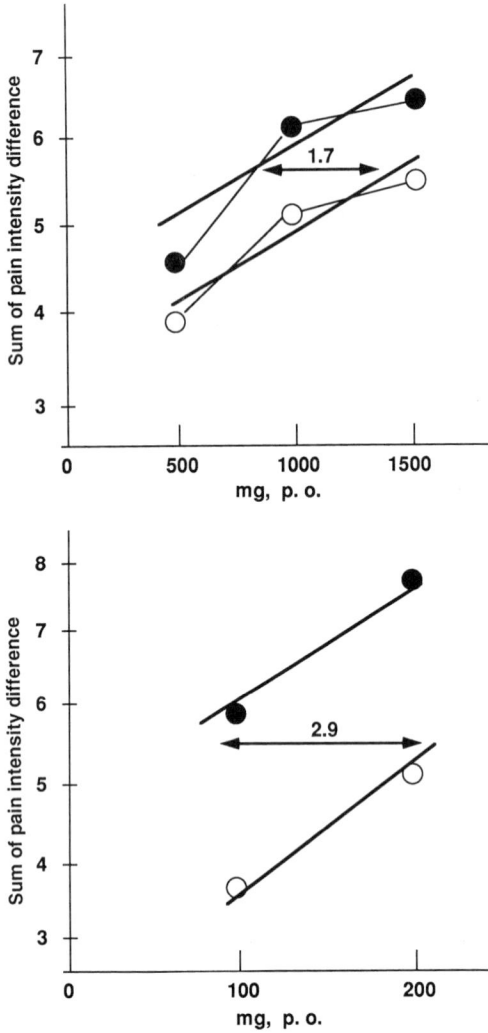

Figure 10.4.   *Use of caffeine as an analgesic adjuvant. (a) (○) Acetaminophen, (●) acetaminophen + caffeine; (b) (○) ibuprofen, (●) ibuprofen + caffeine. Source: Sawynok and Yaksh (1993)*

importance of such combinations reflects the fact that different pain states can, to different degrees, be mediated by different mechanisms that may be caffeine-sensitive, e.g. vasomotor tone, inflammation or acute tissue mechanical distortion.

The prominent role of caffeine with more intense pain may reflect the involvement of specific neural mechanisms, which not only initiate or facilitate the pain message, but are also directly sensitive to caffeine. Although there are relatively few data to define the anti-pain effects of caffeine alone in various human pain states, several studies have shown that caffeine may exert at least a modest anti-nociceptive effect of its own. The underlying mechanisms involved and which specific role they may play are relatively speculative. It is known that during inflammatory conditions adenosine is produced endogenously at peripheral nerve endings via release of ATP or c-AMP. As known, 5′-nucleotidase, converts 5′-AMP to adenosine. Caffeine is known not only to occupy adenosine receptors, but also to inhibit 5′-nucleotidase, which converts 5′-AMP to adenosine. In these ways caffeine could then prevent activation of the nerve ending by adenosine to signal pain.

In addition, although it has been recognized that changes in affective state can alter the response to pain, it remains difficult to translate this into specific insights. The ability of caffeine to produce subtle but discriminable changes in affect and mood may focus the attention of investigators on the way in which drug-induced changes in the affective state can effectively ameliorate a debilitating psychological component of the pain state. Whether this influence on mood rests on the 'stimulant' properties of caffeine or represents a distinct effect remains to be studied.

Auditory Stimuli

After adaptation to the experimental situation and procedure (Bonnet, Webb and Barnard, 1979), six healthy men, aged 21–23, received one 400 mg dose of caffeine or placebo (twice) on nonconsecutive nights. On each night the subjects were aroused five to eight times with an ascending series of 1000 Hz tones from standard segments of stage two sleep. Arousal threshold (tone-evoked response in the EEG) and awake threshold (pushing a button) were decreased by caffeine. In addition, the arousal threshold appeared to be modified in a time-dependent fashion such that extreme effects were found during the first half of the night. However, the awakening threshold was lowered by caffeine throughout the whole sleep period.

Auditory and the Visual Sense Combined

Selective attention was studied by Tharion *et al.* (1993) in a setting in which both auditory and visual stimuli had to be processed after the administration of a placebo or 200 mg of caffeine. The visual vigilance task, which was the main task, required 18 military men (19–28 years) to detect the appearance of a small, dim rectangular target on a computer screen at randomized time intervals over a two-hour period. The importance of this task was explicitly stressed and they were asked to perform to the best of their ability. The participants were told that during performing the vigilance task, there would be a constant and invariant auditory stimulus; this was the secondary or distracting task. As a result of the instruction to the subjects, it was expected that the focus of attention would be on the vigilance task only. Auditory evoked potentials (ERPs) obtained during the performance of the visual vigilance task were examined for changes in response to caffeine (200 mg). The significant increases in the N_1 and P_2 latencies and decreases in amplitude voltage by caffeine were shown over the two hours of the experimental session and can be interpreted as showing that caffeine helped subjects to ignore the distracting auditory stimulation (Figure 10.5).

These changes in latency and amplitude support the conclusion of Lorist *et al.* (1994) that caffeine apparently is able to help subjects to focus attention on the primary task, containing the relevant information, and to ignore the distracting stimulus, that is the irrelevant information. Summarizing the data on effects of caffeine on the auditory sense alone, it seems that caffeine may indeed affect the processing of auditory stimuli.

Taste Effects of Caffeine

The responsiveness of an organism to sensory stimuli is modified by the internal state. To illustrate this, a well-known experience is

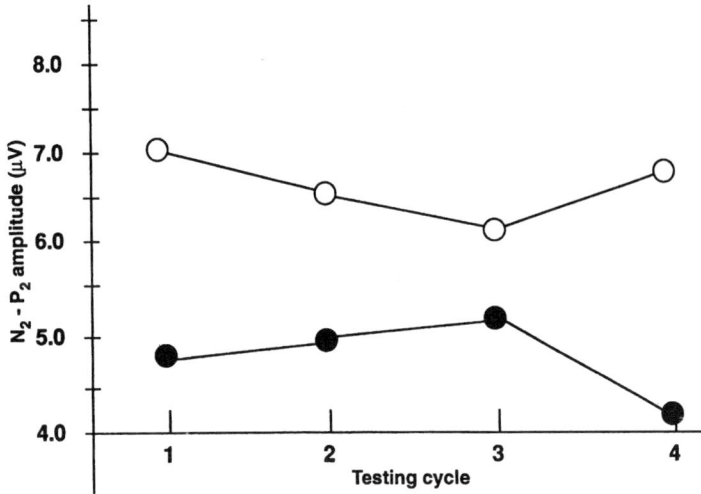

Figure 10.5.   *Results of selective attention experiment: (O) placebo, (●) caffeine. Source: Tharion et al. (1993)*

that hunger or food deprivation selectively enhances pleasantness ratings of the taste of nutritive stimuli, without affecting hedonic ratings of non-nutritive stimuli. Moreover, the increased ratings of the pleasantness of such stimuli occur without changes in ratings of intensity or quality of such stimuli. To give an example, Brauer, Buican and de Wit (1994) refer to a study done by Cabanac in 1979, in which subjects rated temperature-related stimuli as more pleasant when the subjects were cold, yet changes in ratings of intensity or quality were unchanged.

   Reasoned similarly, if the internal state is influenced by a psychoactive drug such as caffeine this may contribute to subjective responses to sensory stimuli. Thus, deprivation of caffeine could result in increased hedonic ratings of those stimuli that have been repeatedly associated with its effects, such as the taste or smell of coffee. Expectations are: (i) that ratings of the pleasantness of coffee taste would be expected to be higher following caffeine deprivation and lower following caffeine administration, (ii) that such changes should be selective to tastes associated with caffeine consumption but not to other tastes, and (iii) that such changes should also be selective to ratings of the hedonic value, to the exclusion of ratings of quality or intensity.

In contrast to these expectations, Schiffman and colleagues (1985, 1986) found that caffeine presented on the tongue produced increases in ratings of taste intensity, with the largest increases in ratings of other bitter tastes and sweet tastes with bitter components. The explanation that the authors suggest is that methylxanthines potentiate tastes by competing with adenosine for receptor occupancy via a local mechanism at the level of the taste receptors in the tongue. In the study of Brauer, Buican and de Wit (1994), 12 regular coffee drinkers took 300 mg caffeine or placebo after caffeine deprivation or non-deprivation. Unexpectedly, the pleasantness of the coffee taste was not affected by caffeine deprivation. However, following caffeine intake the ratings of the bitterness and sweetness of the coffee taste and ratings of a sucrose solution were altered. These ratings were highest when subjects received caffeine on day 1 and placebo on day 2, and lowest when they received caffeine on both days. Caffeine administration on day 1 increased ratings of bitterness/sweetness on the next day, compared with when the subjects received placebo on day 1. Ratings of other tastes, such as quinine and saccharin, were not influenced by the presence or absence of caffeine.

The important difference between the two studies is that in the study of Brauer, Buican and de Wit, caffeine was administered systemically, that is taken up in the body by swallowing gelatine capsules. In the studies of Schiffman and colleagues, caffeine and other taste stimuli were placed directly on the tongue. Studies done by Mela and co-workers (Mela, 1989; Mela *et al.*, 1992) using ingestion of caffeine as the method of administration also failed to demonstrate an effect on taste thresholds. Thus, caffeine may affect taste only when it acts directly on peripheral taste receptors. Although it seems that systemic administration of caffeine does not affect taste ratings, further studies should determine this relationship at varying time points in an effort to assess the issue of time course directly. Also, future studies should evaluate the relationship between blood levels of caffeine and its effect on taste (i.e. pharmacokinetics) and possibly on other senses as well. Since taste does play a role in caffeine self-administration, it seems likely that factors altering the taste of coffee would also alter rates and patterns of self-administration. At this moment, it is difficult to ascertain whether changes in hedonic ratings of coffee taste underlie to some extent increased self-administration, but this relationship is plausible.

Coffee Odour

Laing and Clark (1983) studied olfactory preferences for 10 odourants in 302 young male subjects. The subjects were aware of the supraliminally present odours. A striking change was found from dislike to like for coffee odour from 8 to 16 years of age. This change in coffee liking was the greatest as compared with the change in liking of nine other odourants. No indications were found for the factors that determined this change in liking of coffee. Although studies of adult liking for coffee indicate contextual factors and psychopharmacological effects of caffeine as possible determinants (Cines and Rozin, 1982), no clear explanation exists for the general dislike of coffee by children and the liking by adults. The change in liking of coffee occurs within a narrow age range, which may form a starting point for a study of the physiological and behavioural factors that affect the preferences for a substance appreciated so much throughout the world.

Whether the presence of a liked odour, such as coffee smell, might have effects other than just a change in the extent of liking was studied by Kole, Snel and Lorist (1996) in 11 students, aged 18–25 years. The aim was to investigate whether the presence of a supraliminal olfactory stimulus could influence cognitive task performance and brain activity. Although the smell of coffee was present continuously and supraliminally during the experimental sessions, the subjects were not explicitly made aware of its presence. The experimental stimuli consisted of intact or degraded digits to which the subjects were asked to respond by pushing a button corresponding to the digit, which was displayed on a screen. The presence of coffee odour affected neither reaction time nor the number of errors. However, effects of coffee odour did show up as increased amplitudes of the early ERP components, in particular those between 140 and 180 ms after stimulus onset on parietal, frontal and central scalp sites. There was a robust effect of odour on the P_1 component, independent of 'stimulus quality' (degraded or intact). Together with some shortening of the early ERP latencies, the results suggest that coffee odour induced an earlier and more intense perception of the administered visual stimuli. This energizing effect of coffee odour might be called an arousal effect, in the sense of addressing an energetic mechanism, necessarily involved in the processing of information. Although this study has methodological imperfections and for this reason needs to be replicated, the tentative conclusion is that coffee odour might be beneficial for the perceptual part of visual information processing.

DISCUSSION AND MAIN CONCLUSIONS

Our aim was to investigate whether caffeine—or, more broadly speaking, coffee drinking—could have a stimulating effect on information processing, in particular on perception. The present conclusion is that, indeed, caffeine or coffee seems to have a beneficial effect on perceptual activities. In other words, caffeine apparently lowers the perceptual threshold and by that is beneficial for the processing of information.

However, this conclusion needs some comment. If the sensitivity of sensory systems is influenced by caffeine, one may wonder whether the various sensory systems are differentially affected by caffeine. Theoretical models (e.g. Yingling and Skinner, 1977) say that the thalamus, known as the sensory relay of the CNS, receives its information from the mesencephalic brain arousal system and serves a gating function to the neocortex. If this is true, it should mean that the supposedly lowering effect of caffeine on perceptual threshold must be located in the thalamus, and that its gating function is therefore non-specifically influenced and hence will affect all sensory systems.

On the other hand, the associated effects of caffeine on central mechanisms could mediate the quality specificity of the effects, since caffeine may differentially affect fibres of different diameters and sensory function, impinge on different sensory receptor cell characteristics, such as size, number and distribution, or differ due to the complexity of the addressed neural networks and their quantity or quality of neurotransmitters. Further studies will be necessary to verify these hypotheses.

Although most studies on caffeine have been conducted among young adult subjects, several studies suggest that some senses, especially the olfactory system, show large age-related losses in sensitivity. For example, when presented with coffee-related stimuli, such as coffee odour, young subjects will perceive greater intensities of these stimuli than elderly subjects (Swift and Tiplady, 1988). Thus, given specific stimuli, perceived stimulus intensity levels will be different for young and old subjects. This implies that the context for any given stimulus will be different for young and old, and consequently scores on dependent variables under study will be affected by these age-related differences in context.

Many authors prefer to discuss the effects of caffeine on arousal in terms of the Yerkes–Dodson law, or the inverted U model of arousal. A theoretical problem is the different quality of physiological arousal as a trait variable and the caffeine-induced arousal, which can be seen as a state variable. So, when a state–trait interaction is reported it becomes particularly difficult to adhere to the use of arousal as an intervening variable and a unitary concept. Therefore, one could say that it is not arousal, but rather a complex pattern of activation that determines changes in performance in different physiological states. For instance, based on the work of Pribram and McGuinness (1975), Sanders (1983) distinguished computational or processing structures, involving specific transformations of information, while energetical mechanisms provide non-specific input to these processing structures. Pribram and McGuinness (1975) had already linked stages of information processing to their presumed neurophysiological substrates located in specific brain structures. Since the thalamus apparently plays a prominent role in the processing of sensory information, as does caffeine, studies aimed at assessing the effect of caffeine on many sensory systems at the same time in one study, rather than studying one sensory system at a time, should be preferred.

The summarizing conclusion from the presented experimental evidence suggests that caffeine taken in moderate amounts exerts a beneficial effect on the input side of information processing; that is, on perceptual processes. Keeping this conclusion in mind and considering the positive effect of caffeine on lowering sensitivity to pain, it may mean that caffeine has the potential to optimize processing of sensory information and in this way may form a major contribution to the enjoyment of life.

11

Food, Drink and Mental Performance

Andrew Smith

Health Psychology Research Unit, University of Bristol,
Bristol BS8 1TN, UK

INTRODUCTION

There is now considerable evidence that what we eat and drink can influence our mental functioning. This chapter reviews several areas illustrating this point. The first two sections describe research on the effects of meals, focusing mainly on lunch and breakfast. This is followed by data on the beneficial effects of caffeine in low arousal situations, such as working at night, following prolonged work and after lunch. In real life, we consume a combination of products, and the third area covered is the combined effects of lunch, caffeine and alcohol. As well as considering meals and drinks, it is essential to examine the behavioural effects of factors that we add to influence palatability, such as sugar. Indeed, even the small amount of sugar that we add to a cup of coffee can be shown to influence our mental functioning. All of the above areas have largely involved studies of the acute effects of food and drink. It is essential to consider longer term effects of these and to examine how they interact with factors such as how stressed the person is. The final section provides

Pleasure and Quality of Life. Edited by D.M. Warburton and N. Sherwood
© 1996 John Wiley & Sons Ltd.

an example of this approach by considering the effects of regular levels of alcohol consumption and stress.

EFFECTS OF LUNCH ON MOOD AND MENTAL PERFORMANCE

The aim of the early part of this chapter is to review recent research on the effects of meals on mood and mental performance (a more exhaustive review is given in Smith and Kendrick, 1992). This section considers the effects of lunch, the most widely studied meal, and it is followed by shorter accounts of breakfast and evening meals. Most of the research discussed here has involved laboratory studies of the short-term effects of single meals. It is clearly desirable to extend the research to consider the longer term effects of eating patterns on real-life behaviour. Such research will be expensive and time consuming but it is argued that the information obtained to date makes such an endeavour worth while.

Research both in the laboratory and in real-life settings provides evidence for a 'post-lunch dip' in alertness and sustained attention. Until recently, it was unclear whether this reflected effects of the meal, circadian variation in mood and performance, or both. A number of recent studies have compared performance and mood in the early afternoon of individuals who have either had lunch or abstained from eating. Craig, Baer and Diekmann (1981) examined perceptual discrimination and found clear differences between the lunch and no-lunch conditions, with those subjects who had eaten lunch showing an impairment in their ability to discriminate between successive signals. Smith and Miles (1986a, b, 1987) compared early afternoon vigilance performance in subjects who had eaten lunch with those who had not. The results showed that consumption of lunch reduced the ability to sustain attention, as measured by the number of correct detections of targets (hits) in the task.

The nature and the extent of these post-lunch changes depend on the type of task carried out, the characteristics of the person eating the meal, the nature of the meal and the presence/absence of stimulants after the meal. For example, post-lunch impairments are not usually observed with short tasks unless they are part of a larger battery of tests. People who are low in anxiety typically show a smaller post-lunch decrement than anxious subjects, and eating habits may also modify the changes seen after lunch. For example, people who eat a larger than normal meal are often greatly impaired after lunch, whereas the performance of those who eat a smaller meal than usual may actually improve in the early afternoon. The effects of consuming lunch can be largely removed by increasing alertness after the meal, for example, by drinking caffeinated coffee (Smith *et al.*, 1990).

EFFECTS OF BREAKFAST ON PERFORMANCE AND MOOD

Recent research in our laboratory (Smith, Kendrick and Maben, 1992; Smith *et al.*, 1994) has examined the effects of breakfast on mood and performance of a range of tasks assessing different mental functions. A first experiment demonstrated that subjects who had eaten a cooked breakfast felt more contented, interested, sociable and outward-going two hours after the meal compared to those who had eaten a cereal/toast breakfast or had no breakfast. No differences in alertness or the ability to perform sustained attention tasks were found for the various breakfast conditions. A second experiment demonstrated that eating a cooked breakfast improved recall of a list of words, impaired the accuracy of performing a logical reasoning task but had no effect on the speed of retrieving information from general knowledge.

These results confirm that the effects of breakfast on performance and mood are, like lunch, selective in that they are only observed with certain types of task. However, the effects of breakfast differ from those of lunch in that they appear to be restricted to memory tasks. Other differences between the two meals are that the effects of breakfast are not modified by consumption of caffeinated coffee, neither does the anxiety level of the person eating the meal appear to be important in determining the extent of the breakfast effect. A possible mechanism underlying the effects of breakfast on memory has been put forward by Benton and Sargent (1992). They suggest that breakfast increases the supply of glucose to the brain, which fits in well with evidence that memory performance may be enhanced by increasing the availability of glucose.

There is currently little information about the effects of meals eaten at other times of day or about the effects of snacks. Similarly, our knowledge of the longer term effects of diet on behaviour is slight, and this topic must clearly receive more attention in the future. Further information on the mechanisms underlying meal/behaviour relationships must also be obtained. The results of studies conducted to date do suggest that the behavioural changes produced by meals may be of practical importance. It is also possible that the changes in mood induced by food are important in determining the acceptability of products and subsequent food choice. This means that it is important to consider the relationship between food and mental functioning from both directions so that we not only know what effects nutrition has on our behaviour, but can also understand how a person's psychological state may influence food intake.

CAFFEINE, LOW LEVELS OF ALERTNESS, PERFORMANCE AND MOOD

There has been considerable interest in the effects of caffeine on human performance and mood (see Lieberman, 1992, for a review). This research has often shown that caffeine increases alertness and improves attention, which suggests that consumption of coffee should be especially beneficial when a person's arousal is low. Smith *et al.* (1990) have obtained support for this view in an experiment demonstrating that caffeine removes the drop in sustained attention that is observed after lunch. Arousal may be reduced in a number of ways (e.g. by sleep deprivation, illness, etc.) and studies will be reviewed that considered (i) two working practices that lead to a low level of arousal, namely working at night and prolonged work, and (ii) diurnal changes in alertness.

Effects of Caffeine on Performance and Mood over the Day and Night

Our interest in this study lay in whether the effect of caffeine would be constant, or whether it would be much greater when circadian arousal was decreased (at night). From a practical point of view, it was of interest to examine the extent to which caffeine could reduce the night-time decline in alertness and performance. In addition, the experiment was designed to examine whether the effects of caffeine were global or selective (only apparent in certain aspects of performance).

Method

An experimental study of night work was carried out. Each subject was tested in all of the conditions found by combining day/night shifts with different drink conditions. The order of the conditions was counterbalanced across subjects. Each subject attended for day shifts, from 09.00 to 17.30, and night shifts from 22.00 to 06.30. Before the first test session subjects were familiarized with the testing procedure. The subjects were 24 students (12 male, 12 female) who were all regular coffee drinkers. Half of the subjects were tested in the order day/night and the others in the order night/day. In the caffeinated coffee condition the subjects were given decaffeinated coffee with 1.5 or 3 mg of caffeine tablets added per kilogram of body weight. In another condition subjects were given decaffeinated coffee and in the third they were given fruit juice. The order of the three beverage conditions was counterbalanced across the subjects. The caffeine manipulation was double-blind, with neither the experimenter nor the subjects knowing whether they were given caffeinated or decaffeinated coffee. Subjects were given a drink at the start of the shift, after two hours' work, at the mid-shift meal and two hours after the meal. Subjects rated their alertness using a visual analogue scale (after Herbert, Johns and Dore, 1976). Subjects carried out a range of different tasks on a PC. Simple perceptual–motor tasks are usually impaired at night and it was of major interest to determine whether caffeine removed these impairments. The same applied to tasks involving sustained attention and tasks requiring retrieval of information from general knowledge (semantic memory tasks).

Results

In none of the analyses was there a significant effect of order of beverages. Similarly, comparable effects were obtained for both dosages of caffeine so the combined data of the two groups are presented here.

Ratings of Alertness

Alertness was greater following caffeine at all times. Alertness was reduced at night compared to the day, especially at 03.00 and 05.00. However, when the subjects were given caffeinated coffee their alertness at these times was comparable to the day-time alertness levels of those given juice.

Variable Fore-Period Simple Reaction Time Task

Reaction times were slower at night, especially at 03.00 and 05.00. Consumption of caffeinated coffee improved reaction times relative to the other drinks. This improvement was especially large at 03.00, 05.00 and 09.30. Indeed, after caffeinated coffee reaction times at 05.00 were faster than the day-time reaction times for the other groups. Furthermore, at this time caffeinated coffee was associated with responses that were 20% faster than those found after the other beverages.

Five-Choice Serial Response Task

There was a significant effect of time of testing on the number correct, with performance being impaired at 03.00 and 05.00. Significantly more correct responses were made after drinking caffeinated coffee than after the other beverages. Performance declined over the night shift following consumption of juice and decaffeinated coffee but this was not observed after drinking caffeinated coffee. Indeed, the only time when there was little difference between the drinks was at 22.30.

Semantic Processing Test

Speed of retrieval of information from general knowledge showed a similar circadian trend to those observed in the psychomotor tasks, with performance being impaired at 03.00 and 05.00. Following consumption of caffeinated coffee, the speed of performing this test improved. This effect was especially pronounced at night, and the only time that the beneficial effect of caffeine was not observed was at the 09.30 session.

Logical Reasoning Task

There were no significant differences between the drinks conditions for this task, although numerically the caffeine condition was better than the other two. As expected, there was also no indication that performance of this task was impaired at night.

This experiment has demonstrated quite clearly that caffeinated coffee increases alertness and improves performance on a variety of tasks. These effects were observed across both the day and the night, and the caffeinated coffee greatly reduced the night-time decline observed following consumption of the other drinks. In contrast to the effects of the caffeinated coffee, the differences between the decaffeinated coffee and the juice were small and variable. It would appear, therefore, that caffeine may be of great benefit in reducing the acute impairments associated with working at night. Further research is now required to examine whether it can remove some of the longer term effects, and whether it is also beneficial in other low arousal situations.

The next experiment examined the effects of caffeine on the mood and performance of individuals whose alertness had been reduced by prolonged work.

Caffeine and Prolonged Work

The main aim of the next study was to examine the effects of caffeine on impairments in performance and changes in mood induced by prolonged work (see Craig and Cooper, 1992, for a review of the effects of fatigue on performance). This paradigm has great potential for examining positive effects on performance and mood, for it is possible to see how much recovery is produced by the experimental manipulation. The literature on caffeine suggests that it has selective effects on performance and mood, with some functions being more sensitive than others. This study examined performance of a range of tasks to determine whether these would show similar impairments over a 12-hour period and whether caffeine would produce different levels of recovery in the different tasks.

Method

Each subject carried out three 12.5-hour sessions (from 09.00 to 21.30), with a rest day between each. The first eight hours of each day were constant with regard to beverages consumed, with all subjects being given fruit juice at the breaks. On one of the days subjects were given caffeinated coffee at the end of 8.5 hours, with further caffeinated coffee after 10.5 hours. On the other days subjects were given decaffeinated coffee or fruit juice instead of caffeinated coffee. The order of the different drinks was counter-balanced across subjects. The schedule for each day and the order of the tests within each session were identical to the previous study. After the first four sessions were completed, the subjects had a drink break where either caffeinated coffee, decaffeinated coffee or juice was given. The subjects then carried out the tests again, had another drink break and then repeated the tests for a sixth and final time. In the caffeine condition 3 mg of caffeine tablets per kilogram of body weight were added to decaffeinated coffee. The caffeine/decaffeinated manipulation was double blind. Twenty-four undergraduate students (12 male, 12 female) took part in the study. They were paid for participating. Prior to the start of the experiment subjects were given a familiarization session, during which they practised the performance tasks. Subjects refrained from drinking alcohol for 12 hours before the start of each session and had no caffeinated drinks prior to the first tests. In between test sessions, subjects remained in the laboratory and were not allowed to smoke or eat snacks.

Results

Mood Scales

Caffeinated coffee had a significant effect on the majority of the mood scales. The general effect can be illustrated by considering the drowsy/alert ratings. The caffeinated coffee greatly increased alertness and this effect was apparent at both sessions 5 and 6.

Variable Fore-Period Simple Reaction Time Task

Again, caffeinated coffee improved speed of reactions. This effect was greatest at session 6 but was apparent at session 5 as well.

Five-Choice Serial Response Task

As in the night work experiment, subjects made more correct responses following the caffeinated coffee. Again, this effect was observed at both sessions 5 and 6.

Semantic Processing Task

In session 5, response times were quickest following the caffeinated coffee. However, this was not seen in session 6 and this resulted in a significant drinks/sessions interaction.

Logical Reasoning Task

After caffeinated coffee, subjects performed the logical reasoning task more accurately. However, the effects of drinks just failed to reach significance. Once again, this result follows the general trend of improvement after caffeinated coffee.

This experiment confirmed that caffeinated coffee has beneficial effects on the performance of a range of tasks. Similarly, alertness increased after this drink. These results confirmed that caffeinated coffee can reduce the low levels of subjective alertness induced by prolonged work, and that it can also remove the performance impairments associated with such situations. This has important implications for operational efficiency and safety, and further research is now required to determine what doses of caffeine are successful in achieving these effects.

The next series of experiments examined whether a low dose of caffeine influenced mood and performance when circadian alertness was reasonably high (late morning) and whether different effects were obtained when alertness was reduced after lunch.

EFFECTS OF LOW DOSES OF CAFFEINE

Results from several of our experiments have shown that it is difficult to demonstrate effects of low doses of caffeine (50–100 mg) on mood or performance when alertness is high. However, it is possible that the slight improvements observed following caffeine may have more impact when arousal is low. This was tested in the next experiment, which examined the effects of a low dose of caffeine in the post-lunch period.

The results showed that prior to starting the performance tests subjects in the caffeine condition felt significantly more alert and energetic. After the tests, those in the caffeine condition felt significantly more alert, stronger, more clear-headed, better coordinated, more energetic, more quick-witted, more proficient and more interested. There were no significant effects of caffeine on the free recall, recognition memory, semantic memory, simple reaction time or repeated digits vigilance tasks. However, those in the caffeine condition made significantly more responses in the five-choice serial response task, and also performed the logical reasoning task more accurately than those in the decaffeinated condition. The effects of caffeine on mood after performing the tests were especially beneficial in the early afternoon testing session. Similarly, the effect of caffeine on the number completed in the five-choice serial response task was greatest at this time, whereas this time of day was associated with the lowest level of performance in the decaffeinated group. These effects of caffeine were apparent on both days when lunch was consumed and when the subjects abstained from eating.

This study clearly demonstrates that low doses of caffeine, similar to those frequently consumed by large numbers of people, have beneficial effects on mood, psychomotor performance and the ability to think logically. However, other aspects of mental functioning were not significantly altered following ingestion of caffeine. This may reflect several things. Firstly, low doses of caffeine may influence these functions but a more powerful design (large number of subjects) is required for such effects to achieve significance. Secondly, certain types of performance may be more sensitive to contextual factors associated with caffeine consumption, such as the regular caffeine usage of the subjects, the time of day of administration and other background conditions. Further research is clearly required to determine the impact of such factors. It is, of course, also possible that low doses of caffeine will not influence certain types of behaviour at all. Such a conclusion, however, is premature until further studies with low doses of caffeine are conducted. The present results showed that the effects of caffeine were especially pronounced in the early afternoon testing session. This confirms previous findings obtained with higher doses of caffeine.

COMBINED EFFECTS OF LUNCH, CAFFEINE AND ALCOHOL

This research is described in detail in Smith, Kendrick and Maben (1992). The main aim of the study was to examine the separate and combined effects of caffeine (4 mg per kilogram of body weight), lunch and alcohol (1 ml per kilogram of body weight) to provide further insight into their modes of action and to allow comparison of the magnitude of the effects of the different factors.

The results revealed two different patterns of effects of alcohol, lunch and caffeine. The subjective mood data showed effects of all of the factors but these appear to be largely independent. In contrast to this, the physiological data and performance data showed some independent effects but also instances where the factors interacted. For example, performance of a categoric search task (Broadbent, Broadbent and Jones, 1989) was most impaired in the alcohol/no lunch/decaffeinated condition, an effect that was greatly reduced by consumption of lunch, removal of the alcohol or drinking caffeinated coffee. This demonstrates that any conclusions about the effects of lunch, alcohol and caffeine on performance will depend on the nature of the activity being carried out. Similarly, their effects on physiological function will vary depending on the parameter measured. When one considers a range of functions, one finds that some show no effect of any of the factors, others show independent effects, and interactions are observed in some.

Such results presumably reflect the fact that alcohol, caffeine and lunch have many possible modes of action. For example, it has been suggested that lunch produces its behavioural effects by increasing blood glucose, which in turn leads to a hypoglycaemic state and a reduction in arousal (Karlan and Cohn, 1946). Others (e.g. Woods and Porte, 1974) have proposed that the increased blood glucose leads to a parasympathetic initiation of an insulin surge, which is responsible for the behavioural effects. Other researchers suggest that changes in serotonin (Spring *et al.*, 1983) or cortisol (Follenius, Brandenberger and Hietter, 1982) are responsible for these effects. Caffeine is a stimulant of both the central nervous system (CNS) and the autonomic nervous system (ANS) (Boulenger and Uhde, 1982; Zahn and Rapaport, 1987) and it is known to (i) increase central and peripheral catecholamines, (ii) inhibit phosphodiesterase, the enzyme that promotes degradation of cyclic adenosine monophosphate, and (iii) block many of the peripheral effects of adenosine. Alcohol is a general CNS depressant, and as the dose increases so more primitive brain functions are depressed (Tiplady, 1991). The precise effects observed will, therefore, depend on the factors that influence blood alcohol level and also on changes that produce direct effects on different CNS functions. Further studies are now required to determine what underlies the independent and interactive effects of lunch, caffeine and alcohol that have been demonstrated in the present study.

EFFECTS OF SUGAR IN COFFEE

Recent studies in our laboratory suggest that caffeine is not the only psychoactive substance in drinks such as coffee. Comparison of the performance of those who took sugar in their coffee with the no sugar group has shown that sugar influences performance of logical reasoning tasks and memory-loaded attention tasks. The general trend was for sugar to be associated with slower but more accurate performance. The above data suggest that sugar changes mental efficiency. However, the no sugar/sugar groups were found to differ in personality, with those who took sugar being more extroverted, and this difference could have been responsible for the behavioural effects observed. An experiment was, therefore, carried out controlling for personality to examine whether sugar does change performance. In addition to comparing sugar and no sugar groups, an aspartame condition was also included. This manipulation enabled us to determine whether any results obtained reflected the sweetness or the post-digestive effects of the sugar. The results from the logical reasoning task showed that 150 minutes after the drink, those subjects who had consumed sugar or aspartame performed the task more accurately but more slowly than the no sweetener group. This effect was not modified by the caffeine content of the drink. There were no significant effects of sugar or aspartame on free recall, semantic memory or the number of hits in the recognition memory task.

The results from this experiment confirm our previous observation that sugar improves the accuracy but reduces the speed of logical reasoning. This effect cannot be attributed to differences in personality or to other factors that influence performance in the morning. The effect of sugar is also observed with aspartame, which shows that we have demonstrated an effect of sweetness rather than sugar *per se*. However, as the effects were observed some considerable time after consumption of the sweetener, it is not possible to explain them in terms of short-lived sensory effects. Indeed, it is more likely that the changes observed here are produced by effects that are conditioned responses to sweetness. The precise mechanisms underlying the present results must be determined in further experiments. Similarly, it is important to determine why the effects of sweetness appear to be restricted to the logical reasoning task. Overall, the present results provide further evidence for the view that nutrition influences behaviour. Most of the evidence for this has, until now, been based on studies of the effects of meals (see Smith and Kendrick, 1992), or on the effects of drinks containing psychoactive substances (e.g. alcohol or caffeine). The results reported here show that even small amounts of constituents of beverages can influence performance, and that we must now assess the functional significance and the mechanisms underlying such effects.

REGULAR ALCOHOL CONSUMPTION AND STRESS

All of the previous sections have examined the acute effects of food and drink. It is now important to examine the effects of regular patterns of eating and drinking. Similarly, it is well established that increases in stress lead to changes in alcohol consumption. The combined effects of stress and alcohol consumption were, therefore, considered. An experiment was conducted to examine the effects of alcohol consumption and stress on mood, mental performance and cardiovascular function; 106 young adults (mean age 21.2 years) took part in the study. The results showed that alcohol consumption and stress interact to influence performance but not mood. Different effects were obtained depending on whether one examined the total number of units consumed per week or the frequency of drinking alcohol, but in both cases the effects were selective, being found only with certain stress measures and in some aspects of performance. The pattern of results was, however, consistent enough to suggest that these were not chance effects. The number of alcohol units consumed and degree of negative affect in the last week interacted reliably in analyses of the memory tasks. High scores on both were associated with improved performance (relative to low scores on both), whereas a high score on one but not the other was associated with impaired performance. Two types of effect could be distinguished in these interactions, the first, found in the working memory tasks, reflected the personality differences in the various groups; the other, seen in the episodic memory tasks, was present even when personality and gender were statistically controlled. Frequency of alcohol usage and frequency of negative life events were found to interact in the simple reaction time data, with frequent drinkers who had experienced a large number of negative life events having the slowest reaction times.

CONCLUSIONS

Overall, the studies described here show that what we eat and drink can have effects on our mood and performance. Further research is now required to assess the impact of such effects on our real-life activities. This will require consideration of the contextual factors that modify these behavioural changes. In addition, it is essential to understand the mechanisms underlying the relationships between nutrition and behaviour so that the application of findings can be made in a coherent fashion.

ACKNOWLEDGEMENTS

The research described in this chapter was supported by grants from the Agriculture and Food Research Council, the Physiological Effects of Coffee Research Fund and the Alcohol Education and Research Council.

12

Creativity: Links with Alcohol and Other Substance Use

Geoff Lowe

Department of Psychology, University of Hull, Hull HU6 7RX, UK

INTRODUCTION

In many cultures it has long been assumed that there is a close association between alcohol, drugs and creativity. Creative artists are notorious for their use of psychoactive substances, allegedly to enhance their perceptions and the novelty of their output, but there is little objective evidence for this (Kerr *et al.*, 1991). As Lapp, Collins and Izzo (1994) point out, the precise effect of alcohol and other drugs on creativity is largely unknown. Grant's (1981) review of the alcoholism literature has documented the disproportionate number of recognized writers and other creative persons who drank very heavily. Such an association may be misleading since it could simply reflect the 'eccentric' lifestyle of artists whose alcohol abuse is but one of many 'deviance' patterns almost expected in their unique environment. Indeed, they may well succeed in spite of, rather than because of, drinking. Other researchers have reported links between alcoholism and creativity (Koski-Jannes, 1985), while doubting that alcoholism actually produces creativity (Ludwig, 1990; Rothenberg, 1990).

Pleasure and Quality of Life. Edited by D.M. Warburton and N. Sherwood
© 1996 John Wiley & Sons Ltd.

On the other hand, the popular notion that alcohol has mind-altering effects, often perceived as positive by at least some consumers, suggests the possibility of a more substantial relation between drinking and creativity. The presumption of a positive correlation between drinking/drug use and high creative achievement has certainly been a feature of the characterization of both alcoholism/drug abuse and creativity. Many publications on drinking and creativity reflect only anecdotal accounts and theoretical speculations (Goodwin, 1973, 1991, 1992; Grant, 1981; Ludwig, 1990). Often the case studies suggest that if alcohol is helpful at all, it is as an aid in starting and stopping the creative process. The conclusion that alcohol at best plays an indirect rather than a direct stimulating or inspirational role in creativity can also be drawn from available surveys of artistic people (e.g. Roe, 1946). Few respondents indicate that drinking contributes to the quality of their creative products, although some suggest that it may play a role in the control of the creative process. Others would argue that a presumed connection between alcohol consumption and successful creative work is anomalous in view of the emphasis that occupational alcohol programmes place on the adverse effects of drinking on performance.

Moreover, as Lapp, Collins and Izzo (1994) again point out, the belief that alcohol boosts creativity may well be part of the motivation to drink. For instance, when Newcomb *et al.* (1988) used a scale that measured enhanced positive affect and creativity, the highest factor loadings related to motivation to use alcohol and to use cannabis. Hence the role of cognitive expectancies, in addition to pharmacological actions, of beverages consumed needs to be taken into account. Their impact on evaluated behaviours is well documented (e.g. Marlatt and Rohsenow, 1980). Lapp, Collins and Izzo (1994) used a balanced placebo design to partial out the pharmacological and expected effects of alcohol. Alcohol itself had little effect, possibly because the experimental design required fairly low doses. However, subjects who thought they had been drinking alcohol produced a greater diversity of aesthetic groupings in a picture-sorting task (taken as an indication of greater creativity) than did subjects who expected their drinks to be non-alcoholic, irrespective of actual alcohol content.

LABORATORY EXPERIMENTS

There have been few empirical studies on the alcohol–creativity link, presumably because creativity is difficult to measure (Levine and Levine, 1990; Parke, 1984) and there are too many influences on the creative process (Woodman and Schoenfeldt, 1990). Those that have been attempted seem to indicate rather specific and/or indirect effects. Hajcak (1976) reported increased 'original solutions' in a word-association test after subjects consumed whisky. Lang, Verret and Watt (1984), using a rather low dose (0.6 g ethanol per kilogram of body weight), found no main effect of alcohol on Torrance Creativity Test performance but did observe increased confidence ratings. Adopting yet another measure, Brunke and Gilbert (1992) found greater quantities of creative writing when subjects were intoxicated (1.1 ml ethanol per kilogram of body weight) compared with a sober condition. Gustafson and Norlander (1994) observed impairment effects of alcohol on persistent effort and deductive thinking—processes assumed to be at work during the preparation phase of creativity.

There remain many uncertainties regarding the drinking–creativity relation. For instance, what is the nature of creative ability when such behaviour takes place specifically during—as opposed to surrounding—an actual acute intoxication phase? Hitherto, very little attention has been given to the alcohol–creativity link in 'ordinary' (i.e. not 'established' creative) people. It is not known whether alcohol 'stimulates' creativity in ordinary people to the same extent or even in the same way as it allegedly does in many highly creative artists and writers.

In Study 1, we sought to address such issues in a laboratory-based experiment using a balanced-order, repeated-measures design involving alcohol and placebo sessions. The Torrance Creativity Test was used as a measure of (verbal) creativity because it is a well-standardized test with good validity and reliability (Torrance, 1974). The test assesses originality (the relative unusualness of responses), fluency (the total number of relevant responses) and flexibility (the number of different response categories). In the verbal creativity test version ('Thinking Creatively With Words') there are seven time-limited activities:

1. Subjects write any questions about activities and objects in the stimulus picture.
2. Subjects list the causes for the situation depicted in the picture.
3. Subjects list the possible consequences of the situation.
4. Subjects view a picture of a toy and write down any suggestions for improvement.
5. Subjects list unusual uses for a cardboard box (Form A) or a tin can (Form B).
6. Subjects list unusual questions about cardboard boxes or tin cans.
7. Subjects consider a bizarre situation and suggest possible consequences.

The test has been shown to be sensitive to drug effects. For instance, Warburton (1987b) found that scopolamine produced significantly greater scores for originality and fluency. Like scopolamine, alcohol (in modest doses) also slows electrocortical activity. According to Warburton, slower electrocortical arousal may be beneficial for creative thinking, which does not require focused attention or information retrieval.

Experiment 1a

Sixteen social drinkers (eight male, eight female), aged between 18 and 25 years, volunteered to take part in a four-session experiment. Drinks were administered in the form of 50:50 mixtures of either vodka and tonic (alcohol condition) or water and tonic (placebo condition). Body weights were used to calculate alcohol amounts at 2.2 ml of vodka (37.5%) per kg. This dose (0.83 ml ethanol kg^{-1}) was administered to produce an average 0.08 blood-alcohol concentration (BAC) (the UK legal limit for driving).

Although all subjects knew they were taking part in an alcohol experiment, they were told that alcohol and placebo conditions would be randomized over all four sessions. Thus it was possible that the first two sessions could be both alcohol (A), both placebo (P) or one of each (A,P; P,A). Unbeknown to the subjects, only the latter arrangements were used to run the creativity tests (sessions

3 and 4 were part of another experiment). This procedure was designed to control for 'expectancy' effects.

After the 10-minute drinking period, subjects spent 15 minutes completing personality questionnaires and operating a serial reaction tester while BACs were rising. They were then breathalysed via an Alcolmeter (Lion Laboratories) before completing a 31-item sensation scale (Maisto *et al.*, 1980). The subjects tackled the first four subtests of the Torrance Creativity Test 20 minutes after drinking. They were then breathalysed again before continuing with the last three subtests. Subjects wrote their responses on pages of the test booklet. After a final breathalyser reading, subjects recovered as necessary and left at the end of the two-hour session.

Session 2 was conducted one week later and involved the same procedure except that the (alcohol or placebo) drink, unbeknown to the subjects, was different from that consumed in Session 1, and the alternative form (A or B) of the Torrance Creativity Test was given. Beverage conditions (A or P), test forms (A or B) and sex (M or F) were counterbalanced in the experimental design.

Peak BACs averaged 0.082%, indicating that subjects reached the required intoxication level. Creativity scores were based on three constituent aspects of the Torrance Tests: fluency, flexibility and originality (Table 12.1).

Table 12.1 *Mean creativity scores in Experiment 1a (written response, n = 16)*

Condition	Creativity measures			
	Fluency	Flexibility	Originality	Total creativity
Placebo	74.0	37.0	88.4	199.4
Alcohol	65.3	33.1	75.8	174.2

Total creativity scores between alcohol and placebo conditions were not significantly different. The three component comparisons were also non-significant. Correlational analyses between creativity scores and (i) BACs and (ii) subjective sensation scores revealed no significant relationships. Thus, moderate doses of alcohol, administered under controlled laboratory conditions, failed to produce significant enhancing effects on performance in a standardized creativity test. If anything, there was a slight decrement in performance under alcohol, although this may have been related to the observation that many subjects indicated some difficulty in the actual physical process of writing while intoxicated.

Experiment 1b

A second group of 16 subjects (8 male, 8 female), aged between 18 and 30 years, volunteered to take part in a similar experiment. All the design features were identical, except that instead of subjects writing down their responses in the creativity tests, they were allowed to respond orally into a tape recorder. This modification was designed to overcome the problem of the potential deleterious effect of alcohol on motor performance (handwriting). The results are presented in Table 12.2.

Table 12.2   *Mean creativity scores in Experiment 1b (oral response, n = 16)*

Condition	Creativity measures			
	Fluency	Flexibility	Originality	Total creativity
Placebo	70.8	36.3	80.8	187.9
Alcohol	75.6	37.9	93.8	207.3

Analysis of total creativity scores again revealed no significant difference between alcohol and placebo conditions. The three component comparisons were also non-significant. However, it was noticeable that, if anything, the effect of alcohol was slightly positive (in contrast to the slightly negative effect in Experiment 1a). The largest positive effect was in the originality score (but this was also non-significant).

Over both experiments, there were no significant sex differences overall in creativity, although females tended to achieve higher scores than males, nor were males and females differentially affected by the beverage manipulations on creativity. There were, however, significant individual differences in alcohol–creativity effects. Specifically, in subjects with higher creativity scores (above median) under the placebo condition, alcohol produced significant decrements (mean = –41.25); whereas in subjects with lower creativity scores (below median) under the placebo condition, significant increments were observed with alcohol (mean = 35.25). This would, of course, be expected from a simple regression effect. However, analysis of individual placebo–alcohol differences showed that relative size of increments/decrements was unrelated to absolute score in the placebo condition. Hence, this result cannot be explained simply in terms of statistical regression.

The lack of significant main effects of alcohol on creativity test performance does not necessarily mean that alcohol plays no role in the process of creativity. The present findings merely indicate that under laboratory-controlled conditions the performance of unexceptional subjects on a standardized creativity test is not directly affected by a moderate dose of alcohol. It is still possible that other forms of creative ability may be enhanced. In fact, Brunke and Gilbert (1992) observed a greater quantity of creative writing in their intoxicated subjects.

It is also possible—and perhaps likely—that exceptionally creative people interact idiosyncratically with alcohol and related substances to affect productivity. Post (1994), for instance, argues that a 'causal link' exists between creativity and psychopathology, 'including tendencies towards depression and alcoholism'. One outcome of the present study is the observation of significant individual differences in the alcohol–creativity interaction. Those subjects 'under-performing' while sober improved their performance after alcohol, whereas those subjects with higher scores while sober were impaired after alcohol. This is consistent with the notion of alcohol reducing 'writer's block', or 'loosening up' an individual partially constrained, perhaps, by the demand characteristics of the task. With higher-scoring subjects—not thus constrained—no such scope for facilitation (and hence enhancement) exists. These latter individuals are in a sub-optimal (for them) state when intoxicated, and the net result is deterioration, rather than improvement, of creative performance.

Individual differences crop up elsewhere in the creativity literature. In a study of creativity in alcoholic and non-alcoholic families, Noble, Runco and Ozkaragoz (1993) make the interesting suggestion that alcoholic family members 'may show greater creativity under the influence of alcohol. That is, alcohol may have a on these individuals' creativity, in contrast to a detrimental or, at best, neutral effect on individuals not at risk for alcoholism'. In research on hypnosis and creativity, Ashton and McDonald (1985) also observed individual differences, despite an absence of treatment effects. Hypnotizable subjects achieved higher scores than unhypnotizable subjects. The change to an oral response mode in Experiment 1b (from a written response mode in Experiment 1a) produced higher test scores after alcohol while performance scores in the two placebo conditions were similar. The renowned motor effects of alcohol on handwriting (Galbraith, 1986) may well have slowed subjects' physical production of creative output, and in some cases may have produced frustration. Thus, the improved procedure in Experiment 1b may provide a better test of alcohol's effect on creativity test performance when this is assessed in terms of fluency and quantity as well as originality.

One implication to be drawn from the present results is that creative performance during moderate alcohol intoxication may be enhanced in less creative subjects but diminished in more creative subjects. Such a conclusion—admittedly only tentative at this stage—would tend to contradict much of the alcohol–creativity mythology. However, we have no direct evidence that we were dealing with more and less creative individuals: only that their test scores differed, for some unknown reason, under placebo conditions, and became more similar after drinking alcohol.

JUDGEMENTS OF SUBSTANCE USE AND CREATIVITY IN 'ORDINARY' PEOPLE'S EVERYDAY LIFESTYLES

Laboratory studies are designed to control possible confounding variables but may have little relevance for how people actually use substances in relation to creativity/productivity aspects of their everyday lives. Arising from earlier work with the Mass-Observation (M-O) archive at Sussex University, an opportunity arose for taking this research out of the laboratory. Several of the M-O 'directives' were concerned with people's everyday use of socially acceptable substances (e.g. tea, coffee, chocolate, alcohol, tobacco and prescribed medication). An initial, subjective scanning of the

M-O archive data on stimulants and relaxants suggested that heavier smokers and drinkers were somewhat more likely to be involved in 'creative/productive' activities.

One way around this subjectivity bias would be to have pairs of assessors, blind to the aims of the project, independently read the case material (consisting of respondents' reports of substance use and related everyday activities) and simply rate each respondent in terms of likely creativity. Other pairs of independent assessors would score each respondent (on the basis of the information given in the case material) in terms of their reported drinking, smoking and substance use. The main investigator (the present author) could then analyse the relationships between the measures obtained. We would thus be able to test the above hypotheses and notions more objectively. The aim of the present study, then, was to investigate the relationship between substance use and creativity, based on raters' judgements derived from a blind assessment of M-O archive data.

The Mass-Observation Archive

The M-O archive at the University of Sussex is undoubtedly a rich store of predominantly qualitative material about many facets of life in Britain during the past 50 or so years. During the latest stage, in the 1980s and 1990s, a panel of several thousand M-O volunteers has been recruited. Two or three times a year a special directive is sent out, inviting these observers to write about various aspects of British life and their own everyday lifestyles.

A recent M-O directive specifically featured social drugs and related substances. Respondents were asked to report on their daily and regular use of tea and coffee, which were the most important cups of the day, and to give reasons for their preferences. They were also asked about the when and where of smoking, and of drinking alcoholic beverages, including preferences. Information about individual limits and excesses, pubs and abstention was also requested. Respondents were asked about compulsive eating and irresistible edibles. They were also asked about their experiences with other substances, such as prescribed drugs, cannabis and cocaine, and whether there were (or had been) problems with substance abuse in their families (Lowe, 1994).

The M-O Respondents

The database consisted of a total of 619 written reports (1–20 pages) in response to the directive on stimulants and relaxants. The 619 respondents were 459 women (74%) and 160 men (26%). Their average age was 55.75 years, with an age range from 16 to 92. M-O respondents are mostly middle-aged or older, and in our sample 519 (83%) were in the 40+ age group, and 98 (17%) under 40 years. It is important to note that these M-O respondents were typically middle-aged, middle-class and predominantly female. They were not, therefore, especially representative of the general population. M-O respondents, nevertheless, are typically regarded as being mature, well-seasoned, responsive (and responsible) 'ordinary people', whose attitudes and opinions are valued by social scientists and the media as being somewhat representative of the traditional backbone of British society. How representative these respondents are, however, is not a crucial issue in the present study, since the main focus is on the correlations between raters' independent judgements of characteristics of respondents, irrespective of who these people were.

Raters and Reports

There were eight independent raters: four men (ages 22, 23, 24 and 52) and four women (ages 20, 22, 23 and 50), all with college/university experience. There were eight sets of M-O reports ($n = 77$ approximately), totalling 619 reports altogether. The focus of each report was the typical substance use (stimulants and relaxants) of respondents in their everyday lives. Each report was rated four times—by two male raters and by two female raters—twice for substance use (SU) and twice for creativity (CTY). Judgements of substance use were derived directly from the information given in the reports; subjective judgements of the creativity of the respondent were derived from the style of writing and any other details perceived as relevant to creativity in the reports.

We did not require raters to distinguish between alcohol and other chemicals, since they were simply asked to make judgements of 'substance use' (of whatever kind). Thus, respondents describing frequent use of tea and coffee would be given a higher rating than those reporting 'an occasional cup of tea'. A respondent who mentioned use of cocaine would be given a high rating, since cocaine use generally implies the use of other substances as well (i.e. no one, in our experience, ever uses cocaine without previous experience of some other substances, such as tea, coffee, alcohol, smoking or cannabis).

Procedure

Each independent rater was individually briefed and given a short description of only one dimension to be rated (creativity, or substance use), together with the 9-point rating scale (the creativity scale ranged from 'very low' through 'about average' to 'extremely high creativity'; the substance use scale ranged from 'very minimal' through 'about average' to 'extremely high use'). They were then given their first set of M-O reports (n = approximately 77) to process. All raters were completely unaware of the aims of the study and of the task specifications of other raters. At specified times raters returned their ratings and sets of reports to the author. Within a Latin square, counterbalanced design, each rater processed four sets, using the same rating dimension. Four raters, two male and two female (M1, M2, F1 and F2) rated creativity; the other four raters (M2, M4, F3 and F4) rated substance use. After all ratings had been completed and returned to the author, raters were debriefed in a group meeting.

This scheme enabled us, firstly, to determine inter-rater reliability between pairs of raters (for both dimensions); and secondly to average the ratings from each pair of raters. These averaged ratings were then used as bivariate scores to estimate the correlation between creativity ratings and substance use ratings for each set.

Inter-Rater Reliability

Correlations (Pearson r) were calculated for each pair of raters on each of the two dimensions based on each set of reports (Table 12.3). From this it can be seen that inter-rater correlations were higher on the substance use dimension, but all correlations were significantly positive.

Table 12.3   *Inter-rater correlations*

Set	n	Creativity	Substance use
1	77	M1×M2 = 0.42	M3×M4 = 0.58
2	78	M1×M2 = 0.43	M3´M4 = 0.67
3	77	F1×F2 = 0.58	F3´F4 = 0.69
4	77	F1×F2 = 0.37	F3´F4 = 0.75
5	78	M1×M2 = 0.38	M3´M4 = 0.69
6	77	M1×2 = 0.40	M3´M4 = 0.69
7	78	F1×F2 = 0.53	F3´F4 = 0.70
8	77	F1×F2 = 0.33	F3´F4 = 0.78
Totals*	619	Average r = 0.43	Average r = 0.69

*Critical r = 0.01, 75 df = 0.292.

Table 12.4   *Mean ratings for creativity and substance use (on scale 1–9)*

Scale	All(n)	M(n)	F(n)
Creativity	4.86(619)	4.96(160)	4.85(459)
Substance use	3.93(619)	4.20(160)	3.84(459)

Table 12.4 shows that ratings of substance use were higher in men ($F = 5.33, p = 0.02$), but male and female respondents were not rated significantly differently in terms of creativity.

Averaged ratings (of each dimension) from pairs of raters of M-O respondents provided 619 bivariate values for correlational analysis. The main correlation (creativity × substance use) was positive and significant ($r = 0.275, p<0.01$) but rather low, accounting for little variance. Partitioning the subjects into males and females made little impact (female $r = 0.287, p<0.01$; male $r = 0.213, p<0.01$). Further partitioning the respondents into two age groups—under 40 and 40+—revealed the following positive correlations: under 40 $r = 0.340, p<0.01$; over 40 $r = 0.255, p<0.01$.

Discussion

The resulting positive correlations (of the order of +0.275) turned out to be more significant than anticipated. These analyses confirm links between creativity ratings (as assessed via independent judgements of M-O respondents' reports) and substance use ratings (as assessed via different independent judgements). Those respondents judged to be more heavily involved in substance use (smoking, drinking, etc.) were also somewhat more likely to be rated more highly (by different, independent raters) on a creativity rating scale.

These findings are also in line with previous studies of recognized creative artists, writers and jazz/rock musicians. It is well established that alcohol, smoking and related drug use has frequently played a part in the lifestyles of many such individuals (Goodwin, 1973; Grant, 1981; Ludwig, 1990). The observation there is that those individuals judged (by society, media, cultural consensus, etc.) as highly creative are or were more likely to be involved in heavier substance use (May, 1975).

It must be emphasized, however, that these observed links—even if they were larger and more significant—cannot be used as evidence of a causal relationship. In the case of creative artists, writers and musicians, it may well be the case that creativity comes first, and is a forceful personality characteristic. Substance use may then be a 'coping strategy' in a creative (and possibly unstable) lifestyle. Alternatively, for others, substance use may indeed play a part in stimulating 'creative juices', or at least in disengaging 'creative blocks and barriers'. In the case of 'ordinary' people, lifestyle characteristics common to both substance use and increased creativity may be relevant to any explanations of the links.

It must also be emphasized that, in the present study, the observed correlation coefficients are low. Nevertheless, it may be worth considering possible factors or attributes common to both creativity and substance use. One possibility is risk-taking: both creativity and substance use involve some degree of risk-taking. In terms of creativity, it helps if people are willing to take (more) risks. In terms of substance use, people may be engaging in 'riskier' activities, either because risk-taking is part of their lifestyle/personality, or because they underestimate risks. (It is interesting to note that many respondents mentioned 'trying cigarettes' in their youth 'because it was a bit naughty (or risky)'). Alternatively, since many of the substances reported were stimulants, people may score higher on creativity simply because they are more awake.

The research design seems to have worked well. The essential—and innovative—feature of it was the use of pairs of independent raters. This scheme produced the objectivity required to achieve the aims of the study, and enabled us to determine both inter-rater reliabilities and inter-dimension correlations based on averaged ratings. Inter-rater reliabilities were significant and moderately high, especially in terms of substance use. Those relating to creativity were somewhat lower, perhaps indicating that this was a more complex dimension to judge. Feedback from individual raters suggested that creativity was more difficult to rate and they were generally less confident in their ratings. Nevertheless, significant reliability coefficients enabled us to average raters' ratings for each dimension, and input these as elements in the inter-dimension correlations.

It should again be emphasized that these M-O respondents were not representative of the general population. Many M-O respondents are female, since women are more willing to write about their lives. However, any such bias in the sample of respondents should not affect the main correlational focus of the study since each respondent was independently rated on both dimensions, and we were not using subjective ratings to estimate levels of creativity and substance use in the general population.

Nevertheless, the essential characteristic of this sample is that they are 'ordinary' people, going about their daily lives. The observations from the present study, therefore, are relevant to the daily lives and attitudes of similar people. Moreover, the findings complement those obtained via more tightly-controlled (but more artificial) laboratory-based studies of substance ingestion and creativity, as well as those attempting to investigate the lifestyles and substance use of established creatively outstanding individuals.

CONCLUDING REMARKS

In conclusion, laboratory experiments on alcohol and creative performance have highlighted expectancy as a crucial factor, as well as individual differences. Such expectancy, or belief in positive effects, is likely to have a basis in people's perceptions of the links as portrayed via the media and other anecdotal reports. In the M-O study, we observed some weak (but significant) links between substance use and creativity, even when (subjective) judgements were made independently. Again, this may be less to do with direct pharmacological influences and more to do with the expectancies and beliefs of the independent raters. It may be, for instance, that raters (of 'creativity') simply use observed levels of substance use to infer that the respondent is likely therefore to be more creative. This might explain any positive correlation between ratings of 'creativity' and 'substance use'. This is interesting, since it would indicate that the (largely) anecdotal links between creativity and substance use have encouraged (some) people to identify or judge creativity primarily in terms of substance use (e.g. 'X drinks regularly and uses cocaine, so X must be fairly creative'). In other words, the M-O study may be telling us more about the raters than the respondents (whose reports provided the stimulus material for our raters). So, in an indirect way this study may indicate that perceptions of creativity are indeed linked with substance use. If so, this would be evidence for the perpetuation of mythological causal links between substance use and creativity.

In general terms, if people can achieve increased levels of creativity as a function of their beliefs about alcohol (Lapp, Collins and Izzo, 1994) and related substances, then such substance use could thereby be reinforced because the expected and pharmacological effects co-exist under ordinary circumstances. The perpetuation of this notion is further reinforced by the well-documented links between substance use and creativity, especially in terms of people's perceptions.

13

The Bliss Point and Pleasure

Robert L. McBride

SensoMetrics Pty Ltd, 357 Military Road, Mosman,
NSW 2088, Australia

INTRODUCTION

'Why do you eat what you eat? Is it for nutrition? Well, of course; if you
don't supply your body with fuel you will fail to survive. But is nutrition
foremost in your mind when you choose your food? Not really. It's the
taste, the flavour, the sensory satisfaction. In fact the taste factor takes
priority over nutrition, because if you don't like a food you don't eat it. It
may be bursting with nutrition, but if it doesn't taste right it will never be
part of your diet.' (McBride, 1990)

This principle of 'sensory dominance' holds in other areas of
life. For example, paraphrasing the above:

'Why do you buy the clothes you do? Is it for warmth? Well, of course; if
you don't protect your body you will fail to survive. But is bodily protection foremost on your mind when you choose your clothes? Not really. It's
the look, the style, the sensory satisfaction. In fact the sensory appeal takes
priority over protection, because if you don't like the garment, you won't
wear it. It may provide abundant warmth, but if it doesn't look right it will
never be part of your wardrobe.'

In a previous publication (McBride, 1994), I dealt with the concept
of the bliss point and how it affects our choice of sensory stimuli in
everyday life—whether those stimuli be coffee, chocolate, tobacco,

Pleasure and Quality of Life. Edited by D.M. Warburton and N. Sherwood
© 1996 John Wiley & Sons Ltd.

perfumes or even household products. This chapter is more concerned with the implication of the bliss point, particularly in relation to the things that we eat and drink.

Firstly, I should note that, notwithstanding the tenor of the above quotations, this chapter is not about the denigration of nutrition. Nutritional science has been, and will continue to be, vital to human well-being. However, without adopting any moral stance on the issue, the chapter makes the point that, in everyday life, for most people, sensory pleasure is the prime motivator of food selection, not nutritional status.

THE BLISS POINT

The bliss point concept may be defined briefly as follows. The first requirement is that human response to food be recognized as measurable, quantitatively, on a like/dislike continuum (i.e. a scale), from perfect, unalloyed pleasure at one end, to absolute revulsion on the other. Pleasantness can then be measured by having people score their experience on a scale that reflects the continuum. The 9-point hedonic scale, which ranges from 'like extremely' to 'dislike extremely', is one well-known example.

The human predilection for sweetness is well known and will serve as a suitable exemplar of the bliss point. Humans like sweetness, but how much sweetness? We know, intuitively, that a certain amount of sweetness is pleasant but too much is sickly and unpleasant. The same goes for saltiness; a certain amount enhances the food, but too much is distasteful (and can even function as an emetic if really strong). For all ingredients in food and drink, there is an optimum concentration at which the sensory pleasure is maximal. This optimum level is called the bliss point.

The bliss point concept is shown schematically in Figure 13.1. Let us suppose in this instance that we are talking about the amount of sugar in a soft drink. Starting on the left-hand side, a small amount of sugar in the drink induces only a small amount of pleasure. As the sweetness intensity grows toward the right, the pleasure also grows; the drink tastes better. Then an optimum point is reached: the bliss point. Enjoyment of the drink is maximal at this bliss point level of sweetness. If more sugar is added beyond

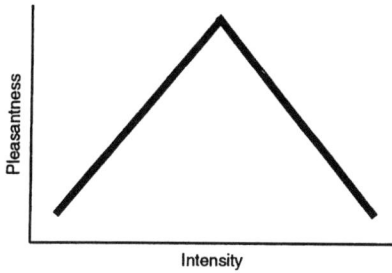

Figure 13.1. *The bliss point (or ideal point) curve is a trademark of hedonic research. There is almost always an optimum level for a sensation, whether this sensation be overall intensity or something more specific, like sweetness. The characteristic shape of the bliss point curve is a trademark of research on food acceptance*

the bliss point concentration, the pleasure actually drops away, until, when the sugar concentration is strong (extreme right) the drink is sickly and affords little enjoyment at all. If you think about your own experience of eating and drinking, this concept will make sense. You will have bliss points for most flavours in food: sugar, salt, acid etc.

The bliss point is not a new concept, nor is it one of my own invention. I have revitalized the concept in recent times, particularly in relation to food and drink, but it was first observed by Wilhelm Wundt, one of the founding fathers of psychology, in Germany over 100 years ago. It is a powerful phenomenon and dictates what we eat and drink more than we realize. Some more examples will make the case.

Suppose you get up in the morning and take a shower. The shower is your first sensory bliss point of the day: you adjust the taps to obtain your desired water temperature—not too hot, not too cold, just right. You take this bliss point for granted but it is the only reason that a shower works! You would not take a cold shower, and you certainly wouldn't take one that was scalding hot. Obtaining a bliss point temperature is a prerequisite. While still on temperature, why do we consume so much food and drink hot (i.e. heated)? Why do we insist on soft drinks and beer being cold? There is no nutritional reason for this. Every year, the world spends many millions of dollars heating (and cooling) food and drink to satisfy the human thermal bliss point.

After the shower there is breakfast and a whole barrage of bliss points. If you have juice and cereal, their sensory characters will have been 'bliss point engineered'—optimized by the manufacturer (there is even a cereal called 'Just Right', implying the bliss point). As for tea and coffee, you will have your preferred temperature, your preferred strength, your preferred degree of milkiness and so on. These examples can sound trivial because the bliss point is accomplished with ease, but it is the bliss points that dictate sensory satisfaction. What about individual difference? There is, for sure, individual variation in bliss points but it is not as great as you might think. The major type of individual difference in food is what might be called 'all or none'; you like peanut butter, I don't; I like avocados, you don't. If, however, we agree on a product that we both like, then we will tend to agree on the optimum formulation. Individual reactions are normally distributed around the bliss point. When you think about this, individual difference could not be too extreme, otherwise we could not have the food industry as we have it today. If individual differences were extreme, there would need to be dozens of formulations within a single brand to satisfy all consumers.

The food industry in the developed world panders to human bliss points, even if they are not always called by this name. Marketeers know that for a product to be successful, it must attract repeat purchase. And, to ensure repeat purchase, the consumer must be more than satisfied with the product; it needs to match, or better still exceed, expectations. It is the percentage of consumers who, after tasting a product, are prepared to respond 'definitely will buy' that will determine the fate of a new product. And every increment in sensory pleasure makes for an increase in purchase propensity. The closer to the bliss point, the better the product, the greater the success. But there are also other factors that conspire with bliss point engineering to make it such an effective determinant of product choice. These factors have profound implications.

THREE DRIVERS OF PRODUCT CHOICE

From the bliss point perspective, three key drivers of choice are flavour intensity, predictability and availability.

Flavour Intensity

Contemporary flavour technology and processing make it a simple matter to manipulate the composition of food, drinks and other products. Just suppose the task is to formulate an apricot flavoured yoghurt. There is no constraint to formulate the product with the same level of apricot flavouring as might occur in a real apricot. If sensory research indicates that consumers like a more intense apricot flavour, then this can easily be attained. And, in fact, the research *does* often find that consumers like flavours that are more intense than is typically experienced in nature. The net effect, then, is that many of the flavours we experience in everyday processed foods are 'larger than life'; they are caricatures of the natural products they represent. The apricot yoghurt, with its high level of apricot flavouring and sugar, becomes 'more apricot than apricot', and the real thing can seem dull by comparison.

If the consumption of unprocessed food is falling, relative to processed food, then this is one reason—the disparity in flavour intensity. Once we become habituated to a diet of processed food, unprocessed food can seem uninteresting; it lacks the 'flavour hit'. I would hypothesize that this is more true of children. The instant sensory satisfaction of fast food and snack food is simply not matched by carrot and celery sticks. A mother remarked to me recently: 'The trouble with pizza is that, once kids get hooked, other food seems too tame.'

Predictability

If flavour affects choice, then predictability (consistency) exerts an even more powerful influence. Before the days of highly processed products, one, or maybe two, generations ago, humans had to rely upon natural produce. The quality of the produce was utterly at the mercy of the seasonal conditions—sweet, succulent fruit one year, a few wizened specimens the next. There was no way of controlling this, so people took it philosophically, like the weather. Then along came processed food, which is always the same. Even if the raw materials are below specification (e.g. sugars too low), the manufacturer has ways to compensate for the shortfall and bring the product up to the same final formulation. So, the consumer buys a product that is constant, day in day out, week in week out, year in year out.

The sensory influence of this is profound. Experiencing exactly the same sensation day after day— and a bliss point sensation at that—etches a 'flavour template' in memory. The consistency makes for familiarity, which in turn is comforting, emotionally reassuring. Marketeers may not have thought about it from this angle before, but it is the sensory consistency that makes a brand feasible. Whether it be cheese, margarine, a snack food, coffee or cigarettes, a brand could not be a brand if the sensory quality were not consistent. Consumers like this predictability; it eliminates uncertainty and fear of the unknown. Staying with the same brand means that the bliss point it evokes is continually reinforced and engraved into flavour memory. Fast-food chains such as McDonald's have exploited this principle, knowingly or not.

So, unprocessed food can lose out to processed food, not only on the basis of its lower flavour intensity but also on its lack of consistency. Alongside consistent, processed food, unprocessed food is now something of an unknown quantity. As an example, compare the appeal, to a child, of two snacks: an apple and a bag of chips (crisps). The bag of chips is predictable in both flavour and texture, guaranteed to deliver. The apple, on the other hand, may be sweet and juicy or it may be floury and dry. Furthermore, the chips are guaranteed to deliver on flavour intensity—the hit—whereas the apple might be bland and tasteless. With an understanding of bliss points, it is hardly surprising that recent surveys indicate children are eating fewer fruits and vegetables.

Primary producers must take heed of this effect. The most effective way to increase consumption of fruit and vegetables is to improve their quality: make them both more flavoursome (i.e. higher in flavour intensity) and more predictable. Then they can be branded, with concomitant adding of value. Similarly, in the meat and livestock industry, animals will increasingly be grown to specification to produce meat of consistent flavour and texture. This will allow meat cuts to be branded and marketed as a predictable product with a tenderness guarantee. It is all quite a revolution, and it is all driven by the bliss point phenomenon.

Availability

For high flavour intensity and predictability to be strong determinants of product choice requires that the product in question be consumed regularly. Thus, availability strongly influences choice (it is trite but true to observe that you cannot use what is not available). Marketeers know full well the pivotal role played by distribution. And this is where bliss point engineered products come to the fore. The type of foods that have made bliss point engineering an art form—the fast foods, snack foods, soft drinks—are available at almost all retail outlets. This ready availability sets up a 'reinforcement loop': the higher flavour intensity and consistency of the processed food makes food more appealing, but its ready availability—the ability to buy and eat it in a variety of occasions—plays an important role in the etching of the profile on flavour memory.

Intensity, predictability and availability are influencing what we eat. The recent phenomenon of 'grazing', for example, is only possible because there are readily available foods on which to graze.

CHOICE AND FLAVOUR SCIENCE

To conclude, I would like to address briefly the impact of the bliss point on food choice and flavour science in general. I have aimed to show here that the pleasure of food is not a diffuse, ethereal concept; it can be measured, just as physical, chemical and nutritional factors can be measured. I hope that, with more concrete status, the capacity of food flavours to evoke pleasure may start to be regarded as a real, tangible property of products. Thus, the capacity of foods to give pleasure will be recognized by food scientists along with its nutritional status.

Until now, it has not been this way; there has been a disparity between food marketing and food sciences. Food marketeers have a better idea of what drives food choice than do food scientists. Most food marketeers are well aware of the pivotal importance of taste and pleasure, whereas food scientists are apt to be more concerned with food safety and nutritional quality. The disparity occurs because the food and nutritional sciences have evolved as spin-offs from the physical, biological and medical sciences. Nutrition science, for example, is inclined to have a 'deficiency orientation'; that is, to focus on the negative (what happens when there is a lack of vitamins, iron, minerals, protein, etc.). This is understandable but unfortunate for its image. Last year I heard a speaker commenting on the stance of the health and nutrition movement that, for them, 'even a happy life can be described as an incurable, sexually transmitted condition' (Skrabanek, 1994, p. 90).

Life is not a disease. If our focus is on well-being rather than on dietary deficiency, we can accord pleasure some status for its own sake and give sensory factors their due in determining food choice. There are signs that greater recognition is on its way. There is now, for example, more of a readiness in medicine to acknowledge 'quality of life' as important, not just longevity. Enjoying food and drink is an important part of quality of life; it warrants more research for its own sake.

Part III

Pleasure and Choice

14

Understanding Risky Choices

Frank McKenna

Department of Psychology, University of Reading, Building 3, Earley Gate, Whiteknights Road, Reading RG6 2AL, UK

From the perspective of public health, people often appear perverse in that they have a great enthusiasm for activities that are harmful. For example, people are frequently confronted with information that smoking is harmful yet they continue to smoke. People are consistently reminded of the dangers of alcohol and overeating, but they continue to overindulge. When public information fails to change behaviour there is often the suspicion that people are denying the risks. However, there are difficulties with the denial argument. In the case of smoking, the denial explanation is difficult to sustain because most smokers do acknowledge the dangers (McKenna, Warburton, and Winwood, 1993).

When public health campaigns fail to produce changes in behaviour the conclusion often is that education programmes simply do not work. For example, Jeffrey (1989) has argued that, 'It has proven difficult to convince a sceptical populace that traditional practices such as smoking, drinking, poor diet and lack of exercise are hazardous to health'. Here it might be important to distinguish between convincing the populace to change their behaviour and convincing them to change their attitude. Because public health campaigns frequently fail to produce major shifts in behaviour they are often viewed with considerable pessimism. However, this

Pleasure and Quality of Life. Edited by D.M. Warburton and N. Sherwood
© 1996 John Wiley & Sons Ltd.

may be an overreaction. It is arguably the case that through public health campaigns people have become much more aware of the dangers of smoking, alcohol, high-fat diets etc., and this is true whether or not they have changed their behaviour.

Although public health campaigns are often targeted at personal risk, they may have an impact on perceived societal risk even if no personal behaviour change occurs. In principle, this could have important practical implications. Effective public policy implementation may require individuals to perceive the need for public measures. For example, even if individuals do not change their behaviour the campaign may produce a re-evaluation of the magnitude of the problem.

Here we might speculate on the contrasting effects of seat belt legislation in the UK compared to motorcycle helmet laws in the United States. In the UK seat belt legislation was preceded by major campaigns aimed at persuading the public to use the seat belts voluntarily. They were not remarkably successful in changing individual behaviour. However, when the law was implemented the compliance was, and remains, high. By contrast, in the USA the helmet laws were not preceded by the same type of campaigns, and when the law was implemented there was so much opposition that many states repealed their laws (Leichter, 1991). The effect of mass media communication on perceptions of personal and societal risk has been addressed by Tyler and Cook (1984). They argued that people separate their personal and societal levels of judgements about a wide variety of risks. They conclude that not only are these two levels of judgement distinct and often independent but also that the mass media exerts its primary influence on societal and not personal risk judgements. In other words, there are circumstances where individuals are sensitive to changes in risk but that they perceive that the change is in the risk to others and not to themselves.

The fact that people do not change their behaviour following a public health campaign does not automatically mean that they have not received and accepted the message. If people have received and accepted the message that certain activities are harmful, why, then, do they not change their behaviour? Although at first sight it might appear irrational for a fully informed individual to engage in an activity that may be harmful, this is not necessarily so. The reason is that individuals are not necessarily pursuing a single goal of risk minimization.

Many activities may involve a tradeoff between health risk and some perceived gain. For example, it is safer to travel by train than by car but many people continue to travel by car. The extra convenience dictates the choice. Here convenience is being traded for health risk. Although many activities involve this type of tradeoff, in some the issue is highlighted. For example, different treatments of cancer have different implications for the tradeoff between quality and quantity of life. McNeil, Weichselbaum and Pauker (1981) contrast laryngectomy and radiation therapy in the treatment of laryngeal cancer. They argue that laryngectomy leads to a three-year survival rate of about 60% whereas radiation therapy has a corresponding survival rate of approximately 30–40%. However, laryngectomy leads to the loss of normal speech, whereas radiation therapy preserves normal or near normal speech. Their analysis indicated that about 20% of people would choose radiation therapy, indicating that length of life is not the only factor taken into account.

Jeffrey (1989) has pointed to the issue of quantity of life as an important criterion differentiating individual and public health perspectives. He argues that the public health, in contrast to the individual perspective, 'is a rationalistic one that seeks to maximize the quantity of life'. The implicit assumption of a connection between maximizing life and rationality is not uncommon but is problematic. How would one compare a long life of misery and pain with a short life of exquisite pleasure? Clearly maximizing life expectancy is a major criterion but the difficulty is in arguing that it is the only criterion. Barofsky and Sugarbaker (1990) have noted that many people rate an extremely limited life as worse than death itself.

In assessing risks, Slovic, Fischhoff and Lichtenstein (1982) have argued that whereas experts' judgements of risk correlate highly with technical estimates of annual fatalities, those of lay people are sensitive to other factors, such as catastrophic potential and controllability. For example, nuclear power is regarded as having high catastrophic potential and low controllability. Slovic, Fischhoff and Lichtenstein are careful to avoid the conclusion that the experts are right and the lay people are wrong.

The fact that individuals persist in the face of harm does not automatically mean that they are denying the risks or are in some sense irrational. One of the factors much neglected in the debate concerns the pleasure that individuals can obtain from participating in risky activities. The obvious, but neglected, point is that people enjoy activities like smoking, drinking alcohol and eating high-fat diets. If smoking, alcohol and high-fat diets could be enjoyed without any negative consequences then everyone would be happy. If a price has to be paid for the pleasure, are people willing to pay? In response to being told that he could add five years to his life by giving up smoking and drinking, Mark Twain is reputed to have replied that five years without smoking and drinking were not worth living.

Whether it is rational to trade-off life-expectancy surely depends on the balance between the costs and the benefits. To provide a computation requires not only knowledge of the costs and benefits but also a means of weighting them differentially. How much pleasure does one require in order to trade-off life expectancy? It has been estimated that a lifetime adherence to a low-fat dietary programme has the potential to extend an average person's life expectancy by only a few months. How reasonable is it then for an individual to adopt a low-fat diet?

Pleasure surely is one of the major factors that make life worth living. In assessing the quality of one's life, happiness must play a significant role. How, then, are we to conceive of pleasure and the pursuit of pleasure? There are at least two conceptions. One interpretation is that pleasure is the subjective experience of positive affect and that the pursuit of happiness is the ultimate goal. Aristippus in the third century BC expressed hedonism in the following way: 'pleasure is the *sole* good, but also that only one's own physical, positive, momentary pleasure is a good, and is so regardless of its cause'.

Aristotle rejected this view of pleasure and argued for a concept that is nearer to what modern writers would recognize as self-actualization. The argument is that happiness is experienced through the fulfilment of personal potentials by developing one's skills and talents. If hedonism as defined above were to be dismissed then the value placed on activities such as smoking and drinking would correspondingly be diminished.

In assessing the societal significance of hedonism and self-actu-alization, one issue that requires examination concerns the oppor-tunity for the experience. It might be anticipated that hedonic enjoyment would arise from a much wider range of activities than self-actualization. In some individuals' lives the opportunity for self-actualization may be very limited. Consider a car worker who has to work overtime to provide enough money to pay for the house and the family's needs. The job may involve tightening four bolts. The person does not move towards the car, the car moves towards the worker. When the four bolts are tightened the next car comes along and the same task is repeated. In this situation the opportunity for self-actualization appears greatly constrained. Even under these greatly constrained conditions, it is possible for people to eat, drink and smoke.

UNDERSTANDING RISK-TAKING BEHAVIOUR

In recent years there has been renewed interest in understanding risk-taking behaviour (see Bell and Bell, 1993; Yates, 1992). One significant feature of work in this area is that a theoretical under-standing of risk-taking behaviour in general is being derived from a number of quite different areas of psychological research.

Gambling

One major paradigm for considering risk-taking behaviour is that of gambling. Lopes (1993) has argued that, 'The formal study of risky choice has, for the most part, concentrated on monetary outcomes presented to subjects in the form of gambles or lotteries'. Although there is an extensive literature in this area there are concerns about the generality of the findings. Even within the gambling area, the correspondence between the behaviour in laboratory games and gambling in naturalistic settings has been questioned (Wagenaar, 1988). There are other reasons for being concerned about the utility of gambling as a theoretical model for all forms of risk taking. For example, one major distinction be-tween gambling and many other forms of risk taking concerns the experience of negative outcome. In gambling people have considerable experience with loss, since this is the most probable outcome, and it is generally of low intensity.

In many other forms of risk taking, e.g. driving, high-fat diets and smoking, people have relatively little experience of the high-intensity negative outcomes. The precise role that experience with negative outcome plays is difficult to determine but at this stage it would be dangerous to assume it had no significance. For example, Kunreuther *et al.* (1978) found that a large proportion of people in flood zones did not perceive floods to be a serious threat unless they had experienced a flood before.

Heuristics and Biases

Another major influence on the study of risk taking has been the work on heuristics and biases in the decision making literature. Here it is argued that when people are making judgements of probability they use heuristics that, though useful, can lead to systematic error. For example, Tversky and Kahneman (1973) have argued that people judge the probability of an event by the ease with which instances can be brought to mind (the availability heuristic). In an experimental demonstration, subjects were presented with lists of well-known personalities of both sexes and then asked to judge the relative frequencies of men and women. In some of the lists, the women were more famous than the men and in others the men were more famous than the women. In each of the lists, subjects incorrectly judged that the more frequent sex was the one with the greater number of famous people.

One of the difficulties that people face in their everyday activities is that of dealing with low probability threatening events. Slovic, Fischhoff and Lichtenstein (1978) argue that in dealing with these events people are more influenced by the probability of occurrence than the magnitude of the consequences. They considered the failure of people voluntarily to use seat belts. They estimated that a fatal accident occurred on approximately 1 in 3.5 million person trips. Here we might contrast the individual and population perspectives. From the population perspective, the use of seat belts aggregated across the community provides a near certainty of a benefit. However, from the individual's perspective the extra effort to protect oneself from an extremely unlikely event hardly seems worth the trouble.

If this analysis is correct then concentrating on the potentially catastrophic consequences of low probability events is not likely to be persuasive. However, Slovic, Fischhoff and Lichtenstein (1978) found that changing the time frame over which people make the judgement can result in a shift in intentions. When subjects were given the lifetime probabilities of a serious accident rather than the per trip probabilities they indicated that they intended to use seat belts more frequently and that they were more in favour of mandatory protection.

The possible specificity of these heuristics and biases to particular groups of people has become an interesting issue. For example, Goodin (1989) has proposed that smokers may suffer from some form of cognitive defect because they believe that they are less likely to suffer smoking related diseases than others. In an empirical test of this proposal, McKenna, Warburton and Winwood (1993) examined smokers' and non-smokers' perceptions of their own health risk and those of the average smoker and the average non-smoker. The findings indicated that smokers rated their chances of developing health-related problems as greater than non-smokers. Smokers also rated the average smoker as being more likely to suffer smoking associated health problems. However, smokers did judge that they personally were less likely to develop health-related problems than the average smoker.

The perception that one is personally less likely to experience future negative events than other people is a pervasive finding. When people are asked to assess their chances of experiencing a negative event such as getting cancer or having a heart attack (Perloff and Fetzer, 1986), being sterile (Weinstein, 1980) or being involved in an automobile accident (Robertson, 1977), it is found that most consider their chances to be less than others. Unrealistic optimism occurs not only in terms of a decreased subjective probability of negative events but also in an increased subjective probability for positive events. For example, Weinstein (1980) has found that relative to their colleagues at the same university, most students considered they had better chances of owning their own home, having a good starting salary and living past 80 years of age.

It seems clear that not only do people have problems with dealing with low probability events, there also seems to be a difficulty in establishing the personal significance of the threat. There are two alternative theoretical interpretations of the personal invulnerability result: (i) unrealistic optimism and (ii) the illusion of control. The illusion of control refers to the finding that people have an exaggerated belief about their control over events, and may even believe that they have control in areas of chance (Langer, 1975). The major distinction between the illusion of control and unrealistic optimism relies on the fact that optimism is concerned with an expectancy for positive outcomes independent of the source of these outcomes. Personal control is not a necessary factor. For example, one might be optimistic about tomorrow's weather without believing that one is exercising any personal control. Optimism may be defined as a generalized expectancy for positive outcomes. Whether this is realistic or unrealistic at an individual level is difficult to determine. However, when as a group the vast majority perceive their chances of a negative event as being less than average, then clearly this is not just optimistic but also unrealistic.

Many everyday activities involve elements of both skill and non-skill factors for success, thus leaving open the possibility that either or both unrealistic optimism and the illusion of control might operate. For example, one might believe that one is less likely than the average driver to be involved in an automobile accident (Robertson, 1977), either because of unrealistic optimism or due to an illusion of control. To examine this issue, McKenna (1993) had drivers make judgements of their accident risk when they had control, for example, when they were driving, and when they had no control, for example, as passengers. It is possible for unrealistic optimism to operate in both the control and no control conditions, but the illusion of control can only operate in the control conditions. The findings provided clear evidence for the illusion of control with no evidence for unrealistic optimism. The extent to which the illusion of control underlies other areas of perceived invulnerability is as yet unknown. At first sight, one's chances of having a heart attack do not seem particularly controllable but perhaps people perceive that by changing their diet and increasing their level of exercise, they are in control.

This research area does indicate that providing the conditions to foster a fully informed decision maker will be a major challenge.

Although the cognitive heuristic approach has generated a good deal of research and has been influential, it is not without its limitations. In particular, the cognitive heuristic approach may explain why people fail to avoid some risks, but it does not provide an explanation for the *active engagement* in the risk behaviours in the first place. While the risk of negative outcome may be very much on the minds of researchers and policy makers, it may not be on the minds of participants in the activity. Most people who engage in activities with some level of associated risk will have successfully completed the activity many times without incident. Take, for example, speeding on the road. Although speeding is associated with higher accident rates, the experience of the individual will be repeated involvement in the activity with reward as the only outcome.

MODELS OF HEALTH BEHAVIOUR

A number of theoretical models have been concerned with risk-taking behaviours that put one's health at risk. These models have been particularly concerned with understanding the factors involved in determining whether people accept recommendations regarding their health and act upon them. The most influential theory has been the Health Belief Model (Janz and Becker, 1984). The theory was initially designed to understand why people accept or fail to accept healthcare recommendations. The major components of the theory are:

- the individual's perception of personal susceptibility to the health threat,
- the perceived severity of the threat,
- the perceived benefits of the recommended health action,
- the barriers the individual foresaw to taking the health action.

Protection Motivation Theory (Rogers, 1983) is similarly concerned with understanding the effectiveness of persuasive health-relevant messages. It is proposed that the effectiveness of persuasive messages is mediated by the motivation to protect oneself, and this in turn is determined by the perceived severity of the threat, the perceived vulnerability to the threat and the belief that the recommended action will reduce the threat. The similarities with the Health Belief Model are apparent.

Maddux and Rogers (1983) examined Protection Motivation Theory by observing the responses of cigarette smokers to a number of communications. The messages were manipulated on the following dimensions:

1. The likelihood that negative outcomes (lung cancer and heart disease) would follow.
2. The severity of the negative outcome.
3. How beneficial it would be to stop smoking.
4. How easy or difficult it would be to stop smoking.

What is perhaps noticeable by its absence is that there is little attempt in the Health Belief Model or in Protection Motivation Theory to understand why people are inclined to engage in risk-taking behaviours in the first place. The perceived benefits of the risky choice are left largely unexplored. A more thorough understanding of risk-taking behaviour will require greater knowledge of the perceived pleasure, happiness, joy and comfort that individuals experience while engaged in activities that may damage their health.

It may be that researchers do have implicit theories concerning the motivations of individuals to engage in risk taking. For example, one implicit theory linking crime and risk taking is that money is the obvious motivation. However, some phenomenologically-orientated studies (Katz, 1988; Lyng, 1993) have challenged this view, arguing that the motivations involved are much more complicated. Lyng (1993) argues that when the subjective experience involved in criminal acts is examined there are great similarities with the experiences described by participants in high-risk occupations (e.g. fire-fighting) and risky leisure pursuits (e.g. skydiving). It is claimed that participants in all of these activities often interpret their experiences as 'magical and sensual'. Katz (1988) has argued that an understanding of the motivations to engage in criminal behaviour has more to do with the rewards of the experience than monetary gain. An understanding of the experiences of those engaged in the risky behaviour may shed new light on these activities or at least reduce the number of misunderstandings.

REDUCING RISK-TAKING BEHAVIOUR

Two factors combine to determine that reducing risk-taking behaviour will be a major societal concern for some time to come. The first and obvious point is that there are links between risk-taking behaviour and negative health consequences. In many societies there is a natural concern with the general health of the nation, and therefore there is some interest in any factors with adverse effects. The second and less obvious point is that from a societal perspective attention is often focused on the negative rather than the positive consequences of risk-taking behaviour. Negative consequences such as accidents or adverse health effects are readily observed and quantified. By contrast, positive outcomes, like pleasure, are less readily observed because they often involve only a subjective experience and are rarely quantified.

The above two factors will mean that there is often pressure to reduce risk-taking behaviour. There is a whole host of methods of attempting to reduce risk-taking behaviour, ranging from education and training, which tend to be uncontroversial, to legal enforcement, which can be very controversial. The difficulty with legal enforcement is that although it is often effective in reducing risk-taking behaviour, it does restrict individual freedom (see Luik, this volume).

One major problem has been identifying criteria that would justify interfering with other people's freedom. John Stuart Mill in his essay *On Liberty*, has argued that there is only one justification:

'the sole end for which mankind are warranted, individually or collectively in interfering with the liberty of action of any of their number is self-protection. That the only purpose for which power can be rightfully exercised over any member of a civilised community, against his will, is to prevent harm to others. He cannot rightfully be compelled to do or forbear because it will be better for him to do so, because, it will make him happier, because, in the opinions of others, to do so would be wise or even right.'

This criterion can go a long way towards justifying many of the interventions that operate in everyday life such as the ban on driving while intoxicated, or the regulations surrounding food production. The importance of the debate surrounding passive smoking can be appreciated in the light of this criterion. Seat-belt legislation is rather harder to justify on the basis of this criterion. Of course, one might reject Mill's criterion and argue that a balance between autonomy and personal well-being should be the aim. Feinberg (1986) has considered this option and rejected it, arguing that when well-being and autonomy conflict then autonomy should take precedence (see Buchanan and Brock, 1989, for an alternative analysis).

Although there is a great deal of emphasis on autonomy in the philosophical literature, interestingly there are some important contrasts with everyday life. Consider something as simple as choice of clothing. One would suspect that undue interference in the choice of an individual's clothes would be unwarranted. However, casual observation of middle class males at work would reveal an astonishing degree of uniformity in that by far the majority would wear a shirt, tie and suit, chosen from a very limited colour range. The fact that the same clothes are not worn at the weekend suggests that the work-day choice is not entirely voluntary. When asked, individuals will indicate that they are expected to wear such clothing and in general express little concern about the violation of autonomy.

One plausible reason for the lack of concern about the violation of autonomy is that for most individuals the issue is not very important and wearing the same type of clothing becomes a habit after a while. Two important issues are worth considering here. The first is that violations of autonomy vary in degree. Some violations appear to leave individuals unconcerned while others have a major impact on the person's quality of life. Clearly, the degree to which individuals value an activity should be considered when depriving them of liberty of action.

Seat-belt laws may provide an informative example. In Britain the majority of individuals did not voluntarily wear seat belts. The law requiring their use was clearly a violation of personal autonomy. For about ten years, successful parliamentary opposition was based on the violation of personal liberty. However, once the law was implemented, people not only changed their behaviour, but showed little concern about the violation of personal liberty that so concerned the politicians. In Britain (although one should be careful not to overgeneralize), the extra few seconds required to use the seat belt did not appear to be sufficiently important to merit serious complaint.

The second point that is worthy of note is that although philosophical discussion places great emphasis on the individual and the right to self-determination, one major problem for this analysis is that people do not lead their lives as individuals. People lead their lives as part of a range of social networks that include family, friends and work. These social networks do have important consequences for autonomy. For example, suppose three friends wish to spend an evening together. They each may prefer a different venue, but through discussion they choose an option that none of them would have individually chosen but which is nevertheless acceptable to them all. In other words, no individual fully exercised their personal autonomy.

Life is full of compromises. Earlier in the chapter, it was noted that it was possible to challenge the doctrine that life should be preserved at all costs. Likewise, it is possible to challenge the view that freedom should be preserved at all costs. After all, we readily accept the restriction of our freedom to drive on the 'wrong' side of the road. The benefits that we gain from sacrificing our freedom seem to be worth it (see the discussion of the importance of decisions being made by elected representatives versus dictatorship, however benevolent; Javeau, this volume).

There are important emergent features of living in a context of many other individuals. If many people choose to engage in the same behaviour there can be consequences that no one would desire and yet, without intervention, no one will change. For example, the pollution caused by coal fires has in the past resulted in restrictions enforcing the use of smokeless fuels. The action of any individual would have had a minimal negative effect on the pollution in comparison to the immediate positive effect in producing heat, so individual action would support continuing the pollution. It is only the collective action of the group that could have a significant impact.

Living in groups almost inevitably involves restrictions in liberty in the form of rules and regulations. The difficulty is in ensuring that these rules and regulations do not needlessly compromise personal autonomy (see Javeau, Luik, this volume). Perhaps greater efforts can be made to deliver personal autonomy while avoiding unwanted risks. Here, it might be noted that many smokers do not wish to damage their health, but they do wish to continue to receive pleasure from smoking. Designing a safer cigarette that delivers the pleasure and minimizes the risk would be one compromise. Similarly, most people who drive cars do not wish to be involved in accidents, but some do enjoy the sensation of speed. At an empirical level, speed is linked to accident involvement, but, interestingly, the sensation of speed is not automatically linked to actual speed. Indeed, it is arguable that car manufacturers and road designers have systematically deprived the driver of cues that indicate speed. For example, major efforts are made to reduce car vibration, engine sound and wind resistance. On the highways, all of the visual information that would provide a visual streaming effect and hence a sensation of speed are eliminated. The driver is left isolated in a comfortable cocoon. An alternative design philosophy would be to introduce cues to speed (not necessarily vibration and engine noise) so that people can get the same pleasure at lower objective speeds.

Is it too much to hope that there are some circumstances where allowing people to have what they want might be in all our interests?

15

The Assault on Pleasure: Health Promotion and Engineering the Human Soul

John C. Luik

Niagara Institute, Box 1041, 176 John Street East, Niagara-on-the-Lake, Ontario, LOS 1JO, Canada

One of the most alarming aspects of most liberal democracies over the past two decades has been the development of government and quasi-governmental agencies for health promotion. While there is some question over what precisely health promotion is, I think that minimally it involves the following strong claims about health:

1. There is an increasing scientific consensus about one healthy way to live that has as its end 'a state of complete physical, mental and social well-being'.
2. Much disease is caused by inappropriate beliefs, unhealthy life choices and behaviours, and so disease can be prevented by appropriate behavioral changes.
3. Individuals have a moral obligation to live their lives in accordance with the societal conception of 'healthy', i.e. to avoid inappropriate life choices.
4. The task of heath promotion is two-fold: (i) to disseminate the truth about health, disease and behaviour with change of both individual and societal beliefs as its end; and (ii) to

Pleasure and Quality of Life. Edited by D.M. Warburton and N. Sherwood
© 1996 John Wiley & Sons Ltd.

provide, aided by the state, the necessary mechanisms for changing individual and societal behaviour with respect to health and disease.

What I wish to argue is that health promotion thus conceived represents a fundamental threat to the values that define a liberal democratic society, namely to science, reason and freedom.

By the values of science, I mean the commitment to empiricism, to the process of marshalling and evaluating the quality of empirical data, to the process of distinguishing facts from fancy in the service of discovering in some sense the objectively real.

By the values of reason, I mean the commitment to reasoned argument, coherent and consistently elaborated propositions, to the development of themes with appropriate supporting claims, to the renunciation of the arbitrary and the authoritarian as the basis of settling disputes between individuals, and between individuals and the community, and as the basis of what is now called public policy.

By the values of freedom, I mean the commitment to allowing all people to order their beliefs, their passions, their ends—in short, their lives—according to their own choices, provided only that they grant others the same right and that their choices do not demonstrably harm others.

HEALTH PROMOTION AND ENGINEERING THE HUMAN SOUL

Of course, there are other values that serve to characterize a liberal society, but it is these that perhaps more than any others shape its substance and its process, and its core conception of what human persons are. For example, if we look to the core rights that attach to individuals in free and democratic societies, they are rights that define an individual, rights that seek to define the inviolable areas. Alternatively, if we look to the democratic process of public policy making, then we find that it is founded upon a deep respect for reason, compelling empirical evidence and objectivity of process.

To say, then, that health promotion is a fundamental threat to the central values of a liberal society is to claim that its aims, its philosophy, its conception of persons, its policies and its methods are incompatible, not in some peripheral way, but in a fundamental way, with the values of science, reason and freedom.

Now, it is a measure both of the vagueness of health promotion and the debased level of their language, that the health promoter will respond to these claims by arguing that, far from threatening freedom, science and reason, health promotion is in reality not merely protecting them but furthering them. It promises not only significant advances in individual and collective health, but furthers science, rational behaviour and genuine autonomy.

THE MORALITY OF HEALTH PROMOTION

All of this suggests that the crucial question about health promotion is not simply definitional but also moral, i.e. what is the moral foundation of health promotion? Why should the state and medicine engage in health promotion? Why should its recommendations become public policy?

I would suggest that health promotion is morally acceptable and that it is legitimate public policy only if:

1. The benefits to be obtained from such promotion clearly outweigh the harms attached to it.
2. The furtherance of health promotion as public policy in no way threatens the core democratic value of autonomy.

Now, I will assert the moral priority of autonomy as a non-negotiable, regardless of health promotion's improvements in health outcomes; in other words, health promotion is not morally acceptable if it erodes individual autonomy. Put most starkly, if pressed to choose between improved health and lessened freedom, I would argue for feeling less well, while being more free.

What, then, are the benefits of health promotion? I will be brief—and, I trust, not overly rash—by saying that apart from the possibility of smoking, and I emphasize, the *possibility* of smoking, there appear to be no substantial benefits that can be traced to health promotion as I have defined it, where benefits are construed as a beneficial improvement on either morbidity or mortality. I am not claiming that this suggests that health promotion, in principle, could not be as beneficial, or even superior to, curative medicine; rather that, in the real world, it is extraordinarily difficult for this principle to come to reality.

Perhaps the most obvious reason for the unfulfilled promise of health promotion is that the causes of the disorders that it seeks to prevent through promoting healthy living are insufficiently understood. Preventive strategies are inescapably linked to a detailed, precise and reliable knowledge of the causes of disease, and this first-order knowledge of causation, not merely association, is a necessary condition for health promotion having any benefits. Thus, this failure to heed the necessary conditions of possible success manifests itself in the fact that the major targets of health promotion, e.g. lifestyle changes with respect to physical activity and diet, have no demonstrated association with significant reductions in cancer and coronary disease (see Skrabanek, 1995). Indeed, the gain in average lifespan to be derived from preventing all cancers has been calculated at only seven months for those aged 15–65.

None of this should surprise anyone, for the major efforts of health promoters are directed to cancer and cardiovascular diseases, diseases that are largely determined by ageing. Indeed, some would argue that the disease interventions of the health promoter are for the most part for diseases that are not susceptible to prevention in as much as their origins have more to do with heredity and chance than to specific lifestyle.

Thus far I have argued that the clinical evidence with respect to improvements in morbidity and mortality due to health promotion is weak. But what of the costs of health promotion? A full treatment of this issue would examine seven costs:

- costs to autonomy and respect
- cost to democracy
- costs to tolerance
- costs to truthfulness
- costs to science
- costs to medicine
- costs to public policy

Given the limitations of space, I will only concentrate on the costs that health promotion presents to autonomy.

HEALTH PROMOTION AS A THREAT TO AUTONOMY

One of the more insidious aspects of health promotion is its claim that through promoting health it actually serves to strengthen and extend the arena of individual and societal autonomy. This claim, however, rests on the faulty assumption that the conception of health used by health promoters is a necessary condition of a satisfying, a good human life, such that a rational person would accord a primacy to health over all other values.

For the health promoter, the logic is simple. If health is a necessary condition for any sort of life, it outweighs any other values that might conflict with it, particularly when health is defined, in the words of the World Health Organization, as 'a state of complete physical, mental, and social well- being, and not merely the absence of disease or infirmity'. But the 'logic' here is flawed. For while it may indeed be true that being alive is a necessary condition for having a life, it is not at all clear that being healthy in that definition is a necessary condition for having a good life.

This is not to suggest that some aspects of health are not an important factor in a good life or an autonomous life; it is rather that:

1. Individuals whose lives do not meet the definition of health favoured by health promoters might still lead rich and good lives, lives satisfactory to themselves and lives freely chosen.
2. People often place a higher value on things other than health.

I will concede that being healthy in the sense of free from debilitating disease can enhance certain kinds of autonomy, but it does not follow that healthy in the all-encompassing sense of the health promoter is a necessary condition of autonomy. Indeed, this sense of the balance between health and autonomy, like the balance between health and the other values of a good life, is determined not by external fiat but by the individual.

HEALTH AUTONOMY AS AN IMPEDIMENT
TO AUTONOMY

What I am saying is not simply that health promotion does not further individual autonomy, but that it actually impedes individual autonomy.

Firstly, its sweeping definition of health allows it to be truly totalitarian. I use that word in its true sense, of a compass of control over individuals.

Medicine's traditional and more limited role of attempting to relieve distress and to bring some degree of physical healing has been replaced with an all-encompassing belief that medicine should bring 'complete physical, mental and social well-being'. As Faith Fitzgerald has written, 'We broadened our horizon from physical problems to character flaws, poverty, crime, unhappiness and even unattractiveness. Internal medicine, surgery, preventive medicine, family practice, paediatrics, neonatology, and especially plastic surgery, genetic engineering, prenatal diagnosis, nutrition, and psychiatry promised potential perfection' (Fitzgerald, 1994, p. 196).

Once health is defined in this fashion, it brings in everything: character, beliefs, habits, pleasures— all of them under the purview of health promotion. Reasoned and careful argument is no longer needed: it is enough to utter the dreaded 'unhealthy' and one has a license to proceed to change not merely eating patterns but thought patterns. Totalitarian is appropriate, then, because the real project is only apparently the physical. The real argument goes much deeper: for to save the body we must literally engineer the soul.

Thus, the health promoter's focus on lifestyle gives away the entire game, for lifestyle is really about nothing more than lives, about how individual human persons choose to order their lives. And the attempt to engineer healthy lifestyles through engineering beliefs is the attempt to engineer the course of human lives. Once health is defined as everything, there is no place for a life that is ordered outside the boundaries of health.

Put so bluntly, it is difficult to understand why health promotion would survive a moment's reflection. We do not, at least in free and democratic societies, allow authority to order our political or religious lifestyles. Why would we allow such authority to order our health lives?

The answer, I think, is to be found in the second sense in which health promotion impedes individual autonomy, and that is that it passes itself off as scientific as opposed to ideological. Whereas politics and religion are matters of personal belief and are not subject to objective analysis, health, and by extension health promotion, is something that is scientifically determinable. Thus, autonomy might reasonably extend to the domains of the ideological, such as religion and politics, but it has no place in the domain of science, that is health.

But is this really the case? Consider the paradigm argument of the health promoter, wherein X wishes to pursue a pleasure Y; the health promoter will say to X: 'Stopping will allow you to live longer. Therefore, you ought to stop Y'. Inasmuch as logic is not the strong suit of health promotion, the health promoter will have neglected the fact that his syllogism is incomplete. He needs a missing premise of the order: X values living longer more than she values Y, her pleasure. But as soon as this premise is added, the scientific character of health promotion is exposed for what it is, a thin cheat.

While it is certainly true that science might tell X that stopping Y will allow her to live longer (if in fact there is good evidence that this is really the case), it is not true that it is science that tells X that she ought to value living longer more than her pleasure. The oughts that are directed to X, whether about wishing to live longer or stopping Y, are addressed to her but by health promotion's version of moral philosophy, not by science.

This is not to imply that they are unworthy of consideration, but merely to suggest that they are the pronouncements of philosophy, not science. Thus, they must be justified, like any other bit of moral philosophy, through careful argument, not through dogmatic pronouncement. Neither medicine nor health promotion has any special intellectual claim for its moral pronouncements, nor is there any evidence that doctors and health promoters live lives of exemplary moral character or insight that would qualify them to determine the moral foundations of entire societies.

In short, the scientific character of health promotion extends at most to its knowledge claims about the causes of ill health. Its pronouncements about what to do with that knowledge form no part of science. Indeed, they are as much a part of the arena of personal beliefs and values as are politics and religion. This means that the entire edifice of health promotion is built on a very shaky foundation, if it has never provided itself with a compelling moral foundation of the kind that would furnish a general argument for the proposition that a life of 70 years full of self-selected pleasures was substantially inferior to a life of 80 years lived without the traditional lifestyle pleasures. It has never shown by specific arguments that a shorter life with some all-important pleasure is worse than a slightly longer life without it.

Now, the health promoter might accept that health promotion must do the hard work of moral philosophy and produce good arguments as to why certain value decisions are better than others. To this extent, health promotion will be subject to the same standards of argument that govern traditional moral claims. Or the health promoter might wish to claim that his moral pronouncements are both obvious and indubitable. In either case, however, he will have acknowledged that a good deal of health promotion is closer to religion and politics than to science.

HEALTH PROMOTION AS HEALTH PATERNALISM

It might be objected at this point that while it is one thing to put forth an overly broad conception of human health, it is another thing to use such a conception to thwart individual autonomy. We can, so the argument might run, allow health promoters their expansive notion of health inasmuch as we know that realizing such a state is impossible. In the end, death and disease are real and they cannot be forever cheated, even by the ideology of health promotion.

Health promotion is not, regrettably, a mere intellectual exercise—its totalitarian definition of health is linked with a genuinely paternalist agenda such that health promoters are invariably paternalist. Such health paternalism is the third way in which health promotion threatens individual autonomy. If health promotion were merely what the words appear to suggest—arguing for health, asking that individuals consider a health perspective in their choices of life—then the health promotion movement would be much less of a problem. Stripped of its scientific pretensions and its official standing, funding and legal sanctions, the moral pronouncements of health promotion would be on a similar footing with those of the Vatican: duly reported, heeded by the true believers and ignored by almost everyone else.

But health promotion does not aspire to the diminished clout of 20th century Roman Catholicism: if anything, it aims for something closer to the political, moral, theological and legal power of the medieval church. Health promotion fully intends that its moral pronouncements about correct lifestyle will be both morally and legally obligatory.

At its core, the health paternalist believes four things: firstly, that there is but one healthy/rational way to live one's life and this way does not include pleasures, activities that entail significant risks to well-being or longevity; secondly, that individuals have a moral obligation to live their lives in this healthy, rational way; thirdly, that individuals frequently have a difficult time living their lives in such a healthy, rational way; and fourthly, that the state is justified, indeed has a moral obligation, to ensure that its citizens conform to this healthy, rational lifestyle, even if they do not wish to or are unable to do so themselves.

The core assumption here is that there is a vast dichotomy of knowledge in society, a dichotomy between those few who know the truth about health, disease, pleasure and lifestyle and those many who are ignorant or knowing but wilful. Failure to heed the admonitions of the health promoters is prima facie evidence either of irrationality or of addiction. It is instructive that at its conceptual core, health promotion, like all forms of paternalism, is unfalsifiable. There is nothing that is allowed as counting to falsify the thesis that those who choose to order their lives against the prevailing dictates of health fashion are irrational or in the compulsive grip of their desires. There simply is no claim of thinking or knowing that counts against the superior knowledge of the health promoter. Given this refusal to specify what in principle would falsify their claims, I would suggest that this is in itself a sufficient reason for rejecting health promotion.

HEALTH PROMOTION AND RISK

The health promoter as a paternalist is thus at pains to prevent individuals—for their own good, of course—from living their lives outside of his conception of the healthy life. The primary conceptual tool in this process is the notion of risk. Indeed, though the ostensible message of the health promoter is about health, his deeper message is almost always couched in the language of risks. What the health promoter as health paternalist argues for is an involuntary process of collectivized risk, not risks that are imposed on others, for which there is a legitimate societal interest, but risks that one assumes voluntarily for oneself.

Health promotion as health paternalism seeks to collectively distinguish legitimate from illegitimate risk and thus remove from the individual the right and the responsibility to make his or her own risk assessments. Such a collectivization of risk is a major infringement of individual autonomy, for our assessment of risk and the manner in which we calculate risk relative to certain benefits is a major component of what we mean when we speak about having a life of our own.

Inasmuch as virtually all human actions, not just pleasures, entail risk, the idea of risk provides at least one dimension against which we can plot what we mean by a good life. In the simplest sense, this can be done through developing a profile of what thing we choose to do in the face of what risks. The calculus of risk and reward—chocolate yes, smoking no, scuba diving no, travel by car yes—is personal, largely *ad hoc* and deeply inconsistent. Equally important, such individual calculi are arational in the sense that they lie outside the bounds of conventional rationality. What I mean by this is that conventional rationality cannot pronounce on the legitimacy of an individual's risk calculus without introducing some prior, external conception of what a proper ordering of risk and reward might be.

But what, it might be asked, would be the foundational principle of such ordering? How would reason simply as reason be able to say to anyone that chocolate yes, smoking no is a rational risk analysis? The answer, of course, is that reason could provide such a critique only in the context of my subjective appraisal of the values of chocolate and smoking and against the value I ascribe to certain other ends such as longevity. Reason, in short, as Hume observed, is the instrumental servant of my passion, or the values that I attach to chocolate, smoking and longevity.

Risk, then, serves as a conceptual shorthand for a complex set of values and choices that are at the centre of what we mean when we speak of having a human life. Risk is the road that takes us to the heart of the soul. Indeed, I would argue that charting the topography of those tradeoffs that an individual has made between risk and reward tells us an enormous amount about what that person considers to be a good life.

The health promoter's desire, then, to manage risk is nothing more than a vast project to usurp not some peripheral but the central aspect of having an autonomous life. What he seeks to do—in the name of enhancing my interests, of course—is to replace my passions, my values, my choices, my weighting of risk and reward, careful or careless as the case may be, with his risk calculus, with his idea of healthy, with his idea of the good life. What he wants to do is to expand reason's province from the instrumental—telling me how I might get what I want—to the morally foundational—telling me what I ought to want. By capturing the definitions of health, risk and reason, the health promoter gains a sweeping power to define and enforce his definition of how personal lives should be lived. Where, within such a vast, ordered and carefully engineered edifice, is there room for the idiosyncratic, the autonomous life? Indeed, what meaning does personal choice, personal value and personal responsibility retain within so sweeping a programme?

The health promoter, of course, might reply that whatever we might think about individual autonomy, his risk calculus, his definition of acceptable tradeoffs, his definition of the good life is not merely different from mine, but better than mine. In what way better? Better in the sense of more rational than mine. But this argument about more rational simply will not work. The health promoter's risk calculus, like his definition of health and a satisfying life, is more rational only if rational is defined as maximizing longevity. And it is this equation of rationality and a good life with a particular kind of long life—one that is without certain values and experience—that requires not dogmatism but argumentation.

It is not obviously true that it is more rational to prefer a slightly longer life deprived of some essential personal good to a slightly shorter one—and, remember, we are not talking about vast differences in years—with that good. Only the one who lives that life has the privileged access to the information about the relative weightings of pleasure Y and risk Z that would allow of such a judgement as more rational; only he can describe how important pleasure Z is in the overall scheme of things.

The health promoter as health paternalist is forced to defend the impossible claim that he knows more about X's values, tastes, beliefs, about what mixture of pleasure and pain gives X's life meaning, than does X himself. He must proclaim without shame that most people do not know what is good for them, that they cannot do well at once the most intimate and exhilarating project of human existence, fashioning their own life.

What makes such arrogant paternalism all the more curious is the fact that its claim to superimpose its own conception of what is a valuable human life and a correct set of value preferences is resolutely opposed in most other areas of medicines. What oncologist, for instance, would adopt the aggressive paternalism of the health promoter and seek to force his terminal patients to accept his value preferences about the benefits and burdens of a particular care regime? Indeed, it is another of the many anomalies associated with health paternalism that it seeks to push its agenda of what a properly ordered life is just as most other areas of medicine are attempting to respect their patients' decisions about how they wish to live their lives and order their dying (see Fitzgerald, this volume).

SUMMARY

Health promotion, then, appears to deliver few benefits, is conceptually incoherent, internally inconsistent and a major threat to the foundations of a liberal society. In the end, it fails to make us better while guaranteeing to leave us less free.

16

Choosing How to Live

Faith Fitzgerald

University of California, Davis Medical Center, Sacramento,
CA 95817-2282, USA

People have always felt compelled to tell other people how to behave, particularly in the areas of food, sex, pleasure and language. Religions, governments, clubs—indeed entire societies—are predicated upon cohesion in these areas. These rules of behaviour are also the manner in which human beings attempt to impose order on a sometimes capricious and ungovernable nature.

With the advent of modern medicine, and its often startling efficacy, as well as the increasing secularization of social mores, those who would govern the behaviour of others have shifted emphasis, at least in some nations, from admonitions that correct behaviour will save one's immortal soul, to similar propositions that correct behaviour will save one's mortal body (see Skrabanek, 1995).

Certainly, the admonitions to correct diet, acceptable sexual partnerships, proscription of tobacco and alcohol, and many of the rituals of preventative medicine are exhorted on the basis that not only is it good for the individual, but because of the cost of the sickness of the individual to society in social medical systems, it is a social obligation (see van Dun, this volume).

It is intriguing that few overtly recognize the division of so-called 'self-abuse' into socially approved and socially disapproved

Pleasure and Quality of Life. Edited by D.M. Warburton and N. Sherwood
© 1996 John Wiley & Sons Ltd.

categories. Exercise, asceticism and chastity are approved; smoking, drinking alcohol, eating as one wishes and sexual indulgence are all disapproved. Yet in their extremes both categories cause illness and ultimately contribute to the death of the individual. Of course, death is inevitable anyhow. Those who claim that, should one follow all of the rules of proper behaviour for health's sake, one will maintain oneself well are suffering a pleasant delusion. What is guaranteed is death; the only question is when and how.

This is not generally accepted. In the United States we have come to a point where dying and death are, in a sense, unnatural acts. We act as if we believe that death is avoidable if only we know enough and behave well as regards diet, exercise, personal philosophy, preventative medicine and the utilization of the recent tremendous advances in medical science. Witness in evidence of this is the fact that Americans are upset when the percentage of people dying of cardiovascular disease goes down only to have the percentage of people dying of cancer go up.

Of course, 100% of dead people died of something, so if one goes down another must go up. But we look at these data in horror and fling ourselves into the battle against cancer, for example. If we win, however, it will happen that as deaths from cancer go down, deaths from yet another cause will rise, and we will have to engage yet another battle. Everyone dies. Last year, the authors of an article in an American medical journal proclaimed that vegetarians had lower mortality than omnivores. The editors did not notice or comment upon this remarkable statement.

Recently, at a national medical meeting, a panel on geriatrics noted that the major causes of death in old, old age—over 80 years—were cardiovascular, cancer and trauma. They then went on to discuss how to prevent all three. I, in the audience, began to wonder: if people in their 80s and 90s are not allowed to die of cardiovascular disease, trauma or cancer, what can they die of? Dissolution?

If we accept that death is inevitable then the proper question to ask as doctors and citizens is not the question of life versus death. It is, rather, how best to accomplish each; what is the good in each, and when and how the one, life, should be surrendered to the other, death.

When one asks people how they want to live they will, in the majority, answer 'long and happily'. Conversely, if asked how they want to die, they generally respond 'late and suddenly'. One man told me he wanted to be shot by a jealous husband at the age of 110. Ideally, then, a man or woman would usually choose to live a full, active and unimpaired life until the instant of sudden, painless death. If this is true it means that we believe the best death is one in which there is no preceding dying. It is dying rather than death that appears to be most painful, socially disruptive, fearful and expensive. This is made clear by euthanasia advocates, who have quite clearly told us that they fear death less than they do dying.

Now, when one begins dying exactly is unclear. Some say it is at birth. Some people who look entirely well are dying. Others teeter on the edge of death for years. Many think of the aged as dying just because they are old. And dying, I propose, is often as much a social as a medical status, and that the position of the dying individual is extremely uncomfortable, not only because of the pains of the illness itself, but also because of the loss of social position and control, its social isolation, and, to an increasing extent—borne of the idea of the preventability of disease and death—blameworthiness (see Fitzgerald, 1994).

Illness, the depredations of age, even death itself are thought by many to be one's own fault because one did not eat correctly, exercise enough or undergo proper preventative maintenance. The aged are even blamed for living too long. As culpable in their own dying, these unfortunate people now also have to bear the extra sin of beggaring the healthcare system. So even if the dying person is held personally innocent for his or her illness, they are nonetheless unarguably a drain upon the state.

Data have suggested that preventative medicine and 'correct behaviour' may actually be increasing healthcare cost, by prolonging the expensive period of dying. The increasing burden of cost for the elderly, for life maintenance in the terminally ill, and for the dysfunction in those who have not died suddenly, has created a conundrum. Sudden death, particularly sudden painless death, as with major strokes, myocardial infarction or trauma, would be an advantage to both the individual who is fearful of prolonged dying and to society. Yet society takes as many steps as possible to prevent sudden death, by imposing strictures upon human behaviour that markedly decrease one's chances of that occurrence.

Of course, sudden death is rare, and the burden of illness—the failure of parts, social status changes, financial burdens, pain, confusion and disability—are the more common modes of exit. Perhaps we should stop all of the argument about how to prolong life, since the paradoxes are insurmountable, and turn our attention as individuals and as social planners to how to guarantee the best death. Of course, there will be influences of individual behaviour, but this must also take into account the biological realities of genetic and social predispositions.

This idea, of recognizing the inevitability of death and of planning for it in a realistic way, is somewhat new. Certainly societies and religions have designed the ideal death for their membership—whether it be glorious death in battle, death by assisted suicide, death by martyrdom, or other ritual formulation—but the tools now of science and particularly of genetic understanding have provided us with a methodology that would preserve individual autonomy (highly valued 'right' in most Western societies) and at the same time approach death realistically, perhaps to considerable cost savings.

In my proposal, which I call 'designer death', individuals would be offered, at the age of cognition, alternatives (according to the best knowledge of the day) for the manner in which they would wish to live their lives, specifically directed at the manner in which they wish their lives to end. For this proposition, the contributions of the human genome project cannot be overstated.

For example; if an individual has a strong family history of heart disease, with death from myocardial infarction in the 40s and 50s, and that same individual, should heart disease be avoided, has a genomic predisposition to colonic carcinoma in the 60s and 70s, or, if that be escaped, Alzheimer's disease in the 80s and 90s, then one could offer that individual the best advice as to how to live his or her life to 'choose' one.

Thus, if one would prefer to die of heart disease at the age of 40–60, current wisdom says one could eat fat-rich foods, smoke heavily and abstain entirely from alcohol. Should one wish to avoid heart disease and live a little longer, taking the chance of

colonic carcinoma, one could be advised to undergo a low cholesterol diet, abjure smoking, drink moderately and maximize one's
chances of getting the colonic carcinoma as opposed to the heart
attack. If, on the other hand, one wants to live a very long time,
but with Alzheimer's as a possibility at the end (since genetic
predisposition may now be influential in that), one would eat a
low fat diet, drink moderately, undergo preventative periodic
gastrointestinal investigations, and hope that smoking might prevent Alzheimer's.

This plan, though imperfect, is, I would put to you, far more
realistic than our current procedures, gives individuals much
more power over their own lives and deaths (acknowledging the
ever present whimsy of nature and of society) and to a degree
removes the 'blame' from those who choose a life full of the
pleasures of alcohol, tobacco and other hedonistic indulgences
since those individuals—by doing so—are contributing to both
their own and society's best interest.

Of course, sudden death is not guaranteed, and premature
death may advantage only a few. Nonetheless, it has become clear
that inordinate prolongation of life and prolonged periods of
dying are opprobrious both to the individual and to society. The
latter is our current system, and we may wish to consider another.
To choose one, such as designer dying, that takes full advantage
of advances in modern medical knowledge, allows chosen self-
indulgence in the pleasures of life, and potentially decreases the
agony of slow and painful death from an undesired disease, has a
certain appeal.

17

Health Scares Are Bad for Your Health

James McCormick

Community Health Unit, Department of Community Health and
General Practice, Trinity College, University of Dublin,
119 Pearse Street, Dublin, Ireland

'Life itself is not the most important thing in life. Some cling to it as a miser
to his money and to as little purpose. Others risk it for a song, a cause, a
hope, for wind in their hair.' (Fox, 1965)

INTRODUCTION

My thesis may be simply stated: the health gurus have diminished
health.

Health is certainly not to be found in the aspiration of the World
Health Organization, as 'a state of complete physical, mental and
social well-being and not merely the absence of disease' (WHO,
1958). It was Henry Miller who said that such a Utopian state was
only achieved in acute mania and at the moment of orgasm.

Probably the most popular notion abroad, although not shared
by the gurus, has something to do with coping. Coping with the
'slings and arrows of outrageous fortune' allows health to the
impaired, the handicapped, and can even envisage dying healthy.
It has to do with maximizing our capacity to enjoy life and to live
it to the full. On the other hand, the health promotion zealots seem

Pleasure and Quality of Life. Edited by D.M. Warburton and N. Sherwood
© 1996 John Wiley & Sons Ltd.

to believe that health is avoiding death. This centres mainly on avoiding cancer and coronary heart disease. As, for the most part, we do not know the cause of these afflictions, we are in a poor position to prevent them (McCormick, 1988).

So, since the end of the Second World War, epidemiologists have turned their attention away from infectious disease and towards cancer and coronary heart disease, and have described associations between factors and an altered probability of developing disease. Something over three hundred risk factors have now been described for coronary heart disease. This is a monument to industry but a reflection of ignorance. However, despite lack of evidence that such factors are causally related, we have been led to believe that modifications to 'lifestyle' can prevent our death. These have concentrated on the avoidance of tobacco, reducing our dietary intake of saturated fats, especially dairy products, increased exercise, weight reduction, and having one's blood pressure and cholesterol regularly checked and often treated with drugs.

MEDICAL HUBRIS

It was Osler who remarked that what distinguished man from the animals was a propensity to take medicines. There is, however, something else that makes the distinction, and it is man's need for explanations. All societies have needed an explanation for our birth, our death and the pain of the journey in between. This is the *raison d'être* for religions. Ridiculously, medicine has become the major religion of the rich world and is believed both to provide explanations and to rid us of disease and discomfort. The high priests of this new religion are the epidemiologists and public health physicians who believe that, for example, coronary heart disease is preventable. Other evangelists would have us believe that 'cancer can be conquered'. The new religion has found fertile soil in the aspirations of politicians to offer a new and better life, especially if it can be provided at minimal cost.

The false promise of salvation has been described by W.H. Carlyon, one-time director of the Health Education Programme of the American Medical Association:

'Constant lifestyle self scrutiny in search of risk factors, denial of pleasure, rejection of the old evil lifestyle and embracing a new rigorous one are followed by periodical reaffirmation of faith at revival meetings of believers ... The zeal with which converts are sought by the recently saved is of awesome intensity ... The self righteous intolerance of some wellness zealots border on health fascism. Historically, humans have been at greatest risk while being improved in the best image of the possibilities as seen by somebody else.' (Carlyon, 1984)

The growth of medical knowledge in my lifetime has been truly amazing. But, as Lewis Thomas has remarked, 'the ship of biological science is under way, but only just'. An increase in knowledge allows a better definition of ignorance but medicine has been deluded into believing that the relative increase in knowledge, dramatic as it has been, has made an appreciable dent in the state of our ignorance. It is this delusion that has led to medical hubris: which has led to false premises and false promises.

As Petr Skrabanek (1995) remarked, 'life is a universally fatal sexually transmitted disease'. Health promotion zealots cannot offer anything other than a prolongation of life. It is not true that they offer a reduction in life's suffering, because not dying of a heart attack allows the possibility of dying of cancer, or the slow death of senescence, often accompanied by Alzheimer-type dementia.

THE ETHICAL DIMENSION

Like other religions, medicine has developed a morality of its own. Smoking, eating white bread, chips, salt and fats, being a 'couch potato', failing to use condoms, drinking, using cannabis, not wearing crash helmets: these things are immoral and 'the wages of sin is death'. Virginia Bottomley, former Secretary of State for Health in the United Kingdom had, in her department, banned not only smoking but also biscuits with coffee (apples were provided). She also informed us that she planned two alcohol-free days a week!

As Mencken pointed out, 'hygiene', now known as preventative medicine:

'is the corruption of medicine by morality. It is impossible to find a hygienist who does not debase their theory of the healthful with a theory of the virtuous. This brings it, at the end, into diametrical conflict with medicine proper. The aim of medicine is surely not to make men virtuous; it is to safeguard and rescue them from the consequences of the their vices. The true physician does not preach repentance; he offers absolution.' (Mencken, 1923)

Health promotion in the 1990s is value-laden and insecurely based. There is no justification for concern over diet unless it is so bizarre that vitamin deficiency becomes a real possibility, with the conceivable exception that women who contemplate pregnancy might wish to ensure that their foliate stores were adequate. Fat, a word redolent of sin, salt, fibre, white bread etc.—there is no good evidence that they matter a hoot! Although the evidence that moderate alcohol intake protects against coronary heart disease is good, health promotion never advocates its use, presumably from fear that use equates excess.

In 1971, Cochrane and Holland, in a paper entitled 'Validation of screening procedures', had this to say:

'We believe that there is an ethical difference between everyday medical practice and screening. If a patient asks a medical practitioner for help, the doctor does the best he can. He is not responsible for defects in medical knowledge. If, however, the practitioner initiates screening procedures he is in a very different situation. He should in our view, have conclusive evidence that screening can alter the natural history of disease in a significant proportion of those screened.' (Cochrane and Holland, 1971)

While Cochrane and Holland were talking about screening, it can readily be argued that the responsibility for conclusive evidence should apply to the whole field of public health. If a doctor advises or treats a patient in ways that are not effective or are harmful, only that patient suffers. If public health policy is ineffective or harmful, whole populations run the risk of diminished health. It follows that the degree of certainty that is required in relation to matters of public health needs to be of a greater order than that which governs the conduct of the individual consultation.

This creates a dilemma, recently stated by Cecily Kelleher, a professor of health promotion:

'What needs to be resolved about basic scientific arguments on any issue, health promotion or not, is at what point can action be taken to translate existing knowledge into policy and whose responsibility is it to take the consequences of that decision.' (Kelleher, 1995)

In arguing on ethical as well as pragmatic grounds for a high degree of certainty that the outcome will be beneficent, I run the risk, with which I am very comfortable, of being labelled an 'abominable no-man' (McCormick, 1990).

Returning to Professor Kelleher, she writes:

> 'Public health guidelines, as opposed to guidelines for specific individual management, are all broadly in agreement on advice to eat a balanced diet, take more exercise, and reduce the relative fat intake in favour of fruit and vegetables. While these may be argued as vague or aspirational by some, it is unlikely from any known evidence that qualitative advice of this kind could translate into a nutritional catastrophe'.

This unexceptionable statement does, however, ignore the extent to which inappropriate concern about diet has diminished people's enjoyment of food, added to maternal anxiety and may have encouraged eating disorders.

There is another ethical dimension that concerns the imposition of moral overtones upon health education. Health education should be about the sharing of information. It should not be offered unless there is certainty about the truth of the information, accepting that in science truth is a best available approximation. If there is uncertainty, it should be shared. People should be informed about risks as well as benefits. Risk should be stated in absolute and not in relative terms. Health education eschews words such as 'good' or 'bad', 'better' or 'undesirable'. It provides information, which people may choose to use and so reduce the chances of disease. It respects individual autonomy and leaves it intact.

Health education has a place. It should be concerned with informing the public of those things that are known to be dangerous to health and the magnitude of the risk that is run by ignoring the information. It must be securely based. It should be free of moral overtones; it should provide useful information but respect the individual's right to choose to take risks. It must not become a justification for victim blaming, for denying life-saving surgery to smokers ('Smoker dies after test denied', *The Times*, 17th August 1993), for regarding AIDS as retribution, for failing to provide clean syringes to those who choose to inject drugs.

Health gurus, on the other hand, promote a morality based upon what is seen as a desirable lifestyle. Smoking has moved from normative to deviance, to sin. Health zealots proscribe certain foods, extol the virtues of being slim and of taking regular exercise, and label sinners as 'couch potatoes'.

EXAMPLES OF TAKING HEALTH AWAY

Fatness

The Royal College of General Practitioners advises in its guidelines for the management of hyperlipidaemia that those whose body mass index (BMI) is more than 25 should be counselled (Royal College of General Practitioners, 1992). BMI is a method of controlling weight for height and is calculated as weight in kilograms divided by height in metres squared. It is a useful way to compare the nutritional state of populations but has no relevance to the individual. Prospective studies have shown that the plump, if anything, live longer than the thin, and that the ill effects on mortality of fatness are not apparent until BMI exceeds 30 (Rissanen *et al.*, 1989). Those whose BMI is in excess of 30 are obviously fat and aware of their body shape. They need sympathy and understanding rather than chastisement.

Alcohol

A large number of studies have consistently shown that moderate drinkers live longer and die less early, especially of coronary heart disease, than teetotallers or drunks. The most recent has been Sir Richard Doll's long prospective study of British doctors (Doll *et al.*, 1994a). As a result of the mounting evidence the 'wise men', who formerly set the upper desirable limits as 21 units a week for men and 14 units a week for women, re-convened recently and plucked out of the air some other figures which are more generous (28 units for men and 21 for women). Despite the evidence, the health gurus have shied away from encouraging drinking for fear that we shall all become drunks.

Cholesterol

Randomized controlled trials of cholesterol reduction have shown no benefit in symptomless populations (Ravnskov, 1992), and lowering cholesterol by drugs has, if anything, an adverse effect upon total mortality (Rissanen *et al.*, 1989). Furthermore, individual cholesterol levels are both variable and largely independent of diet. Even strict dietary regimes have little effect on cholesterol and there is no evidence that they prolong life. It now appears that dairy fat may be good for you and that older formulations of certain unsaturated fat spreads, for example, may have been harmful (Elwood, 1991; Mann 1994). Yet, and this is characteristically an American phenomenon, thousands upon thousands are worrying about what they eat, rather than enjoying their food. Incidentally, the guidelines of the Royal College of General Practitioners (1992) recommend counselling for those whose cholesterol exceeds 5.2 mmol/ litre—that is, most of us!

Tobacco

Cigarette smoking is associated with an increased probability of relatively young myocardial infarction (heart attacks) in men: this effect tends to disappear with age and is not apparent in women (Seltzer, 1989). Cigarette smoking is also strongly related to the probability of developing lung cancer and chronic bronchitis. In contrast, pipe and cigar smoking seem relatively innocuous (Doll *et al.*, 1994b). Yet, is it not extraordinary that, as most smokers find giving up difficult, those who fail are never encouraged by the health gurus to transfer to a safer habit? Perhaps we should be promoting pipe smoking for women! This failure seems to be analogous with the reluctance to promote alcohol and has much more to do with a moral position than the giving of good advice.

HEALTH PROMOTION IN THE UNITED KINGDOM

Band 3 of the Health Promotion Bands, for which general practice in the United Kingdom is being rewarded, has the aims of 'reducing coronary heart disease and stroke by a programme of primary prevention'. The objectives are to 'collect relevant information on the target population (aged 15–74) and carry out a programme of life-style interventions for those at risk, concentrating on priority groups'. The tasks are to 'collect information on blood pressure, smoking, body mass index, alcohol, family history and monitor diet and physical activity, offer advice, appropriate intervention and follow up' (Department of Health, 1992)—all this without a mandate from the person, restyled patient, or without 'conclusive evidence that screening can alter the natural history of disease in a significant proportion of those screened'. With two exceptions, lowering very high levels of blood pressure and stopping cigarette smoking, there is no good evidence that alteration in risk markers for coronary heart disease alters the probability of developing disease. At least one multiple risk factor intervention study has demonstrated increased mortality in those who were subjected to the intervention (Strandberg *et al.*, 1991). The final irony is that two major randomized controlled trials in the United Kingdom have demonstrated that health promotion as currently practised has negligible effects on risk marker status, at least in the short term (Family Heart Study Group, 1994; Imperial Cancer Research Fund, 1994).

As David Mant has reported, 79% of the subjects of the British Family Heart Study were labelled as unhealthy and merited follow up for one or more risk markers (Mant, 1994). Four out of five people faced the possibility of diminished health to no purpose! Such an activity must be deemed both unethical and ineffective.

The health promotion lobby has offered false promises of salvation not supported by evidence: belief has displaced science. We now have a body of useful knowledge about disease but that knowledge is far less perfect than we are led to believe. Nonetheless, most people in the rich world are living out something approaching their biological lifespan, which is probably of the order of 85 plus or minus 7.5 years. That is, some of us are programmed to die before our 70th birthday and a few to reach 100. Unfortunately, those who do not die of a suddenly fatal myocardial infarct may live to die the slow and painful death of senescence. Those anxious about our health seldom talk of alternative modes of death, if indeed they were to be successful in eliminating, for example, coronary heart disease.

A major precondition of health is a sufficiency of money to do more than meet the bare essentials. Poverty is, apart from genes, the major predictor of premature mortality. A more equitable distribution of wealth would do far more for the health of the nation than squandering resources on mindless health promotion and screening tests that do more harm than good. The other major precondition of health is being loved.

CONCLUSIONS

Alas, the prospects for the death of medicine as a religion are poor; even the suggestion that it worships false gods is widely regarded as heresy. As a result, believers will continue, from the best of motives, to damage our health.

While many, possibly a majority, will ignore the warnings of the health gurus, others will become unnecessarily concerned about their weight, their diet, their lack of exercise and sometimes their blood pressure. This will undoubtedly diminish their health. As we have suggested previously, (McCormick and Anderson, 1992), it would surely be better were we to encourage people to live lives of modified hedonism so that they may enjoy to the full the only life that they are likely to have.

18

Prohibiting and Taxing Everyday Pleasures

Christie Davies

Department of Sociology, University of Reading,
Reading RG6 2AL, UK

One proof of the importance of pleasurable substances to every-day life lies in the very severe problems that arise when attempts are made to ban sources of everyday pleasure such as alcohol, tobacco, tea, coffee or chocolate or to impose upon them an excessive burden of taxation. As will be shown below, the ordinary, moral, law-abiding citizen refuses to comply with attempts made to coerce his or her behaviour in this way. As a consequence, there is an escalating threat to law and order and public morality and, indeed, in the longer run to basic human and legal rights, should the state continue to pursue such an unacceptable policy.

Quite simply, these everyday pleasures are so basic to people's quality of life that ordinary citizens will defy the state rather than have access to them denied or severely restricted. If the state chooses to ignore their strongly held preferences, now manifest in 'deviant' behaviour, it will provoke a severe moral and social crisis. Given that such resistance is possible, indeed likely, why, then, are the rulers of states so keen to tax the substances that provide everyday pleasure? The answer to this question during most of the history of the civilized world is that such substances are taxed precisely because they are so important.

Pleasure and Quality of Life. Edited by D.M. Warburton and N. Sherwood
© 1996 John Wiley & Sons Ltd.

Rather than give up their favourite substance or drastically reduce their consumption of it, citizens are willing to pay considerable sums in tax and to cut down on other aspects of their expenditure; the demand for pleasurable substances is inelastic, which makes them an ideal target for taxation. Also, they are very widely consumed; they are the luxuries of the poor. This means that a tax on such substances has a very broad base. Furthermore, whereas to tax necessities such as food or fuel is apt to produce moral and political objections because of the regressive impact of such a tax, no such objection is made to the taxing of mere pleasure, however strong the sense of deprivation felt by those on whom the tax impinges most. In the twentieth century a new and even stronger pressure for high taxation has come from those who see the consumption of pleasure-providing substances as unhealthy and who wish to use punitive rates of taxation to reduce overall levels of consumption. They advocate rates of taxation that are much higher than the ones needed to maximize the raising of revenue for the state, for much the same reason that the marginal rates of tax on income in left-wing social democratic countries are sometimes so high that the actual total tax yield falls. In either case, the aim of taxation is not to pay for schools or hospitals or machine guns, but to use taxes as a means of coercion for ideological reasons. In the name of healthism, the level of taxation on the targeted pleasurable substance is raised to the point where it becomes little different from a prohibition and the same unpleasant consequences are likely to follow.

THE CONSEQUENCES OF PROHIBITION

The problems inherent in attempting to prohibit the use of a pleasurable substance that is widely enjoyed in a society have been clear to most people since the failure of Prohibition (of alcohol) in the United States (Block, 1976; Davies, 1975). Consumers do not accept the legitimacy of such attempts to control their personal behaviour by state legislation and seek to continue purchasing the forbidden item, thus making it possible for a black market to develop. In the case of Prohibition, illegal supplies of alcohol rapidly became available through smuggling, illicit brewing and distilling, and the misuse of industrial ethanol. The gap between the high price consumers were prepared to pay for a now scarce commodity and the much lower costs of production and importation made this kind of large-scale illegal trading inevitable. In this way the first level of damage to morality and society was done; very large numbers of ordinary, normally law-abiding, citizens were drawn into breaking the law, a process that was bound to undermine respect for the law generally. Further problems arose as the authorities took forceful steps to prevent the illegal importing and production of alcohol since this led to violent clashes with the bootleggers, who were often unwilling to surrender their illicit cargoes, stocks and stills peacefully. In this way a second blow was dealt to law and order.

Additional violence arose between different gangs of alcohol dealers due to disputes over territory, unpaid debts and other essentially commercial problems. Once the sale of a pleasure is prohibited it becomes impossible for those involved in it to settle their disputes by law and they turn to violence instead, as often happens in the case of, say, gambling or prostitution. There has been no proven case in Britain of a consumer of pornography going on to commit murder in consequence but I have interviewed a person whose conviction for a murder was a direct result of the censorship of pornography. The person concerned made pornographic videos at great expense and then discovered that a rival pornographer was making copies of his work and selling them cheaply; he was unable to sue for breach of copyright and in an ensuing dispute his rival was stabbed to death; one more source of damage to law and order generally.

A fourth kind of undermining of public morality arises, and indeed arose during Prohibition, when those involved in illegal dealing in pleasure seek to corrupt those whose task it is to enforce the law by bribing police officers, customs officials and judges.

A final set of problems that can arise from the prohibition of pleasure by law results from attempts by the state to regain control of a by now lawless situation through taking on new powers *vis-à-vis* the ordinary citizen such as enhanced powers of search and seizure, the power to intercept mail and tap telephone lines or the power to inspect bank accounts and financial transactions, all of which infringe the individual's basic right to privacy. Prohibiting pleasure by law thus tends to undermine liberty, privacy, rights, morality and order, i.e. all of the most basic elements of a democratic society. It may well be that there was some overall degree of improvement in the health and welfare of the American people as a result of the prohibition of alcohol but this was overwhelmingly and inevitably offset by the moral and political disasters it generated.

THE CONSEQUENCES OF TAXATION

Taxation is often both seen and advocated as a more subtle and problem-free means of curbing pleasurable indulgence than prohibition. In order, for instance, to reduce the incidence of the health problems linked to the smoking of tobacco (such as lung cancer, heart disease, bronchitis, emphysema and peripheral neuritis), the anti-tobacco lobbies have sought to reduce the consumption of tobacco by having very high taxes on tobacco. It is hoped that some smokers will choose to give up and that others will smoke less in order to avoid increased expense. Higher tax rates equals higher prices, equals lower consumption, equals more health—or so it is believed. The purpose of such taxation is not the mere raising of revenue (indeed, the tax rates may well be set much higher than those that would maximize revenue to the state) but an attempt to force people to change their personal choices and behaviour. John Stuart Mill denounced the use of taxation in this way as being not an alternative to prohibition, but an alternative form of prohibition:

> 'To tax stimulants for the sole purpose of making them more difficult to be obtained, is a measure differing only in degree from their entire prohibition and would be justifiable only if that were justifiable. Every increase of cost is a prohibition to those whose means do not come up to the augmented price; and to those who do, it is a penalty laid on them for gratifying a particular taste. Their choice of pleasures, and their mode of expending their income after satisfying their legal and moral obligations to the State and to individuals, are their own concern and must rest with their own judgment.' (Mill, 1983)

Mill accurately pinpointed the similarity of the threat to liberty posed by the disproportionate and discriminatory taxation of pleasurable substances and by their prohibition. However, heavy taxation and prohibition also resemble one another in terms of their negative implications for the maintenance of public morality and order and of civil liberties. Parallels with the problems caused by American Prohibition are now to be found in countries like Canada and Singapore, which have greatly increased their taxation of tobacco as part of a national assault on smoking driven by authoritarian ideology of a healthist kind. Singapore has recently tightened its anti-smoking laws to prevent smoking in 'air-conditioned offices, factories, stairways, enclosed elevators, lobbies, toilets and storerooms', i.e. 'almost everywhere except outdoors or in special smoking rooms' in an attempt to become the world's first smoke-free nation. As part of this drive it has imposed a very high import duty on cigarettes so that they cost the consumer $US 30 a packet compared with a basic pre-tax price of $US 8 paid if they are bought overseas (Joshi, 1995). Such a gap in price has inevitably led to a massive rise in smuggling from such adjoining countries as Malaysia and Indonesia.

A similar situation arose in Canada in the early 1990s where the tax on cigarettes was raised by 400% between 1984 and 1993, making tobacco twice as expensive as it was south of the border, in the United States. Given that the vast majority of Canadians live close enough to the border to be able easily to visit the United States, a rise in smuggling was almost inevitable; by the 1990s one survey suggested that perhaps one in two of Toronto's smokers bought smuggled cigarettes, occasionally at least. The speed with which smuggling developed, its enormous extent and the degree to which ordinary people were willing to buy and sell smuggled cigarettes undermined law and order to the point where the Canadian government was forced radically to cut the tax on tobacco and to induce the individual provinces to reduce their tax levels also. In consequence, in Quebec the price of a carton of 200 cigarettes was nearly halved from Canadian $45 to about Canadian $24 a price roughly similar to that prevailing across the border in the United States (Nicholson, 1994).

The Canadian government's decision to retreat from its untenable position was a wise one, for serious problems had developed involving smuggling by organized gangs and the use of violence. Mafia, Triad and Vietnamese gangs became involved in the smuggling, sometimes through the Mohawk Indians' Akwesane reservation, a tax-free area that straddles the Canadian–US border. (This remarkable example of multi-cultural cooperation and ethnic enterprise does not seem to have inspired praise from Canada's politically correct community.) There have even been reports of the Mohawks arming themselves with AK-47 rifles to protect their valuable stocks of cigarettes and tobacco and becoming involved in shoot-outs with the police (Nicholson, 1994). The problems that emerged in Canada due to a crass attempt to cramp people's access to one of the more widespread pleasures of everyday life is by no means a new one. Similar consequences have often arisen in the past whenever the state has attempted to raise too large a portion of its revenue from the taxation of everyday pleasures, only to provoke smuggling and in turn violence among otherwise peaceable and moral citizens. Adam Smith, writing about eighteenth-century Britain, noted that:

> 'The hope of evading such taxes by smuggling gives frequent occasion to forfeitures and other penalties which entirely ruin the smuggler; a person who, though no doubt highly blameable for violating the laws of his country, is frequently incapable of violating those of natural justice and would have been in every respect an excellent citizen, had not the laws of his country made that a crime which nature never meant to be so ... Not many people are scrupulous about smuggling when without perjury they can find any easy and safe opportunity of doing so. To pretend to have any scruple about buying smuggled goods, though a manifest encouragement to the violation of the revenue laws and to the perjury which almost always attends it, would in most countries be regarded as one of these pedantic pieces of hypocrisy which, instead of gaining credit with anybody, serve only to expose the person who affects to practice them to the suspicion of being a greater knave than most of his neighbours. By this indulgence of the public the smuggler is often encouraged to continue a trade which he is thus taught to consider as in some measure innocent; and when the severity of the revenue laws is ready to fall upon him, he is frequently disposed to defend with violence what he has been accustomed to regard as his just property. From being at first rather imprudent than criminal, he at last too often becomes one of the hardiest and most determined violators of the laws of society.' (Smith, 1902)

It is no accident that Adam Smith—like John Stuart Mill, one of the classic expounders of the virtues of a free society—should have concentrated his attention on the dangers of excessively taxing the pleasures of everyday life. For Mill, such a tax undermines one crucial moral basis of society: personal autonomy; for Smith it undermines another equally important basis of the social order: respect for the law and for the monopoly of violence granted to the state in order that we can enjoy state protection. From their arguments we can see that the substance pleasures of everyday life are definitely not trivia to be dismissed as unimportant items that can be recklessly taxed in the name of a higher morality of coerced survival.

ENFORCEMENT OF TAXATION

For well over 20 years (Brandon and Davies, 1973) there has been considerable controversy in Britain over the rights of the accused *vis-à-vis* the criminal justice system culminating in the recent wrangles (1994–1995) over the abolition of the 'right to silence', which has been seen by many as an oppressive augmentation of the power of the state over the individual citizen. Yet, where questions of revenue raising are concerned, the entire matter had long before been resolved in favour of the state. In 1973 Mr Justice Ackner said in a famous judgment that:

> 'The so called "right of silence", currently alleged with emphasis and fervour by many lawyers as going to the very root of British notions of justice, seems to find no place in the field of tax avoidance – a fortiori where tax evasion is concerned. Mr. Potter tells me that in the field of Value Added Tax the inquisitorial powers of the Commissioners of Customs and Excise far exceeded those of his clients. If it is an essential of our principles of jurisprudence that silence should be sanctified, I pause only to wonder why, when it comes to the detection of deceptions practised upon the Commissioners of Inland Revenue and Customs and Excise, those principles have no application. Indeed, so far from being entitled to remain silent, the individual is subject to penal sanctions if he refuses to supply the very information that may lead to his conviction. Had such powers been reserved for use in the detection of the most serious offences in the criminal calendar, doubtless there would have been, not acclamation, but a public outcry.' (Board of the Inland Revenue, 1974)

Mr Justice Ackner's criticism is directed against any excessive powers granted to tax-raising agencies in general but it is clearly one that is likely to have a particular reference to the taxation of pleasurable substances since the rates of taxation are high; so too are the opportunities for and the temptations of evasion, notably through smuggling. At present, the smuggling of pleasurable substances into Britain from the other countries of the single market European Union is becoming easier and more profitable, yet the British government is employing fewer customs and excise officials to monitor its frontiers. Accordingly, a crisis is likely to arise in the near future, with the government seeking to grant drastic powers to an inadequate rump of officials faced with a flood of smuggled substances. A similar situation occurred in 1972 when Value Added Tax was introduced, probably without adequate reparation. The sometime Chancellor of the Exchequer, Mr Dennis Healey, then in opposition, declared that the Conservative government of the time could only operate the tax effectively 'if they confer on Customs and Excise powers which have made the heads of the legal profession shiver at the affront to our traditions' (Hansard, 1972). What inspired this outburst was the granting to the Customs and Excise of totally unlimited powers to enter and inspect any premises, regardless of whether it was concerned with the provision or receipt of taxable supplies. It was the proposal to grant these and other similarly intrusive powers that led the Chairman of the Bar Council and the president of the Law Society to declare:

> 'We are of the opinion that these provisions ... represent an unwarrantable extension of the powers necessary to be conferred on a government department for the enforcement of a comprehensive tax ... [these] provisions constitute an infringement of the liberty of the subject in a most significant manner.' (Hansard, 1972)

In the mid-1990s the situation is once more critical, this time in relation to the movement of alcohol and tobacco into Britain in large quantities by private individuals who have bought these commodities cheaply in low tax countries such as France. Is it even smuggling, if the carriers can claim it is for their own use or that they are merely acting as pre-paid agents for a neighbour or acquaintance? Faced with a major loss of revenue and a severe slap in the face for its healthist tax policies, the government is likely to introduce legislation to obstruct its own citizens' freedom to purchase pleasurable substances in adjoining European jurisdictions, and thus to provoke a disagreeable confrontation with the countries supplying these commodities. If anyone thinks that the taxation of pleasurable substances is not a matter of sufficient importance to provoke an international crisis, they might do well to remember that there was once a Boston tea-party; the world has still not recovered from its consequences.

CONCLUSIONS

There is a clear link between the small important things in life such as the pleasure derived from tea, coffee, chocolate, alcohol and tobacco and the big important things in life such as the freedom of the individual, the state of law and order and public morality, and the need to constrain the power of governments and their officials. Attempts to prohibit or excessively to tax widely used and accepted everyday pleasures are not only an attack on the freedom of the individual, but also tend to lead to an erosion of respect for law and order, a decline in public morality and the granting of excessive powers of coercion to the state.

19

The Economics of Pleasure Choices

Chris Gratton and Simon Holliday

School of Leisure and Food Management, Sheffield Hallam University,
City Campus, Pond Street, Sheffield S1 1WB, UK

The subject of this chapter is an analysis of the question: Can economics help us to understand how consumers make choices about pleasurable products and activities? The answer we suggest is 'No, not without incorporation of other social science disciplines'. We build our argument on the work of other economists who have attempted to broaden the economic analysis of consumer choice to a more interdisciplinarian approach and we concentrate on two major choices: firstly, the choice to consume a particular good or service for the sole purpose of the generation of pleasure; and secondly, we look at the decision that is logically prior to this, the choice of how to allocate our time between work and leisure.

UNDERSTANDING CONSUMER DECISION MAKING

Our starting point for the analysis of consumer behaviour is the theory of consumer demand. This has remained virtually unaltered for over a century. It is a theory developed from the nineteenth-century economist Alfred Marshall. The consumer is regarded as having a given set of tastes and preferences, and,

Pleasure and Quality of Life. Edited by D.M. Warburton and N. Sherwood

facing a given set of prices of goods and services, allocates income in such a way as to maximize utility, which results in a spending pattern where the relative marginal utilities of different goods are equated to relative prices. Economic theory concentrates on such 'rational' maximizing behaviour.

This approach to the analysis of consumer behaviour has not escaped criticism from within the economics profession. Hosseini (1990) comments:

> 'Neo-classical economic theory has been founded on the assumptions that economic agents are omnisciently rational and that they are always optimising ... These assumptions are questionable. When we deal with collective decision-making, individual objectives might be in conflict, or, individual preferences might very often be inconsistent, fuzzy and changing over time. It can also be argued that as human beings, while engaged in decision-making, we often ignore our own fully conscious preferences. Instead of maximising rationally, we often follow rules, traditions, hunches, and advice and actions of others.'

Fine (1990) points out how the economic approach prevents a broader analysis of consumer behaviour and shifts the emphasis away from the individual and on to the commodity markets:

> 'By homogenising and setting aside non utility maximising behaviour as "irrational", economics precludes the possibility of an inter disciplinary theory of consumer behaviour and heavily discourages even a multi disciplinary approach. In addition, the economic theory of consumer behaviour focuses attention away from individual acts of exchange. These become of no interest in their own right, since each is meaningless in isolation from the others. Only bundles of commodities give utility, so that the individual acts of obtaining and enjoying them become irrelevant.'

In this chapter we do make an attempt to explain non-utility maximizing behaviour. To do this we have to go beyond the boundaries of economics and into areas of psychology. Psychology adopts a more general approach to consumer behaviour than economics. It concentrates much more on the individual consumer than on the commodity, and it concentrates much more closely on the process by which a consumer obtains satisfaction (and sometimes dissatisfaction) from consumption. The approach draws on the work of two economists, Tibor Scitovsky (1976, 1981, 1986) and Peter Earl (1983, 1986), both of whom have developed approaches to consumer demand that use psychology in the analysis.

THE NATURE OF DEMAND FOR PLEASURABLE GOODS AND SERVICES

Scitovsky criticizes neoclassical theory of consumer demand, indicating that at best it can contribute only to a partial analysis of consumer behaviour. He particularly criticizes the assumption of a given set of preferences, and the model of a rational consumer who knows what he wants and fails to achieve it only for lack of means. For Scitovsky, to understand demand one has to understand the motive force behind behaviour; that is, we need to investigate how preferences are formed. To do this his starting point is psychology, and in particular the theory and concept of arousal.

The theory of optimal arousal as a basis for analysis of behaviour is broader than the economic approach, although there is a considerable overlap. Economists see consumer demand as want satisfaction. If an individual is deprived of food, he experiences discomfort in hunger (i.e. he becomes over-aroused). Consumption of food relieves the discomfort and lowers his arousal level back towards its optimum level. Comfort is the feeling that results from being at the optimal level of arousal; pleasure, on the other hand, results from moving towards the optimal level from an over-aroused level. However, pleasure may also follow from moving from a low level to a higher one; e.g. the relief of boredom. Scitovsky criticizes economists for considering only the want satisfaction (lowering too high arousal) aspects of demand and completely ignoring stimulation-seeking behaviour (raising too low arousal).

The basic source of stimulation is experience that is new, unexpected or surprising. Unlike want satisfaction, these experiences require perceptual, cognitive and memory skills to be enjoyed. Scitovsky uses an example of listening to classical (serious) music to illustrate the concept of skilled consumption:

'For example, when I first listen to a complex piece of music with a large information flow, my brain automatically keeps the subjective information flow within the limits of its capacity by blocking out part of the harmonic complexity. Only as repeated hearing reduces the subjective novelty of what I have already heard and so frees part of my brain's information processing capacity so I begin to notice the complexity I have previously missed. This enables one to listen to the same piece of music repeatedly with undiminished or even increased enjoyment, because the increase in subjective redundancy does not diminish the flow of subjectively new information I perceive at successive hearings. Also, the more-than-manageable inflow of information which I receive on first hearing complex music creates a mild frustration or disorientation, whose resolution, and my expectation of whose resolution, is an important part of my enjoyment. Novelty creates a problem, and its enjoyment comes from the resolution of the problem.'

The main question addressed in *The Joyless Economy* (Scitovsky, 1976) is why, in the USA, increasing affluence does not seem to have led to increasing happiness. He argues that a major reason for this is that there has been too much emphasis on the acquisition of production skills and not enough on the acquisition of consumption skills. Consequently, American consumers seek pleasure through want satisfaction rather than stimulation seeking, since they do not possess the skills to 'enjoy' the stimulation. However, once the basic demands for material goods have been met, there is less and less opportunity for pleasure through want satisfaction. Hence the overall picture of an affluent, but bored, joyless society (Javeau, this volume).

A major avenue to pleasure comes through stimulation seeking. Such stimulation can be obtained through interesting and challenging work, again conflicting with the economist's categorization of work as disutility. However, for many it is through their leisure activities that we would expect to see stimulation seeking behaviour.

A more detailed analysis of the way in which certain activities generate satisfaction and happiness is Csikszentmihalyi's 1975 study into man at play, entitled *Beyond Boredom and Anxiety*. The aim of his study was to explore why people took part in activities that yielded no extrinsic rewards. He referred to such activities as autotelic, which he defined as an activity that required formal and extensive energy output on the part of the actor yet provided few, if any, conventional rewards. Thus, he was interested in why people spent a lot of their time in activities that an industrial society would regard as unproductive. He attempts to describe the nature of autotelic experience:

'It is easier, at first, to say what the experience is not like. It is not boring, as life outside the activity often is. At the same time, it does not produce anxiety, which often intrudes itself on awareness in "normal" life. Poised between boredom and worry, the autotelic experience is one of complete involvement of the actor with his activity. There is no time to get bored or to worry about what may or may not happen. A person in such a situation can make full use of whatever skills are required and receives clear feedback to his actions; hence, he belongs to a rational cause-and-effect system in which what he does has realistic and predictable consequences.'

Csikszentmihalyi refers to this 'holistic sensation that people feel when they act with total involvement' as flow. He describes the relationship between flow and skills:

'at any given moment in time, people are aware of a finite number of opportunities which challenge them to act; at the same time, they are aware also of their skills – that is, of their capacity to cope with demands imposed by the environment. When a person is bombarded with demands which he or she feels unable to meet, a state of anxiety ensues. When the demands for action are fewer, but still more than what the person feels capable of handling, the state of experience is one of worry. Flow is experienced when people perceive opportunities for being evenly matched by their capabilities. If, however, skills are greater than the opportunities for using them, boredom will follow. And finally, a person with great skills and few opportunities for applying them will pass from the state of boredom again into that of anxiety. It follows that a flow activity is one which provides optimal challenges in relation to the actor's skills.'

This quotation adds a greater insight into Scitovsky's concept of skilled consumption, and it also explains why such skilled consumption can generate high levels of consumer satisfaction. Moreover, Csikszentmihalyi argues that normal life experiences rarely have the ability to provide such enjoyment. This is because in many everyday experiences we do not have the control to make sure that challenges match skills. Also, most activities in life are not experiences in the sense that they are 'interactive sequences with a beginning, a middle, and an end, which provide a clear cognitive or emotional resolution.'

Csikszentmihalyi's description of flow activities emphasizes that in flow consumers lose their sense of time. Total involvement in autotelic experiences detaches the individual from time:

'Another common feature of flow experience is a "distorted" sense of time. When consciousness is fully active and ordered, hours seem to pass by in minutes, and occasionally a few seconds stretch out into what seems to be an infinity. The clock no longer serves as a good analogue of the temporal quality of experience.' (Csikszentmihalyi, 1992)

Thus the flow experience, a peak of pleasure, requires the individual not to consider the time input to the activity. Rationing the time input may itself prevent the flow experience.

IMPLICATIONS FOR THE ANALYSIS OF PLEASURE CHOICES

In affluent societies, conventional consumption patterns may lead to less and less generation of pleasure, and more and more comfort. As affluence allows us to satisfy more and more of our basic wants, additional increases in incomes may generate less and less additional pleasure. Opportunities for pleasure are available in 'stimulation-seeking' behaviour, but less so through 'want satisfaction'. Achievement of peak experience, or flow, requires the investment of time in skill acquisition and the unconditional commitment of time to the activity. In this context, the time input may be more important than the money input.

The conventional economic analysis of a rational, fully-informed consumer spending income in order to maximize satisfaction ignores these two essential ingredients to the achievement of flow: skills and time. Lack of either, or both, can prevent the generation of flow. Conventional economic analysis may be steering the consumer to a life of comfort rather than of pleasure.

As we have indicated, the time input is crucial to the consumption of pleasurable commodities. In order to have time available for such consumption, individuals must decide how to allocate time between work and leisure. The framework for the analysis of this choice has conventionally been an economic one: the income/leisure tradeoff. In the analysis at its simplest, an individual derives utility from the income gained at work in what he or she consumes in leisure-time, but is constrained in the achievement of ever higher utility by the rate of pay per hour (or year) and by the finite amount of time available.

A rise in the wage rate triggers off two effects:

1. It increases the price of leisure, which is the income foregone. This causes a rational individual to switch his or her choice to consuming more work and less leisure because the

opportunity cost of leisure is more expensive. This is known as the substitution effect.

2. It increases the real income to such an extent that more income and leisure time can be achieved, if desired. Which of these actually increases depends on the preference pattern of the individual, who may choose to exploit all the potential advantage in the form of increased income, but who more typically is likely to exploit some of the potential advantage in the form of increased leisure. This effect is known as the income effect.

So, the substitution effect means that a change in the relative prices causes a switch away from the more expensive commodity (in this case leisure), towards the relatively cheaper commodity (work and income). The income effect means that the individual's real income changes, which can affect consumption of both commodities. If leisure is a normal good then a rise in real income, caused by a higher wage rate, will lead to a rise in demand for leisure.

This analysis is possible only with the support of some important assumptions about consumer behaviour:

1. The consumer is rational and interested in maximizing utility. If this is not the case, then sub-optimal choice will result.
2. The allocation of time is an individual decision. It is more likely that such decisions are, to some extent, household ones.
3. Time is divided into paid work and leisure. More realistically, time is spent in a variety of ways, some of which are neither paid work nor leisure, e.g. housework, eating, travelling.
4. Work generates disutility, for which compensation is necessary in the form of income. This simplistic assumption ignores the utility that work generates aside from income. It also ignores other rewards for work, e.g. regularity of employment, probability of success, responsibility and skill acquisition.

As indicated above, whether leisure time increases or decreases as wage rates rise is not answered by the economic analysis. The income and substitution effects pull in different directions and it is an empirical question as to which effect dominates. The evidence suggests that over the past 100 years or so the income effect has dominated. This is certainly the conventional wisdom, and there are several leisure-time indicators that suggest this: the reduction in daily and weekly working hours; reduced male activity rates in the work-force for both younger age groups (longer time spent in education) and older age groups (earlier retirement); and large increases in paid holiday entitlement. On the other hand, there are other leisure-time indicators that provide evidence in favour of a dominant substitution effect: increased female activity rates; more overtime working; and increased second job holding and 'moonlighting'.

We argue here that since the early 1980s this increase in leisure time for many sections of the population has been reversed and increasingly workers have little choice over the hours they work. The conventional economic model is less and less appropriate for the description of people's leisure time choices, and as a result opportunities for the generation of pleasure may be severely constrained as the time input into consumption is rationed more and more.

Schor (1991) showed that in the USA the long-term decline in work-time has now been reversed. She shows that, against the conventional wisdom, since the late 1960s work-time has been steadily increasing. According to these estimates, the average employed person worked 163 hours longer in 1987 than in 1969, or the equivalent of an extra month a year. The increase in employed women's hours is greater, at 305 hours, over the same period.

Recent evidence shows that in Europe, and in particular in Britain, similar trends are emerging. Figure 19.1 looks at working hours for full-time employees across the European Union (Watson, 1992, 1993). It shows that the average worker in the UK was working 43.7 hours per week in 1992. Working patterns in terms of hours in the UK bear little, if any, resemblance to the majority of EC nations. The majority of European nations now have average working weeks of below 40 hours. The EC nation that has the lowest average number of working hours is Belgium, where the average number of weekly hours worked in 1992 was nearly six

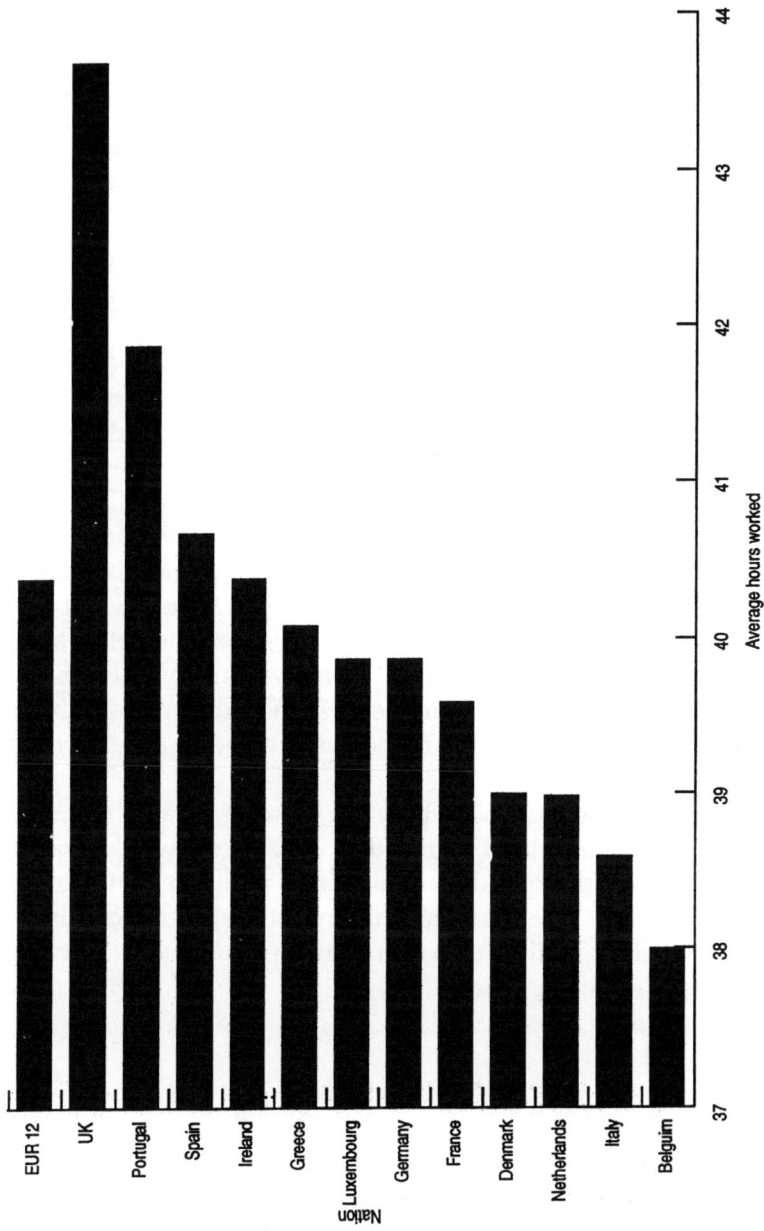

Figure 19.1. *The average total usual weekly hours worked by full-time employees. Source: Eurostat (1992)*

fewer than in Britain. Britain, Spain and Portugal are the only countries in the EU with working hours above the EU average.

The same pattern is revealed by the other Eurostat (1992) indicator used, the proportion of employees who usually work over 48 hours per week. Figure 19.2, if anything, shows the UK to be more of an exception than Figure 19.1 did. Again, the pattern in the UK appears to be more reminiscent of Schor's (1991) US picture rather than the European case. As many as one in six of British employees usually work over 48 hours per week.

In terms of the proportion of employees usually working over 48 hours per week, only Ireland in addition to the UK displays characteristics that are in excess of the EU's average. Even in France, whose workers are the most likely on the continent to be found working more than a 48-hour week, the occurrence is only a third of what it is in Britain. In fact, in the vast majority of EU nations less than 5% of employees work in excess of a 48-hour week.

A study conducted by the *Observer* newspaper (1994) and other recent evidence (Freeman and Bell, 1994) indicate that this move to increasing working time in Britain and in other European countries for particular groups in the population (the better educated, better paid), is not a choice by the worker for less leisure time. Rather, it is driven from the demand side of the labour market by the increasing drive for competitiveness caused by the globalization of markets.

This constraining of leisure time by those most able to make choices for pleasurable consumption (i.e. those with enough money to have an expanded choice and with an educational background that is likely to equip them with relevant consumption skills) puts a further constraint on the ability of economic growth to generate happiness.

CONCLUSIONS

We have argued in this chapter that the conventional economic analysis of consumer choice is inadequate if we are to understand consumer behaviour, particularly in the area of pleasure. The choices that economics analyses, the allocation of money income

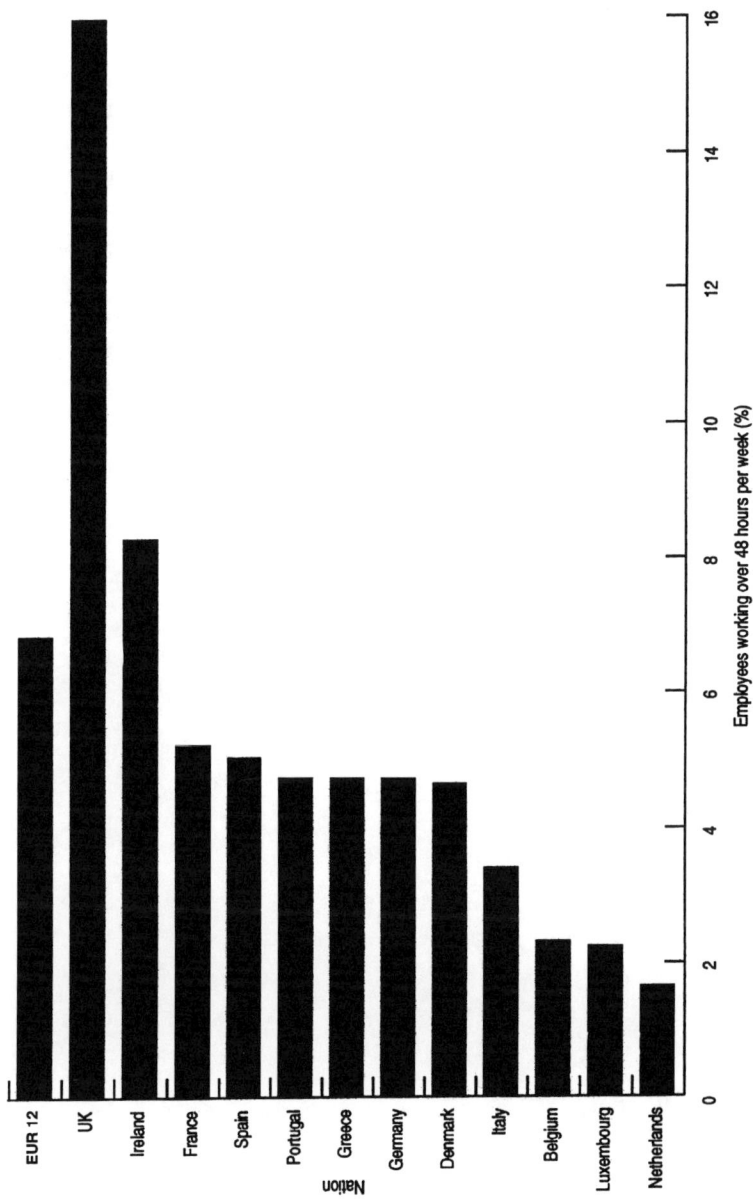

Figure 19.2 *The proportion of employees who usually work over 48 hours per week. Source: Eurostat 1990 data*

over a basket of goods and services, concentrates on the production of comfort rather than on the production of pleasure. As societies become more affluent, time rather than money is the most crucial allocation decision.

We have presented evidence to show that many individuals' control over the time allocation decision is becoming more and more constrained by the demand side of the labour market (i.e. employers) so that, again, the conventional economic analysis is less and less appropriate.

As we approach the end of the twentieth century, it is appropriate to ask the question of why we should continue to place the emphasis on the growth of economic indicators that have less and less relevance to pleasure and happiness. What is the point of working longer hours, in increasingly insecure and stressful working environments, to generate higher incomes, the spending of which does little to increase pleasure, happiness and quality of life?

20

Whence the New Puritanism?

Keith Botsford

120 Cushing Avenue, Boston, MA 02125, USA

INTRODUCTION

I am asked to explain why and how our times have become—through the media as well as in government, science and
the academy—censorious in the extreme: not just of our living
habits and private pleasures, but of our social behaviour. My
purpose is to shed a little light on the intellectual underpinnings
of this development, which is sufficiently organized and militant
to be considered a new ethical system. In schematic form, its
essential tenets are:

- the overriding interests of the biosphere
- the primacy of public policy over private behaviour
- an attack on 'impartial' science
- sexual androgyny
- the rise of human 'rights' to an absolute and their extension
  to the rest of the physical world

OF THE MEDIA, THEN AND NOW

The how, the mechanisms by which the new morality is disseminated, often in apocalyptic, millenarian terms, are not hard to

Pleasure and Quality of Life. Edited by D.M. Warburton and N. Sherwood
© 1996 John Wiley & Sons Ltd.

discern. A simple history of the media in our century will show how our media have changed. Before the 1914–1918 war, the function of the media was to convey information. Information was both necessary and useful, and some of it was called 'news': people, ideas and events influenced all of us, so we needed to know about any change in our daily environment. The Boer War and mankind's descent from the apes were both significant. Information was also useful; it was educational. In this regard the media continued a great nineteenth-century tradition of vulgarizing (in the high sense) and simplifying information. The media, it was thought, contributed to intellectual enlightenment.

In retrospect, it seems an admirable epoch. It was not value-free, for it was supported by eternal verities that seemed to be accepted by all, but it was animated by a virtuous desire to develop independence of mind and informed judgement, regardless of class or income. It was obviously not opinion-free, but science and rationality were its models. Argument and evidence were to be taken seriously. It was an age of fact and of debate about facts, not about opinion. Just how little a personal opinion was valued was demonstrated by the anonymity under which journalists wrote.

The media considered their function to be that of mediator between the leaders and the led. The appropriate medium was print, since that was the form in which knowledge was collected and disseminated. To perform this task satisfactorily a skill was required: that of using a common language clearly and intelligibly. In return, its audience was required to confront texts, to deal with serious 'ideas', to absorb information and to apply it to their own lives. However, between then and now, a remarkable change took place. In cursory fashion, the principal stages are discussed in the following subsections.

Technological Progress

The proximity of facts or events and the interest aroused by them has multiplied exponentially. First the photograph, then the radio report (the eye witness), the newsreel and television brought the remote into our ears and eyes. If what we heard or saw was objective, what we made of it no longer was: we could pass judgement on it, feel for or against it—whether or not our feelings or judgements were sufficiently informed. There was still selection (of what is news, or what part of it should be shown) but there was not time, or mental space, for prolonged consideration; the media were no longer mediators, but simply presenters, peeping Toms, our ears and eyes. Obviously, this brought about certain changes in our perception of 'information'. It became of more intimate concern; it aroused, as was expected, passions pro and con. Print, that elemental medium for analysis, lost ground in the presentation of news and events. Quite naturally, it turned to opinion, to 'background', to more detailed analysis at some distance from events.

Competition

Competition, between the different media and within each medium, established a series of specialized audiences. The visual media engaged the attention of those who wished to be 'present' at historical events; radio pioneered the dramatic confrontation of conflicting views and had the advantage of speed over its rivals. But all the media diversified, not so much by what they covered, but by the way, the slant, with which they covered it. The media had discovered their power in moulding public opinion. Ownership of the media was coveted. Greater audiences meant greater influence. In my view, the competitive struggle for an audience, and even the profit motive, is much less important than influence. The circulation of newspapers and magazines, as a proportion of the whole population, has remained stable or has fallen slightly since 1914. Technological advances are slow to have an impact on the great public: it took decades before a majority of people owned a radio or a television. The influence of the media, however, has shown a constant increase. It may well be that competition between conflicting views is in part responsible for this. It followed that privately owned media could only survive by following their audiences. Where Lord Reith thought he knew what the public should be given, media barons sought rather to give the public what it wanted.

The Rise of 'Issues'

Between the two wars in this century, the media remained reasonably stable, though increasingly available to propaganda (and not just in totalitarian countries, where it was at the service of the state). The mobilization of the masses in the Great War (war as a by-product of the industrial process) had shown that these were a mere human lump that could be manipulated with relative ease. It followed that in democratic nations, as in undemocratic ones, the media could be used to advance causes, to sponsor 'campaigns', to sensitize the public to 'issues' of public policy, to mobilize opinion.

Personalization

The media person as star was a natural outcome of a romantic focus on the individual: as creator and protagonist—not the North Pole, but its explorers; not a natural disaster, but those who suffered from it; not flight but Lindbergh; not the discovery, relativity, but its discoverer, Einstein. From this to pairing reporter and event was but a step. By the 1940s, such coverage was no longer limited to events, but became part of the debate; issues became as important as events.

The Democratization of the Media

Finally, when the groundwork for this apparently libertarian interaction between media and audience had been completed, the media made it possible for, literally, a hundred or a thousand flowers to bloom. The democratization of the media had been completed; the people had their media; one idea was as good as another. It shows all events and personalities, all ideas and 'movements' in terms of easily-accessible images and ideas, none of which, at their origin, is much more important than any other. Multiplicity of access has meant no more than plurality of views.

THE NEW MORAL STATE

As a historian, I should first perhaps state my assumption, which is that the definitive moment in the destruction of many aspects of the old order was the 1914–1918 war. The carnage of the war, the bolshevizing of Russia, the corporatism of fascism all reveal a profound doubt, both on the part of individuals and on the part of governments, that the individual is the best judge of his own life and fate. These new totalitarian regimes, ensuing on a war that enslaved a whole generation to destruction and then spewed them up in a new and unfamiliar world, were deeply moral. They believed that there were clear distinctions between the right and the wrong in social and political life, and that these were demonstrated in the corruptions of the past. Only a new social order could save us from our own worst instincts. They likewise believe that there are no aspects of individual behaviour that do not impinge on the welfare of the generality. If the effect on regulation is to be taken as a benchmark of totalitarianism, the sorry truth is that there is not much to distinguish the developed 'democracies' of the Western world from either fascism or communism. They share the same assumptions, only use different means to use the same ends.

The new 'moral' state is a Puritan state, with some millennial and apocalyptic traits. It is, of course, not really a moral state, but a moralizing state. It preaches what it does not necessarily practice. As with the self-righteous in general, it is governed by fear and guilt. While seeking its new god in Nature, it does not wish to recognize in the physical world what past generations saw—a universe proceeding under inexorable law in an uncertain direction—but rather a species of 'childhood of man', an innocence just waiting to be rediscovered. This, too, derives from the disillusionment of the Great War. The past, to this historical generation, is how its parents fouled up the world for them, is how that old world is perceived by the new to be 'out of touch' with modernity. This would be all right, one could live with it as yet another passing phase, if it were not that the new 'moral' state seeks legitimization through a revived theocracy, and casts its god in the guise of Nature. A more appropriate word would be a 'gurocracy'. A theocracy supposes a god and his appointed ministers; a pantheistic, animist, ecological world cannot have priests—the sources of its priestly power are too many, too variable and too diffuse. Instead it has gurus. Each teaches his own way.

PURITANISM, SCIENCE AND PUBLIC POLICY

Classical Puritanism is a self-enclosed doctrine; it is a form of purist apartheid that took root in the new American colonies and primarily in the Commonwealth of Massachusetts. There are five principal characteristics of the Puritan mind and ethic

1. The absolute sovereignty of God (for which, in the new dispensation, read Nature).
2. The total depravity of Man.
3. The importance of the personal religious experience
4. The concept of God's elect.
5. Following from this, there must be an union of church and state, a new theocracy.

I hold that our present political and post-religious (in the classical sense of religion) attitudes and precepts, our rules, derive, as the original Puritan revolution did, from a profound reaction against the existing order. What should concern us here are the control mechanisms through which this Puritan order imposes itself on us.

All of the principal Puritan doctrines come together when science is combined with public policy. By definition, policy is directional; it is a vector; it has an aim, an end. This aim—which increasingly resembles a secular form of immortality—like salvation, is beneficial. Public policy claims to know what is good for us and to achieve a 'good' society in which all shall be saved. Public policy incarnates the absolute sovereignty of God; it believes that man is fundamentally depraved; it offers us the personal religious experience; it is administered by its own elect; and there is no doubt that it tends to union between religious purpose and state control. If we eat fewer chocolates, if we avoid cholesterol, if he eschew so-called 'known' carcinogens, if we rear our animals (and presumably our vegetables) humanely, if we abandon our vices, if we never have sex without explicit consent, if we abandon the motor-car, if we exercise more, then we will not only feel better, but we will be in harmony with God. The state may enforce part of this code of behaviour (when it is noxious to others), but that inner harmony and that concord with the natural world will not be achieved without a personal conversion: you, the state insists, and only you, can change the world. Start now. Just say no. Or yes, whatever the desired or undesirable may be.

Public policy is about what is desirable; it is not about what is. This alone should reveal its origin in religious sentiment. Hence, in my view, the corruption of science by state policy. State influence on individual behaviour, whether by prohibition (alcohol, certain classes of drugs, smoking) or by enforced admonition (health warnings issued via the media, or on packaging) or by so-called 'scientific study' (not a week goes by that some new study of the 'dangers' of this or that substance is not released) is all created in view of an optimum to which society should be aiming; it is impartial neither at source (the commissioning of a study) nor in diffusion (hence the frequent rejection or suppression of data which contradicts government policy.) Once the all-powerful state has determined, for instance, that the social benefits of policy X outweigh the disadvantages (interference with freedom of choice), science will be found to show that the state is correct. The Volstead Act, like its intermittent Russian or Scandinavian counterparts (prohibition), or the more common 'sin taxes' against products determined to be harmful (in excess), are an expression of this quasi-eugenic desire to create a 'better' people.

Although the combining of the two words 'public' and 'policy' is relatively new, the idea of polity is not. The sovereign state has always had a polity: one that governed its relationships with other states (war or peace) and another that created the rules (law) under which it could demarcate between those things that were a part of individual choice (e.g. the choice of whom to marry) and those that pertained to civil society (e.g. under what circumstances and by whom). Quite clearly, as the state extended its powers, individuals were increasingly circumscribed by an ever-growing sense that the number of autonomous actions that an individual may perform are limited: by the interdependence of all members of a civil society and by the requirements of the state. How these requirements of the state were determined depended largely on the nature of individual and social behaviour. In matters that affected the law, economics and politics, the principal ideological thrust of public policy has been, for some centuries, utilitarian: the greatest good of the greatest number. In other fields, especially health, the arbiter of that greatest good has been science.

The question is whether that arbitration of science is still representative of 'good'—that is, objective, verifiable—science or whether science has not now become, in many fields, a hand-maiden of state policy. A secondary question is how those who disagree with state science (Trofim Lysenko) are going to make themselves heard. There have been a few interesting cases recently in the Puritan state of Massachusetts, including suits by those confined to psychiatric hospitals, against the general smoking ban (imposed by the Massachusetts Council of Hospitals in response to state pressure). As one of the several known beneficial effects of smoking is relief of stress, and that is the ostensible purpose of hospital care, the threat of such suits has caused some psychiatric hospitals and transient facilities to provide smoking areas. Need-less to say, the likelihood is that this will be overturned by person-nel claiming a threat to their health from their patients' smoke.

A fundamental difference between the older policy and the most recent is that where in the past it would never have occurred to science to provide the answers required by the state, this has now become commonplace. By 'most recent', I mean in the past twenty or so years, largely (and puzzlingly) led precisely by those nations with the highest ostensible regard for individual 'rights'. This ceases to be puzzling when one considers that 'rights' now include a putative right to be free of the violation of those 'rights' by others. An outstanding analysis of this was offered by Luik (1993), who traced much of the current agenda of public health science to Brice Lalonde, the former Canadian Minister of National Health and Welfare. Lalonde, Luik points out, argued that health messages must be vigorously promoted even if the scientific evi-dence was incomplete, ambiguous and divided. Health messages must be 'loud, clear and unequivocal', even if the evidence did not support such clarity and definition. The only logical result of such a policy is the corruption and discrediting of science. The result is analogous to the numerous studies on cholesterol and its dangers. These were so contradictory, and yet so menacing, that the public eventually ceased to listen to the message.

There are, of course, many reasons why the new morality pro-pounds its message. There are livings to be made and celebrity to be enjoyed in missionary work (as the clergy learned in its day.) In the advanced societies, the state is far and away the largest source of funding for science in general. Major charitable organizations devoted to single-issue science, such as the American Cancer Society or the Heart Society, come next. How many independent scientists are likely to be funded if they wish to test the accepted, state-enjoined hypotheses? How many will risk future grants by challenging the assumptions of the science clergy? Private research does go on, but it is perpetually menaced by the clamour of the new Puritans, and when funding is provided, for instance on food issues, by those who have an interest in the outcome, the hue and cry is immediately raised that these cannot be objective studies, because they are supported by those with an interest in the outcome. A similar cry is not raised, save by groups such as ARISE, against the 'interest' of the state in promoting its own kind of science. In short, as the law has taken precedence over legislation as a way of solving a perceived problem, so public policy now rules over much of science, nowhere more so than in epidemiology or public health.

CONCLUSIONS

Given the circumstances I have described, the conversion of the media and the perversion of science to a new religion, perhaps in the United States one might consider a suit based on Article One of the Constitution, which holds, *inter alia*, that 'Congress shall make no law respecting an establishment of religion'? Of course, such a suit is unlikely: not least because the climate of opinion created by the New Puritanism and imposed on public consciousness by a compliant media makes it almost impossible to fight back, as we ought, against the corruption of the law, science and gender relations.

It has to be said that of all the institutional structures of the modern world, business and trade have been the least prescient about an attack that is striking at the very heart of the world's economy. Short-sighted as ever, competitive with each other to the point of mutual destruction, none of the industries under attack by the New Puritanism—whether agrarian, like the livestock, coffee, cacao and tobacco industries, or urban, like transport and distribution—have shown any coherent strategy. What they do not seem to realize is that the current rumblings from the Anglo-Saxon world are merely a foretaste of what is to come, when the new morality proceeds systematically down its shopping list of human depravities. That these attacks are ideologically inconsistent (how does one 'protect' the environment by destroying the livelihood of third world countries who depend for their survival on raw materials and agricultural products?) is of no matter to the priests of the new morality. Our supine attitude should indeed concern us.

From Man as 'victim', we have progressed to 'sentient' nature (animals). Already the rough beast of this New Puritanism is slouching towards its new Bethlehem: all of Nature must be preserved, as is, and Man be damned. No wooden houses, no roads for no cars, no planes, no aerosols, no chemical pharmaceuticals. New ethical systems feed on their intellectual environment. Early Puritanism's revolt against the sinful condition of Man systematically increased the definition of sin. We can be sure that this new puritan system will do no less.

21

Pleasure Products and Sociability

Christie Davies

Department of Sociology, University of Reading,
Reading RG6 2AH, UK

INTRODUCTION

In Europe and North America tea, coffee, alcohol and tobacco are products extensively consumed because of the pleasure they give to the users, not just as individuals but in groups. Tea, coffee and alcohol are the foundation of much sociability, for typically they are consumed in company and are the basis both of social invitations to people's homes and of spontaneous but regular meetings in pubs, coffee bars and tea shops. They are all drinks that are easy to prepare or purchase. In other societies, tobacco is used in the same way and a collectively-used, substantial tobacco pipe may be passed around as a sign of amity much as a hookah is in the Middle East.

It is often conventionally accepted on such occasions that payment will be on the basis of sharing rather than individual calculation, as when a person buys a round of drinks or offers a packet of cigarettes around a group before taking one for himself or herself. Or again: 'Your coffee is delicious, Mrs McNulty, I must have had four cups of it'. 'You've had six, but who's counting?' They are hospitality goods rather than mere items of individual consumption. Their significance can be seen by substituting vari-

Pleasure and Quality of Life. Edited by D.M. Warburton and N. Sherwood
© 1996 John Wiley & Sons Ltd.

ous pleasing but inappropriate items of our diet for them in standard forms of invitation:

- 'Why don't you drop in for cabbage at about eleven?'
- 'We always take muesli and zinc supplements at four o'clock. Do join us one afternoon.'
- 'How about another round of skimmed milk?'
- 'Would anyone care for a cod-liver oil capsule?'

The importance of social product use can be inferred from the behaviour of those who decline to take part or who break the rules in some way. These exceptions enable us to understand the importance of routines in our lives that we would otherwise take for granted. The most drastic version of refusing to take part and partake occurs when a particular group of people such as a sect tells its members that alcohol, tobacco, tea and coffee are banned and forbidden, as is the case, for instance, with the Mormons and the Seventh-day Adventists.

These bans are an important means of setting the members of these sects apart as an exclusive group, by ensuring their withdrawal from everyday patterns of sociability, which nearly always involve consumption of one or more of the forbidden products.

MORMONISM

A divine revelation given to Joseph Smith, the founding prophet of Mormonism in 1833, forbidding tobacco smoking and the drinking of alcohol, tea and coffee is recorded in Section 89 of the Doctrine and Covenants known to Mormons as the 'Word of Wisdom' (O'Dea, 1957):

> 'That in as much as any man drinketh wine or strong drink among you, behold it is not good, neither meet in the sight of your Father ... And again, tobacco is not for the body, neither for the belly, and is not good for man, but is an herb for bruises and all sick cattle, to be used with judgement and skill ... And again hot drinks are not for the body or belly.' (Smith, 1845)

It is to be doubted whether the devout Mormons of today wash in whisky or elastoplast cigarettes to bruised limbs; rather it is the restricting of these products to such minor and peripheral uses that is significant. Indeed, abstention from tobacco, coffee, tea and alcohol is required for full membership of the Mormon church. As Thomas F. O'Dea, one of the leading sociologists of religion to have studied the Mormons, has noted:

> 'Admission to the temple and hence permission to take part in the ceremonies performed there—temple marriages, sealings, baptism for the dead—are denied to Mormons who do not abide by the proscription of smoking and the command to abstain from coffee, tea and liquor. Moreover, this commandment has become for Mormons a most salient mark of their membership in the Church ... Abstention from the practices forbidden in the Word of Wisdom appears to have replaced plural marriage as the badge of Zion, the sign of the gathered, in these days of accommodation to and integration into the larger gentile community. Frequently defended and rationalized in terms of bodily health and hygiene, the Word of Wisdom is the symbol of Mormon concern with the things of this world.' (O'Dea, 1957)

At an earlier time, the prohibitions might have been somewhat less central and important to the Mormons (Anderson, 1942; Shipps, 1985), who initially had sought to preserve their distinct identity through geographical isolation, by building a religious community with its own laws and way of life in the remote deserts of Utah. Now that Utah is fully integrated into the political, economic and legal institutions of the United States, and Mormons in Utah and elsewhere have to live alongside the 'Gentile' (which, significantly, is the term they have chosen as their word for non-Mormons), the control of individual social behaviour plays a vital part in helping to maintain a separate group identity. Since 'Gentile' leisure-time social interactions are, to a large extent, structured around the sharing of alcohol, tobacco, coffee and tea, a ban on these products ensures that Mormons will spend their free time with other Mormons, rather than with Gentiles. Thus, the ban serves to maintain and strengthen the boundaries and separate identity of the Mormon people.

Although the rules are stated, 'defended and rationalized in terms of bodily health' (O'Dea, 1957), it would be pointless to expect an orthodox Mormon to abandon them in the light of evidence that moderate tea and coffee consumption is harmless, that those who regularly drink small quantities of alcohol live longer than teetotallers or that alcoholism is more common among

Mormons (Helman, 1984) than among groups who permit and control the use of alcohol.

To do so would be to undermine the Mormon collectivity, and it is the survival and integrity of the group, rather than of the individuals who constitute it, that is the more important function of their prohibitions on products. That the Mormons should place such great emphasis on the banning of all product use indicates how very central such items are to ordinary social life, for those who wish their members to avoid and withdraw from the common life of the 'Gentiles' achieve this end by means of an attack on alcohol, tobacco, tea and coffee.

SEVENTH-DAY ADVENTISM

The Seventh-day Adventist prophet and leader, Mrs Ellen G. White, likewise attacked the use of alcohol, tobacco, tea and coffee in her essay, 'Spiritual gifts' of 1864, concluding:

> 'Those who indulge a perverted appetite, do it to the injury of health and intellect. They cannot appreciate the value of spiritual things. Their sensibilities are blunted and sin does not appear very sinful and truth is not regarded of greater value than earthly treasure.' (White, 1864)

For Mrs White, even moderate drinkers of alcohol eventually degraded themselves 'lower than the beasts', those who had fallen victim to the 'slow poison' of tobacco 'could hardly expect eternal life' and she was adamant that 'tea and coffee drinking is a sin' (Lindén, 1978). There seems to be some doubt among Seventh-day Adventists as to whether her writings should be regarded as those of a divinely inspired prophet that are not to be questioned, or merely as the respected views of a charismatic leader, but either way they remain influential.

Given the remarkable degree of dedication to medical work within the Seventh-day Adventist church (Bull, 1990), it is interesting to see what happens when there are conflicts between her ideas, or indeed those of the Bible, and the findings or ambitions of Seventh-day Adventist doctors. The pioneering transplant of a baboon's heart into a human being in 1984 by Seventh-day Adventist doctors (Bull, 1990) is at odds with her fundamental belief in the keeping of the categories of creation pure and distinct. She would have seen this blending of the human and the animal as especially abominable, however potentially therapeutic it may have been. Parallels for many of Ellen G. White's ideas can be found in the writings of various secular health faddists of the mid- and late-nineteenth century but she found her main inspiration in the Bible, notably in the Jewish dietary rules, the purpose of which was social, not medical. She was against the eating of meat and in principle favoured vegetarianism, but condoned the eating of 'clean' meat under certain circumstances on a pragmatic basis. Her notion of what constituted clean meat was based on the dietary laws of the Old Testament. Just as the Seventh-day Adventists celebrate the Sabbath in the Jewish fashion from sunset on Friday to sunset on Saturday, the seventh day of the week, so too their leader taught that the dietary laws laid down for the Jews in Leviticus were still in force for Christians (Lindén, 1978), even though they had been explicitly repudiated in the New Testament (1 Corinthians 10: 25).

For the Jewish people, the observation of the Sabbath and the dietary rules were, and are, a means by which the Jews, a holy people, kept themselves apart from the heathen (Davies, 1982, 1983; Douglas, 1966, 1975). Mrs White saw quite clearly the significance and importance of using the words 'Seventh-day' in her sect's title as a means of setting it apart decisively from other churches. She wrote: 'The name Seventh-day Adventist is a standing rebuke to the Protestant world. Here is a line of distinction between the worshippers of God and those who worship the beast and receive his mark.' Lindén comments on this passage: 'the denominational name is lauded as a kind of separating line between Civitas Dei and Civitas Diaboli'.

JUDAISM

The dietary rules of Leviticus may well have appealed to Mrs White for the same kind of reason, for their explicit purpose was to preserve the distinctive religious and ethnic identity of the Jewish people at a time of exile (see Davies, 1982, 1983; Douglas, 1966, 1975). They are one of the most detailed and subtle sets of dietary rules there are, for they not merely prevent orthodox Jews from eating at the tables of non-Jews, but their very structure emphasizes the importance of maintaining categories and boundaries (Douglas, 1966, 1975).

The blood (life) must be removed from meat before the meat (lifeless) can be eaten; milk products (life) must not be consumed with or at the same time as meat (lifeless); birds, fish and animals may only be eaten if they are not carnivores and belong clearly to their proper sphere of the air, the sea or the land, respectively. Only animals that have a cloven hoof and chew the cud may be eaten; ambiguous animals such as the pig that have one of these characteristics but not the other are strictly forbidden (see the Books of Leviticus and Deuteronomy; see also Douglas, 1966, 1975; Soler, 1973).

In obeying such rules, orthodox Jews observe boundaries and keep categories every time they eat and are thus reminded of the need to keep the boundaries of the Jewish people intact and to preserve their separate identity under the difficult conditions of exile. Most minorities in exile fade away in time as they inter-marry, adopt the way of life of their neighbours and disappear. The ancient Greeks, whose settlements once stretched from Marseilles to Peshawar, are now but fodder for archaeologists. The Jews, by contrast, have survived as a distinct people, despite repeated exile and persecution, i.e. their religion and laws have worked as they were intended to do.

The Jewish dietary rules were edited and codified during their exile in Babylon (Porter, 1976), based on the traditions of their earlier period of exile in Egypt, and have remained potent during their most recent diaspora. They are a set of internal social boundaries that serve as a substitute for the geographical boundaries, isolation and sheer numbers that are the basis of the identity of static and undisturbed peoples, such as the Chinese or the French, who will eat almost anything and have become cooks to the world.

CHRISTIANITY

When the early Christians decided to admit and recruit Gentiles (non-Jews) to their new Church, they specifically and deliberately repudiated the Jewish dietary taboos, which, though vital for the religion of a people, were a hindrance and a source of division for a proselytizing church. It is a measure of Mrs White's obsession with the creation of new boundaries to set the Seventh-day Adventists apart from other Christians that she should have considered bringing back the Jewish dietary rules in defiance of the teachings of St Peter and St Paul (1 Corinthians, 10: 25). The Mormons, the other Christian sect to have banned all manner of product use, were likewise inspired by the traditional Jewish emphasis on being a distinct and bounded people, and sought to recreate Zion in Utah, where they set up temples, sacred places surrounded by secrecy, which only truly worthy believers may enter (Anderson, 1942).

We may reasonably deduce that there is a strong connection between the Mormon and Seventh-day Adventist bans on product use and their wish to maintain a very separate social existence from other people. Since their bans on product use are aimed at keeping people apart, it is clear that product use must be a very important means of bringing and holding people together and a marker and heightener of significant social occasions.

Unlike the Jews, the Mormons and Seventh-day Adventists are proselytizers seeking new members and, therefore, needed a universal rationale for their restrictions on what may be taken into the body so as to justify them to potential converts. A similar problem faced the rationalist Jewish sage, Maimonides, when involved in arguments with disputants from other religions, and he tried to solve it by justifying the peculiar Jewish dietary rules as being rational, empirically-based health precautions. It was not a persuasive or convincing argument and his thesis is heretical in its content and subversive in its implications for, if true, it would undermine the special and holy quality of the Jewish people.

For proselytizing sects such as the Seventh-day Adventists and the Mormons, however, the health arguments provide a perfect rationalization for their extensive bans on product use. Mrs White even argued in the manner of Maimonides that pork, an abhorrent form of 'traif', or prohibited food for the Jews, was harmful to health. 'Pork-eating', she declared, 'is still causing the most intense suffering to the human race'. She further asserted that:

'Swine's flesh above all other flesh-meats, produces a bad state of blood. Those who eat freely of pork cannot but be diseased ... but it is not the physical health alone which is injured by pork-eating. The mind is affected, and the fine sensibilities are blunted by the use of this gross article of food.' (White, 1865, cited in Lindén, 1978, p. 320)

It is striking to note, once again, her blurring and combining of secular issues of health with questions of spirituality that conventionally belong to religion. Mrs White, according to Lindén, 'also knew why pork was so dangerous'; it was because swine feed on 'every detestable thing' and wallow in 'filth', that their flesh became extremely harmful. Consequently, this kind of meat caused 'scrofula, leprosy and cancerous humors' (White, 1865, cited in Lindén, 1978). Lindén comments dryly on this last point: 'To my knowledge this idea has not yet been substantiated by scientists' (Lindén, 1978, pp. 320, 331).

It might be added that neither have many of Mrs White's other ideas, such as her view that female orgasms were debilitating and that female masturbation led to 'imbecility, dwarfed forms, crippled limbs, misshapen heads and deformity of every description' (cited in Lindén, 1978, p. 325), as did the wearing of wigs (Lindén, 1978, p. 327). What those Orthodox Jewish women who routinely wear wigs as a religious duty thought of Mrs White's theory is not recorded. Fortunately, it is unlikely that it was ever brought to their attention.

I have stressed these somewhat eccentric opinions about pork, sex and wigs (which, in fairness, were shared by various contemporary secular health reformers) to show that it is misleading to represent the Seventh-day Adventist bans on product use as part of a rational and beneficent health movement in advance of its time. On the contrary, Mrs White's philosophy is full of peculiar ascetic, puritanical and restrictive ideas about product use. Asceticism about eating meat and the various forms of product use are, in one form or another, to be found in other religious traditions. In the nineteenth century, especially in America, this religious tradition of restrictive puritanism was often combined with a radical boundless, utopian optimism, to create secular pseudo-scientific movements of the militantly pleasureless. These secular versions of the ancient tradition of obtaining merit through abstinence in turn fed back into and informed the beliefs of the sects.

Hence, we find that Mormon children were taught to sing 'In Our Lovely Desert' to the tune of 'The Little Busy Bee':

'That the children may live long,
And be beautiful and strong,
Tea and coffee and tobacco they despise.
They drink no liquor and they eat
But a very little meat;
They are trying to be great and good and wise.
(Anderson, 1942)

This could, in principle, be a secular health song for godless infants but is, in fact, a training in their sect's rules, regulations and prohibitions which serve to maintain its segregated integrity (Anderson, 1942). Most of the forbidden fruits listed are, of course, also the obsessions of modern 'scientific' dieticians, though it should be noted that sugar and chocolate are omitted from the list, which may account for the quantity of sweet cakes on offer at Mormon social occasions and the striking girth of many middle-aged Mormons. Mrs White, likewise, arbitrarily exempted cocoa and chocolate from the list of drinks forbidden to Seventh-day Adventists (see Lindén, 1978, p. 330).

A negative and ascetic attitude to alcohol, tobacco, tea and coffee may well also be a key aspect of sectarian behaviour because such products are rival sources of exalted moods, either strictly excluded from, or safely incorporated into, a religion. Sectarians and ascetics also dislike meat because they see it as having been produced by aggression against animals and because they believe that it increases people's sexual appetites; they seek to minimize intense feelings and excitements of this kind so as to eliminate the carnal rivals of religious ecstasy and to suppress any forces that might disturb the controlled and regular routines of religion.

Similar doubts about the validity of pleasurable indulgence may well also have influenced both the ways in which scientific research into product use is chosen and funded and the manner in which the results are interpreted. If this is the case, then it would be reasonable to predict that:

1. Far more research will be conducted into the supposedly harmful effects of alcohol, tobacco, tea and coffee than into

any beneficial effects they may have on people's health and well-being, and very little publicity will be given to any negative correlations with disease or mortality that such product use may have. Already the finding that those who regularly drink small quantities of alcohol live longer than teetotallers seems to have been proved a grave embarrassment to the health scare industry.

2. Research into product use will tend to treat it as a mere case of drugs being ingested by isolated individuals and then to measure any changes in physiological functioning. Such a procedure would fail to pick up the benefits to the health and well-being of individuals that accrue from the way in which such products facilitate sociability. As a consequence, their key function in society will be ignored.

3. Relatively little research will be done into the possible harmful properties of the alternatives that religious sectarians or secular nature-faddists employ as substitutes for alcohol, tobacco, coffee or tea. Herbal infusions or smoking mixtures, low-alcohol or completely soft drinks and decaffeinated coffee will not be exposed to the same intense scrutinies as the products for which they are substituted, yet they may well be harmful when regularly consumed over a long period of time.

4. Groups, such as the Mormons and the Seventh-day Adventists will be used as a kind of 'natural laboratory' for measuring the supposedly evil effects on others of the products they eschew. However, less investigative effort, thought or publicity will be given to the examination of any causes of death or debility among these groups that are more frequent than in the population at large. In particular, there will be little incentive to investigate the social and psychological impacts, both positive and negative, on a person's health or well-being of belonging to an exclusive group that controls and restricts the social life of its members to the extent of instituting bans on product use.

Health surveys of Mormons or Seventh-day Adventists are likely to be restricted to those who remain members in good standing throughout their lives. However, some of those who have been raised as Mormons or Seventh-day Adventists may find membership and its restraints too restricting and either secretly indulge in the forbidden products, possibly to a reckless extent, or drop out of their religion altogether.

The health and happiness of these 'rebels' and 'failures' from puritanical homes are as much a consequence of the existence of absolute bans on product use as are those of untroubled conformists. To grow up in a teetotal home, for instance, can be a cause of alcoholism in later life, for such a person has never learned how to exercise moderation (Anderson, this volume). One lapse and they are lost, much as their own self-confirming morality would have predicted.

Health scare attacks on alcohol, tobacco, tea and coffee are also assaults on our dominant patterns of sociability. At least in the case of the Mormons or Seventh-day Adventists there was, and is, on offer a rewarding alternative pattern of fellowship and a rich variety of leisure activities, as well as the satisfactions of religion and good works. Modern secular health scares, by contrast, may merely snatch individuals from customary conviviality and turn them into anxious calculators, worried about how many months of lonely senility they may be losing at the end of their lives through companionable indulgence in cheering products today.

Alternatively, they may take on a religious fervour and become a source of tight moral and social control more appropriate to a sect. Health crusaders purport to be rational, objective and scientific but they have much in common with the true believers of sectarian religion, notably in their lack of scepticism, their failure to distinguish between fact and value, and their division of their fellow humans into an enlightened elect who have the true faith, diabolic doubters who are unconvinced and the ignorant masses who must be forced to accept their truth.

22

Gluttons, Soaks and Boors: The Regulation of Pleasure

Digby Anderson

Social Affairs Unit, London, UK

Readers of P.G. Wodehouse will know how eager Bertie Wooster was to spend weekends at Brinckley Court. This was partly because he was very attached to his Aunt Dahlia who lived there. It was even more because he was very attached to the cooking of Aunt Dahlia's chef Anatole, 'that wizard of pots and pans'. Anatole could prepare a dinner such as:

- Le Consomme aux Pommes d'Amour
- Les Sylphides a la creme d'Ecrevisses
- Les Fried Smelts
- Le Bird of some kind with chipped potatoes
- Le Ice Cream

But the pinnacle of Anatole's achievements was sweetbreads, ris de veau. When Tuppy Glossop wants to show how in love with cousin Angela he is, Bertie suggests that he reject his dinner untasted:

'Push my dinner away, eh? Yes.
Push away a dinner cooked by Anatole? Yes.
Push it away untasted? Yes.
Let us get this straight. Tonight at dinner, when the butler offers me a *ris de veau a la financière* or whatever it may be, hot from Anatole's hands, you

Pleasure and Quality of Life. Edited by D.M. Warburton and N. Sherwood
© 1996 John Wiley & Sons Ltd.

want me to push it away untasted?
Yes.
He chewed his lip. One could sense the struggle going on within. And then
suddenly a sort of glow came into his face. The old martyrs probably used
to look like that.
All right.
You'll do it?
I will.'
(Wodehouse, 1934)

The best authorities of French cooking enthuse about sweetbreads (the thymus gland). Calves' sweetbreads are best, but
lambs' sweetbreads and even beef breads are also good. Curnon-
sky's *Cuisine et Vins de France* gives several delicious recipes, in
butter, with mushrooms, in creme. I personally love them with a
soubise sauce. Enough. The point I am making is that those who
know about grub, know that sweetbreads are among the best
dishes. One of the few dishes that is better is brains—either in black
butter or blanched and in *beignets*. They are a valued dish in North
Indian cooking too (brains massala).

In the early 1990s, the British government banned them both.
To be more accurate, it banned the sale of calves' and beef sweetbreads and brains. There is no proof that they are a danger. There
is a remote possibility. But the Government did not just warn
consumers or say you buy them at your own risk. It, a group of
politicians, forbade gourmets to eat what they chose. Its statement
did not mention sweetbreads in soubise sauce or *beignets* of brains.
It did not appear to be aware that anyone valued these dishes or
know of sweetbreads' culinary reputation. It spoke of them purely
as a remote health hazard.

Subsequently, government interference has closed down scores
of UK slaughterhouses so that eager cooks cannot now get blood
(for boudins), tripes, chitterlings or the variety of abats and ex-
tremities that good cooking needs. Egg producers have been
curbed. Seafood vendors are forced to boil their cockles twice,
removing their taste and leaving them tiny, wrinkled and dry.

And all this is part of a wider interference with the products
of pleasure, things that are consumed usually in private premises and were once thought to be a private matter. Now, the
politicians have their big feet in the shopkeeper's shop, the
restaurant owner's restaurant and they are walking all over

private houses strutting about the kitchen telling us what we may buy, cook and eat, drink and smoke.

The past years have, then, seen increasing government attempts to intrude in the legal sale and consumption of pleasurable products, especially alcoholic drinks, cigars, cigarettes and food. This has been portrayed by its opponents as an interference in the liberty of the individual to take his pleasures how he may.

I suggest that it is more than that. And if you ponder my opening remarks about sweetbreads, you may see what this extra dimension is. The pleasures that the individual takes are in fact social activities, not necessarily in the sense that he does them with others but, in the sense that they have been developed by past societies and are hedged with social norms and manners. These norms and manners are about taste, excellence, ways of preparing and enjoying products. What is being interfered with are social institutions, many of them social institutions of quality and civilization. Moreover many of them are to an extent self-policing. By interfering with them, government may damage valuable aspects of civilized life and destroy sources of social order and restraint.

Let me give a rather different example. Kevin is a 17-year-old manual worker from Coventry in the British Midlands. He has all of the awkwardness and uncertainty of his age. When he goes to the pub, which he does on Saturdays with his friends and once or twice in the week on his own, he passes for 18. Eighteen is the minimum age for buying and consuming alcoholic drinks under British law.

Sometimes, on Saturdays, he and his friends used to drink novelty drinks, those ghastly drinks that somehow suddenly acquire cult status among teenagers, such as the disgusting cider with blackcurrant juice. Once, Kevin ordered a cider and blackcurrant when he was on his own in the pub on a Thursday. Immediately he was embarrassed by the laughter of the older men. No more cider and blackcurrant for Kevin. Now, he drinks what the older men drink, lager or bitter.

Before he started going to the pub, Kevin and his friends used to buy the strongest cider from off-licences and down a few cans quickly, trying competitively to get drunk as rapidly as possible. Somehow that did not seem to be the thing to do in the pub. Not only did he learn to make drinks last and enjoy a couple of hours drinking and talking, but he became aware that being drunk, at least noisily drunk, was not appreciated. One of his friends had been barred for a month for swearing while drunk. All right, he and his friends still boast afterwards about how much they had downed last Saturday, but actually on Saturday and in the pub, their efforts are directed in precisely the opposite way, trying to appear sober.

Something similar happened to the way they bought their drinks. In the early days, he had paid for his own drink. He and his friends would come in. The landlord would ask the four of them what they wanted and each would reply for himself and pay for his own drink. But it seemed a time-wasting system. They became conscious of being looked at as each repeated the same order. Indeed, Kevin used to have the correct change ready before he went in so as to get the process over with as fast as possible without blushing. Gradually, they fell in with the custom of buying rounds—even if they did argue afterwards about who owed whom some money back.

Within a year, Kevin and his friends are drinking in much the same way as the older men. Indeed, he now chats happily with other drinkers of all ages. Kevin has become 'a regular'. There is a code of drinking behaviour in pubs. It varies, of course, from pub to pub, but young people learn this code by going to pubs. The code concerns acceptable and unacceptable drinks, amounts to drink, the pace of drinking, the spirit in which drink is taken. It is about matters of taste and conviviality.

There is no blackboard in the pub to teach the code. It is learned by watching what others do. That does not make it weak. It is backed up by sanctions. Infractions of taste—the cider and blackcurrant—are laughed at. The young men are embarrassed into conformity by mockery, mutterings and raised eyebrows. Infractions of the social code—getting noisily drunk—are punished by ostracism or banishment. Offences against taste or conviviality are remembered—some of the same drinkers are in the pub most evenings—and reputations get established. This provides the possibility for shame. And there are positive incentives, too—not least the approval of older men and established drinkers, indicated by acceptance into conversation. The code may be learned by such sanctions external to the individual. But the sign that it is well and truly learned is when the external sanctions are internalized, when Kevin ceases to look about him for mutters and glances, and drinks convivially and tastefully because he himself would be ashamed or ill at ease if he did not. By now social control has become self-control and is institutionalized into habit.

Drinking can make a few drinkers aggressive, silly, tiresome or maudlin, but it usually does not do so. Most drinkers in pubs are not tedious soaks, let alone violent aggressors, but rather good fun to be with. The socializing process is to be thanked for this, the institution of the pub itself, or in other societies, the cafe. This is not to say that the code taught is necessarily all good. Round drinking, for instance, can lead to involuntary over-consumption and over-expenditure. It is simply that by drinking with older others, Kevin's drinking is civilized.

Pubs and cafes are usually seen as opportunities for pleasure, for relaxation, letting yourself go. And so they are. But sustained communal pleasure, like sustained communal anything else, requires order and rules. And relaxation needs the comfort of assured expectations and habits. In short, the pub or cafe regulates pleasure and thereby makes its repeated, comparatively secure indulgence possible.

This is textbook sociology and psychology. Look at any such textbook prior to the 1960s and you will find a similar account of socialization. It contains two insights, both of which became obscured in the 1960s. The first is that order and habit and inhibition and tradition are not the enemies of liberty and true self-expression and pleasure, but its preconditions. Drinking as much neat spirit as fast as possible on your own in a darkened garage provides neither the sensory nor the social satisfaction to compare with three leisurely gin and tonics with friends in the Red Lion.

The second insight is that the various sources of regulation do not necessarily involve explicit regulation, let alone government regulation. The nearest Kevin's pub code gets to explicitness is when the landlord shouts, 'Any more swearing and you're barred'. All the other disciplines are implicit or tacit.

The widespread view among social scientists used to be that this informal order, the operation of social control and self-control by shame and example, and by habit and manners, was much more powerful than political regulation. If a society was fortunate enough to have its eating, drinking, smoking, courting and other pleasures controlled by informal habits and heightened by civilized taste and manners, then it should be grateful and not seek the heavy hand of government regulation or explicit codes of political correctness.

The 1960s, in the name of pleasure and personal autonomy, launched an onslaught on this precious informal social order. Manners were ridiculed as artificial. Freedom was seen as freedom from tradition, habit and informal social control. This liberation in the name of pleasure gave pleasure a bad name and opened the way to government intrusion. What we have seen since the rise of licence in the 1960s are calls for more political regulation to make pleasure safe and sociable. I discussed in an earlier paper the calls for advertising bans and penal taxes on pleasure goods, and for government advertising campaigns to promote healthy living (Anderson, 1994).

The older view was not only that explicit laws and codes such as those of the healthiest or politically correct activists are poor substitutes for the informal regulations of manners and self-control, but that excessive or mistaken government regulation subverts informal regulation. To refer to the previous example, Kevin is not taught how to drink with taste and sociability by the law. On the contrary, he learns how to drink in the pub.

The reaction to the 1960s threatens genuine freedom to enjoy pleasure in many ways. It sees pleasures as unordered indulgences rather than as taste-governed, convivially-organized and traditionally restrained activities, results of a civilizing process. Having subverted it by turning it into anomic licence, it then invites political repression to contain the disorder and danger that it has itself unleashed. Firstly, it tells you to stop fussing with your cigar guillotine or passing the vintage port and instead get stoned on your own in the lavatory, then, having conceptualized the traditional pleasures as mere drug taking, it invites in the health police to persecute them as such.

Let us summarize where this takes us in 'political' terms. Some commentators object to politicians interfering in pleasures and excessively regulating pleasurable products on the grounds that this interferes with individual autonomy. The picture that they so often imply is of individuals waking up one day with various desires, animal desires or desires of whimsy, and the politicians trying to stop them. By what right do they do so? What business is it of theirs how they find their pleasures, provided always that they do not hurt others?

Such commentators are wrong. Individuals do not establish the institutions of pleasure every day, themselves, for 'another first time'. They inherit them. They inherit the pub, the cafe and the coffee house and the ways of behaviour that go with them. Tradition gives them these wonderful things. And pleasure does not lie in the litre of ethyl alcohol swigged in the garage or the nicotine patch strapped to the arm or the sugar solution fed through a rubber hose direct to the stomach. It lies in the aged brandy, the cigarette after the breakfast coffee with the newspaper, and the dinner party prepared by a domestic 'Anatole'.

Sometimes such pleasures are enjoyed alone but they are no less 'social' for that. Even if not actually with other people, friends, colleagues, family, they are the products of, and are maintained by, social institutions with rules, rules to pace the consumption, to suggest what might be taken with it, what is not acceptable. The best pleasures one can wish for depend on social institutions including regulations.

It is when government regulations interfere with these that the trouble really starts. When it comes to pleasurable products, the government has a supply-led model. Its interference with the pleasure industries implies that if harm comes from the 'wrong' use of pleasurable products, then that is the fault and responsibility of the producers, not the consumers. The model assumed is one in which the industries inflict products on a confused or gullible consumer. Hence the obsession with advertising and labelling controls.

When a government starts to speak of fine wine, casks of ale, bottles of whisky, good cigars and fine cigarettes, and sweetbreads as if they were just alcohol and nicotine and health hazards, it starts to see their use purely as 'health' matters. The effect of the government's intrusion is *uncivilized* public perceptions of drinking. It is to reduce drinkers to soaks and eaters to gluttons. When the traditions of the restaurant, the pub or the cafe are reduced in policy terms to nothing more than places where potentially harmful products are sold, then we have government undoing civilization.

Let me repeat it again because so few understand it today, at least in government. Pleasure involves more than a consumer and a supplier starting from scratch on each exchange. The very product has been developed over history, been informed by canons of taste, is sold in social situations and mediated by social expectations, manners and habits. Pleasure depends not just on a free exchange between buyer and seller but on some continuity of the social institutions that make pleasure pleasurable, what I have called civilization.

In summary, there is, then, a social fabric on which civilized pleasure rests. It is a fabric largely separate from government, consisting of formal and informal institutions, families, shops, pubs, traditions, habits, manners. There is not much government can do to strengthen it, but it can undermine it. It has indeed undermined it by fiscal and intervention policies, which have been obsessed with suppliers rather than purchasers, and by a view of pleasure products as health matters that has totally failed to see the connection between pleasure and civilization.

23

The Choice of the Pleasures of Life and the Defence of Democracy

Claude Javeau

Department of Sociology, Université Libre de Bruxelles,
Avenue Jeanne 44-CP124, 1050 Brussels, Belgium

INTRODUCTION

Critics of post-modernity are prone to assert that our society is a hedonistic one, which means for them that the prime goal, for which our contemporaries strive, is pleasure. This aim has been inferred from the constantly changing means of entertainment, such as the expansion of the media and mass tourism, but not, notably, from increased happiness. It is true that what has been customarily termed leisure has been based for some decades past mainly on entertainment, of which relaxation is a part. The huge productivity gains of the modern economy enabled the authorities to promote non-productive activities and implement the welfare state. This has led to a style of living in which free time takes, in a quantitative as well as in a qualitative way, a major share.

The producer who in the past was the symbol of the capitalist system, has given way to the consumer as the symbol of the welfare state. The welfare state, while remaining in essence capitalist, has altered the mode of production towards the protection of the salaried workers. The primacy of consumption has taken precedence over cultural things. Nowadays, our contemporaries,

Pleasure and Quality of Life. Edited by D.M. Warburton and N. Sherwood
© 1996 John Wiley & Sons Ltd.

in their free time, which is of a far greater personal importance than their working time, are consumers of acultural messages, especially from television.

Nowadays, the individual is heaped with goods and services, is bombarded by all kinds of information, and is shielded by various protective agencies (especially for health). Of course, this picture of our lifestyle is a caricature and many individuals do not conform to the stereotype, such as recent immigrants and the poor. Nevertheless, it is true that the ideology of post-modern culture is based above all on both total material and mental well-being.

This ideology does not aim to prepare us on Earth for the Kingdom of Heaven, as in the Middle Ages; nor, as in the time of the Renaissance, to open the realm of knowledge to those who want to submit to the empire of Reason; nor, as in the nineteenth century, to work for the collective emancipation of an oppressed class; nor, as in the present century, to bring about the triumph of a Master Race as in fascism or to promote an equal distribution of resources, as in communism. Today, the prevalent ideology is 'selfish hedonism' within the framework of free market economy. The ideology of this hedonism, as described, is that of extracting the maximum benefit, quantitative and qualitative, from that potentially available.

POST-MODERNITY, REALITY AND DE-REALITY

If modernity can be defined as achieving the conjunction of *mouvement* and *incertitude*, post-modernity, at least for those who advanced this notion, would be above all characterized by the final arrival of the *absence de sens* (Balandier, 1988). For example, when the Berlin Wall fell, demolishing with it the reign of terror, one could witness the revival, in Europe and elsewhere, of old nationalistic demons that were believed to have been conquered.

It is in this atmosphere of instability that the hedonistic quest must be undertaken. The post-modernist age, fraught with insignificance and insecurity, favours a so-called hedonistic ideology based on a popular culture of constant varying entertainment. Post-modern people are invited to participate in an apparently endless feast, but which is at the same time threatened with a sudden end. Their horizon is a surfeit of images of overriding realism, and even superseding surrealism. This world's emotional load must be constantly renewed if it is to be maintained. The social order, which is indispensable for the survival of an economy, can only be guaranteed if all emotions are repressed and inner control is exerted by the majority of individuals. Control is focused chiefly on the body, since the human mind has, in general, renounced its critical capacities.

In our Western cultural system, subjugation of the body or 'domestication of the body' (Elias, 1939) has been aimed for a long time to some idealistic goal, with or without a religious connotation. In the Middle Ages, the body was compelled to subjugate the degenerate dispositions that would interfere with the ascent of the soul to Heaven, while now the same unholy desires must be controlled in the interest of the state. Today, the legitimacy of this control is supplied by Medicine, in the name of the Ideal of Good Health, linked with the state's obligation to provide social order and security. This Ideal is supposed to be founded upon a rational concept of 'The Good Life'. Those who do not conform risk the censure of the Health Police.

Medical power subjugates bodies through the dictates of preventative medicine. In order to counteract the prevailing hedonistic tone of contemporary culture, the person and the body must be subjected to a constant monitoring, with the aim of preventing, or at least delaying, the onset of diseases, such as cancer or cardiovascular illness. Prevention implies relentless self-supervision, with respect to various products and practices that are claimed to be dangerous to health, such as alcohol, cholesterol, salt, sugar, sunbathing and tobacco. Constantly, the need for control is repeated in the media, in advertising and from government ministers. Life is lived as if the pleasures of life are confined to fantasy, never to find concrete expression.

A significant example is that of tobacco use. Firstly, it was an emanation of the devil, then a symbol of wisdom, and even a hallmark of manhood (hence its symbolism for women's liberation). Now, tobacco has become the subject of ever-growing repression; smokers are harassed and branded as air polluters and purveyors of illness to non-smokers, and squanders of health funds. In the UK, doctors have refused to treat patients, on the grounds that they had not taken enough care of their own health by being smokers. These attitudes are justified on economic grounds, but their real meaning is subjugation of the body, which, as personal health is claimed to be its sole concern, can only be morally positive.

On the pretext of prevention, liberty is being restricted, by placing so many safeguards against neglect or ignorance in the fields of health or security. An atmosphere of constant concern has been generated, whether it be the fear of suffering or the fear of the Health Police, or *L'angélisme exterminateur* (Slama, 1993). Sooner or later, democracy is threatened by this 'preventionism', as much as by that de-reality culture that is its corollary.

LIBERTIES: POSITIVE AND NEGATIVE

I have borrowed from Sir Isaiah Berlin the distinction between 'positive liberties' and 'negative liberties' (1969). For Berlin, the positive meaning of the word 'liberty' is included in the answer to the following question: 'Whereon can be established the authority that can force someone to be, or to do, this rather than that?' The meaning of negative liberty is found in the answer to the following question: 'What is the framework within which a person—either individually or collectively—must or should have to do or be whatever he or they are capable of doing without another's interference?' Simply, positive liberty is the state interference in the interest of individuals while negative liberty refers to individual freedom.

If, as Berlin shows, individual freedom (which is the subject matter of negative liberty) and democracy are not necessarily balanced, nevertheless it is in a democratic system that individual freedom is spread widely and non-arbitrarily. On the other hand, positive freedom has often been formalized in one or other form as a collective body by dictators who claim to exert their power from the will of the people.

In parliamentary democracies, positive freedom is guaranteed by a power whose legitimacy is based on the votes of electors as well as on the likelihood of the rejection of the voters if they lose confidence in the ruling group. The law of the majority is acceptable only if there is no compulsion for all to conform and that citizens have self-determination. They are responsible for any infringement of these laws, but will be answerable only to a judicial system that they have themselves made legitimate by the electoral process.

However, the advent of the great modern bureaucracies has reduced the scope of negative liberty, by multiplying the barriers to choice. The increase in regulations (a source of unending harassment), the appropriation of a person's time, administrative inertia itself (exacerbated by incompetence), have moulded the world into an obstacle course. The invasion of medical power into collective life has reinforced this disastrous state of affairs.

The multiplication of prohibitions is advantageous for the citizen, if the price for wide protection is less than that paid in the event of their non-existence. This price is the limitation of individual freedom (negative liberty), which attains its true aim only when prosperity has reached a rather high level (Berlin, 1969).

But there comes a time when the price gets to be too high. The protection is replaced by the infiltration of medico-police power into the most commonplace events of everyday life. When all is said and done, this power, is only another arm of the political power, whose main concern is to guarantee a generalized health protection. This is when democracy finds itself in great jeopardy, without the citizens being aware of it.

LIBERTY AND THE PLEASURES OF LIFE

Democracy is founded upon a majority will from citizens who are free and equal. They are free in the sense that they are capable of self-determination and are limited in this autonomy by powers for which the majority have voted. They are equal in the sense that there is no difference between the rights of each citizen. To this equality of rights, the modern democracies, which have given birth to the welfare state, have added the equality of conditions, i.e. solidarity (which in the republican tradition is called fraternity). Free, equal, but bound together: the balance between these three attributes of the citizen in a democratic system is difficult to obtain. These liberties will always be conflicting by definition, for solidarity imposes on the state duties of protection, which even though they limit positive liberty in some measure, hinder much more seriously the exercise of individual freedom (negative liberty).

Here intervenes the dreadful power of the bureaucracy, which creates restrictions and harassment in the areas reserved for self-determination. The expansion of the bureaucratic supervision results in the transition from a society with a contractual foundation to a society with a statutory one. Paradoxically, within this statutory framework are revived various forms of personal allegiances, which are reminiscent of feudal systems.

One is reminded of Alexis de Tocqueville's (1981) pertinent prophecy at the end of his masterpiece, *On Democracy in America*. Above the mass of men who are free and equal rises an immense and guardian power, which alone undertakes to provide for their enjoyment and take care of their destiny. It is steady, provident, gentle, but absolute. It would look like a parental power if its purpose were to prepare people for adulthood, but it seeks only to maintain them irrevocably in their infancy.

This benevolent despot foresees and supplies their needs, manages their principal affairs, runs their businesses, settles their successions, shares out their inheritances. It likes the citizens to find enjoyment, provided they have no other goal. It willingly works toward their happiness; however it wants to be the sole agent and arbiter of this pursuit. It provides their safety and it wishes that it could remove the shame of having to think along with their pain of living. One cannot help being startled by the grave relevance of Tocqueville's premonition of the modern state with its culture of entertainment and its active 'infantilization' of people.

To ensure its survival as a democracy, the democratic state must be animated (by that I mean, receiving its soul) by citizens who have the ability to determine themselves, to accept risks measured by the yardstick of requisite responsibilities. In this connection, the theme of 'the pleasures of life' is quite an illuminating topic. While it may not be superfluous to search for the deep motivations that lead individuals to the quest for this or that pleasure, it looks to me sufficient to point out that when individuals are left to their own sense of obligations, the field of individual freedom is enhanced and the democracy is promoted.

Of course, one cannot condone drunken driving, or transforming public places into spaces reeking of tobacco smoke; I am only proposing that the use of products that the medical authorities frown upon should be left to the free choice of their users, provided they have an accurate assessment of the risks and benefits thereof. One can drink alcohol in company with others and so strengthen sociability, without reaching the debasing stage of intoxication and posing a danger to others.

CONCLUSIONS

The modern state, promoting a culture of enjoyment on the one hand, assures social order on the other through constraints on the citizens, for which it is responsible. It is a price required for guaranteeing the security of its citizens, but it is at a price that lets democracy (as Tocqueville had forecast) run the risk of becoming despotism, gentle though it may be.

If hedonism is to exist, its birth has to take place in the private realm of responsible choices. To promote a sensible, therefore rational, quest for 'the pleasures of life' leads to a reaffirmation of democracy. Allowing a person to negotiate his association with others—whether it be for consumption of goods, driving a motorcar or having sexual relations—is more favourable to this reaffirmation than a host of restrictions, which have been invented by so-called 'experts', without political supervision, and engineered by their own autonomous bureaucracy.

Responsible citizens, as co-contractors of their public and private spaces, are the living source of a true democracy, that which is able to reconcile (except for unavoidable conflicts) the state controls (positive liberties) and individual freedoms (negative liberties), for the greatest good of the greatest number of people.

24

Pleasure and Political Culture

Frank van Dun

University of Limburg, Maastricht, The Netherlands

'It has always been difficult for man to realize that his life is all an art. It has been more difficult to conceive it so than to act it so.' (Havelock Ellis, *The Dance of Life*)

INTRODUCTION

A key element in liberal political thought is the so-called neutrality thesis. It expresses the idea that law should be a neutral framework, within which people of various religious and moral persuasions can live and work together on peaceful terms. Effective constitutional safeguards should keep the power to coerce out of the hands of those who would use it to impose their own preferred normative and value-judgements, codes of conduct or lifestyle on others. However, it has never been easy to implement the condition of the neutrality of law, also known as the Rule of Law.

In many countries, a number of political campaigns ostensibly devoted to improving the quality of life have resulted in a flood of legislation and often burdensome fiscal and administrative regulation. Despite their efforts to present their programmes as having a solid base in 'scientific findings', the term 'morality campaigns' appears to be an appropriate generic name for these political movements because of the nature of their rhetoric and the objects of their ire. Common to almost all of them is a tendency to

Pleasure and Quality of Life. Edited by D.M. Warburton and N. Sherwood
© 1996 John Wiley & Sons Ltd.

attack what are, for many people, the simple pleasures in life: drinking alcoholic and caffeinated beverages, eating sweets, potato chips, red meat, butter and cream, and smoking tobacco. With wild exaggeration and little contradiction, these and other recreational activities, which many people affectionately call their 'small vices', have been denounced in the public media as unhealthy, alienating, bad for the environment, barbaric, degrading, irrational and evil.

From a liberal point of view, this moralistic aspect of the health campaigns would be merely annoying, if it did not have such a regrettable influence on public opinion, debate and policy. With their dramatic stories, scary statistics and stern warnings of impending epidemics, these morality campaigns have created an atmosphere of anxiety, guilt and intolerance, the very opposite of the liberal ideal of a relaxed, tolerant society.

Disregarding the obvious social, psychological and therapeutic functions of the simple pleasures, these campaigns focus on various possible risks to health. However, their message is not that it pays to be aware of risk information, but that the very act of engaging in the censored activities is a symptom of grave moral deficiency, requiring either Draconian preventive legal measures or compulsory treatment.

A message like that is not conducive to enlightened public debate. Rational discussion of the relations between means and ends is difficult with people who believe that they are defending moral absolutes that should on no account be compromised, no matter what the costs. How does one argue with people who take their own visions of imminent apocalypse as sufficient proof that the time to act is now, no matter how uncertain or contested the science (if any) behind their predictions?

Of course, no liberal would deny anybody the right to adopt or experiment with any particular way of life, no matter how puritanical or ascetic, or to advocate and promote its adoption by others. In this sense, the morality campaigns are protected by basic liberal rights of freedom of expression and freedom of association. However, the campaigners are all too willing to deny the same rights to others. Betraying a firm commitment to the theory and practice of political paternalism, they not only claim to know better than other people what is good for them, they also claim the right to use coercive means to discourage or suppress disliked lifestyles.

But it is the relative ease with which the morality campaigns have been able to press their proposals through the political and legislative machinery of the welfare states that should give a person of liberal persuasion the greatest cause for concern. It is indicative of a serious weakness in the political constitution of the modern state. After all, the very idea of constitutional government is to keep the power of coercion out of the hands of those who seek to impose their own value-judgements on others, when there is no clear and compelling public interest at stake.

The aim of this chapter is to investigate to what extent the morality campaigns of the present day can justify the policies they propose as serving the public interest. Later, I shall turn to the concept of the rule of law in order to clarify liberal opposition to the political designs of the morality campaigns, even in cases where the latter profess to protect the innocent or the larger public interest. However, I shall begin with some remarks on the political paternalism of the morality campaigns, especially the health campaigns.

HEALTH PATERNALISM AND THE QUALITY OF LIFE

Obviously, the people behind the morality campaigns are sensitive to the charge of paternalism. Over the years the rhetoric of the campaigns has shifted from unmistakable direct paternalism ('coercing a person for his own good') to claims about protecting the innocent or even society. One example is the shift from the claim that smokers harm themselves to the claim that they harm some other people by 'passive smoking' and to the claim that they harm everybody ('society') by driving up the costs of healthcare. Because no man is an island, it is almost always plausible to argue that a person who harms himself also harms others: the high alcohol consumer who destroys himself also threatens others with his drinking: his wife, his children, his employer, road users and so on.

Despite their tendency to cover their programmes with the veneer of 'defence of the public interest', the morality campaigns are often deeply committed to direct paternalism. For example, it is unlikely that the anti-smoking campaigns would disintegrate if the public were to reject the thesis that 'passive smoking' is a problem requiring government action, or the thesis that smokers impose some of the costs of their habit on others. It is more likely that they would continue to press their original claims about the moral duty of the government to take action in view of the 'unacceptable health risks' of smoking.

Direct paternalism rests on the claim that the superior knows better what is good for his subordinates than they do themselves. Let us grant at the outset that such a claim may be justified. However, we should add immediately that it is likely to be justified only when it is made with respect to some specific aspect of life. That is why so many people can earn a living as professional consultants.

But direct paternalism is not to be confused with the practice of consulting. People are free to seek advice or not. They choose whom they will consult, and decide for themselves whether to follow the advice given to them. And rightly so, because the advice, even when correct within its own frame of reference, may still be inappropriate 'all things considered'. Paternalism, on the other hand, implies that only the ruler is competent to select experts, and that he has a right to impose his experts' advice on others as a binding and enforceable norm, regardless of the others' consent.

Liberalism objects to political paternalism, not to consulting. It rejects the idea that there is any other definitive test of claims about what is good or useful for a person than personal experience. Contrary to what is sometimes suggested, the argument is not that a person is *ex ante* the best judge of his own interests (though that is often enough the case). It is that a person is *ex post* the best judge of his own interests. Therefore, the danger of paternalistic rule is not only that it prevents people from learning from their own mistakes, but also, and far more importantly that it compels them to suffer at the hands of perhaps well-meaning but inevitably fallible rulers for as long as the latter remain convinced of their own superior judgement.

Health paternalism seeks to transform the doctor–patient relationship into a ruler–subject relationship. But this makes sense only if one assumes one of the following implausible and mutually incompatible propositions: (i) that advice on health has no bearing whatsoever on other aspects of life, or (ii) that it is somehow all-inclusive, so that there simply are no other things to consider. If either of these propositions were true, politicized health paternalism would be unobjectionable: for then not to follow the advice given by an adviser more competent in his field than oneself would indeed be irrational.

The proposition that health authorities are competent to give advice on the best way to order one's life 'all things considered' is part of the official ideology of the health movements. As defined by the World Health Organization, health is 'not merely the absence of disease, but a state of complete physical, mental and social well-being'. Health, in short, is the highest all-inclusive good, or something very close to it. If WHO's experts were truly experts on health defined as a 'state of complete well-being', who could reasonably object to their assuming command over his life?

However, the relationship between health and well-being is far from clear. True, other things equal, being healthy is better than being sick—taking the words 'healthy' and 'sick' in their ordinary meaning. If other things are not equal, lack of health can be compensated in many ways. For example, for many people, the diagnosis of a disease may be an asset: all of a sudden one has something important to talk about; one gets to meet people: doctors, nurses, orderlies, fellow sufferers; one gets sympathy and consideration, respect, and a hard to ignore excuse for getting out of a number of unpleasant obligations; with some luck one gets a card certifying one's status as a sufferer or victim, and privileged access to all sorts of things. 'On indefinite sickness leave' sounds better, and often pays better, than 'permanently unemployed'. And so on. It is not absurd to assume that some people may actually experience an increase in the quality of their life as a result of a diagnosis of illness.

On the other hand, the dogged pursuit of health may leave little time or energy for the other interesting things that enter into the balance of one's quality of life or well-being. The man who goes to see his doctor every week, only to be told that there is nothing wrong with him, or to be pacified with massive quantities of placebos, may be healthy—but how does the quality of his life compare to that of the person who will not allow an occasional fever or headache or backache to detract him from his calling? 'Maximal health', like 'a pollution-free environment', is an absolute and probably meaningless concept. It is not the same thing as 'optimal health', a relative concept, relating one's physical and mental conditions to the many dimensions of the experience of life.

Rather than acknowledge the formidable complexity of what makes up a person's quality of life, the morality campaigns often tend to fall back on the other proposition noted above, that their advice is valid no matter what the other particulars of a person's life may be. This strategy is obvious in the many campaigns concentrating on single issues (i.e. on the health risks of particular activities). By making these foremost in the public's mind, the campaigns aim to dim the public's awareness of other relevant factors. It is suggested that changing one item in one's way of life will dramatically improve the quality of one's life by reducing the associated risks. The message is neither subtle nor tolerant: 'Smoking tobacco, drinking alcohol or eating fat will kill you. To do such things is as irrational and stupid as playing Russian roulette'.

But the benefit of the bullet is instantaneous death. Tobacco, alcohol and fat yield their benefits in this life. Even if it were certain that they reduce one's expected lifespan, their use could not for that reason alone be called irrational. The rationality of using such substances depends on one's valuation of whether the extra time that can be gained at the end of one's life is worth the benefits foregone during the rest of it. The claim of irrationality only succeeds if there are bound to be no benefits, only costs, or if one assumes that in terms of quality of life the extra time necessarily shows a positive balance. This is, in fact, what the morality campaigns intimate. For example, anti-smoking campaigns emphasize the risks of smoking (lung cancer, cardiovascular diseases) and the health benefits of giving up the habit. No mention is made of the benefits of smoking: the pleasure it gives, the way it helps people to relax, alleviate stress, concentrate, or even reduce the risk of contracting certain diseases, such as Alzheimer's disease and Parkinson's disease.

Because of their unwillingness to concede that smoking may be beneficial, the campaigns also remain silent on the costs and risks associated with alternative ways in which people might seek the benefits they now derive from tobacco use. The campaigns are also unwilling to concede that the amount of tobacco consumed, and the form in which it is consumed (smoking cigarettes, cigars or a pipe, or chewing tobacco), could make a difference to the statistical health risks. Instead, they tend to portray all use of tobacco as excessive use and all smokers as people who have lost control over their lives. Similar argumentative strategies have been used by anti-alcohol crusaders, most of whom simply ignore evidence indicating that moderate use of alcohol is actually good for one's health, or that moderate drinkers tend to outlive both inveterate drunkards and teetotallers.

Given the theoretical and practical difficulties of measuring the quality of life, it is not surprising that science has to make do with crude indexes, data (such as records of age at time of death) that are then hypothetically interpreted as related to less tangible aspects of life, e.g. health. However, age at time of death is not a straightforward indicator of how healthy one's life has been. A person who is under treatment for one disease after another for 90 years of his life cannot readily be said to have had a healthier life than the person who never had any complaints but suffered a fatal stroke at the age of 65. (As the centenarian with a black sense of humour remarked, 'I wish I had AIDS, for I am told that an AIDS patient still has seven years to live.').

Postponing the moment of death with a few weeks or months or even years by itself does not guarantee that the extra time will be in any sense a gain. Ageing takes its toll, even if one stops short of senility and other debilitating afflictions. To outlive one's own purposes in life, or to come to resent one's dependency on others, even for the simplest things, is more than most people can bear with equanimity. And the question is usually not about actually postponing the moment of death, but about reducing the statistical risks of a shorter lifespan. One can only do this, if at all, by manoeuvring oneself into other categories defined by the statisticians. But the costs may be great, and there is no guarantee that the effort will result in a longer, healthier life. Nor are the classification systems of the statisticians guaranteed to remain constant over time. A determined person who would try to live a healthy life by continually adjusting his lifestyle according to the latest findings on who outlives who would probably have a very varied existence. Whether it would be a long and healthy one is another matter.

Health statistics are no substitutes for the experience of living. To live is to make choices. These choices cannot be considered *in vitro*, apart from the full experiences of the persons making them. People are different: they have different genetic constitutions and personal histories, different personalities, ambitions, expectations, values, preferences, tastes; some may be risk-averse with respect to some risks, which others perhaps love to take. Consequently, what one classifies as a cost, another may see as a benefit. One man's 'pleasure' is another's 'pain' (or 'sin').

True, quality of life as experienced by a person is largely a matter of his having made the 'right' choices. But all choices, no matter how well-informed, are speculative. There is no *a priori* 'right' choice. Because of this, the political aspect of making choices comes to the fore: who should make the choices? The person who will in any case suffer the consequences, or someone else? Compared to one who rules others for his own benefit, the paternalistic ruler may seem an attractive alternative. But he remains a ruler who self-righteously believes that the purity of his own intentions is sufficient justification for exposing others to the risk of having to suffer from his mistakes.

THE RULE OF LAW

The idea of the rule of law is at once familiar and little understood. It is almost universally accepted in the field of criminal law, where it is embodied in that great pillar of criminal justice: the presumption of innocence. We take it for granted that a person should not be convicted and punished for a crime unless his guilt has been proven in a public procedure subject to strict standards of proof and method. The burden of proof should rest with the accusers and prosecutors. The benefit of the doubt should go to the accused, even in the face of hostile public opinion. Whatever the technical legal definition of 'crime', to punish an innocent person is itself a crime. There is no justification for arbitrarily subjecting a person to punitive measures or to harassment and intrusions into their private affairs. Under the rule of law, coercion is acceptable only in defence of one's rights, and then only against those involved in violating them. Defence is no valid pretext for aggression.

The idea of the rule of law applies to all cases where injury is done, regardless of who does it. The law it refers to is the fundamental law of society: to protect people against those who would injure them. It antedates the distinction between ruler and subject, magistrate and citizen, and remains oblivious to it. It protects society as such, rather than any particular manifestation of it. The ultimate standard is and remains the fundamental law itself. If that standard is met, the degree to which people mutually allow each other to cope with life, both individually and in association or cooperation with others, is at a maximum (relative to the technical and social skills available to the people in a particular historical context). In the words of Democritus, 'The custom laws would not prevent any one of us from leading his life according to his own powers and opportunities, if it were not the case that one injured another'. The rule of law is the condition that allows us to be free to make the best of our lives, i.e. to enjoy our natural rights, provided that we do not harm others (see John Stuart Mill, 1983).

Since one's faculties are embodied in one's means of action and life, i.e. in one's property, the basic requirement of law translates into respect for persons and their property, their body and other means. Law, in this naturalistic sense, requires no metaphysical essences, no knowledge of the good. All it requires is a capacity to distinguish one person from another, and one person's actions from the actions of another. Law is something everybody may be presumed to know and understand.

THE METHOD OF LAW

In order to institutionalize the rule of law, it should be made to apply to political and legislative decisions in order to check that they do not 'harm the innocent in a legally relevant way'. Thus, before a certain type of activity can be restricted or forbidden by some form of coercive regulation we should expect proof:

1. either that it (i) is in fact harmful to third parties in a legally relevant way, or (ii) does create an unacceptable risk of legally relevant harm;
2. that the measures proposed are needful, i.e. that the harm to be prevented or reduced is caused under circumstances that (i) make it practically impossible for the victims to seek redress through the usual channels of law, or to avoid the harm through alternative contractual arrangements, and (ii) cannot be removed by alternative measures with less burdensome implications for the enjoyment of one's rights than the proposed regulations and restrictions;
3. that the measures proposed are legitimate, i.e. have a defensive character, and are likely to be effective and efficient.

The burden of proof should rest with those who propose such measures (members of the legislative or executive branches of government), because they are in effect accusing others of socially unacceptable behaviour and suggesting that those people should to some extent be deprived of their rights. The arguments should be open to challenge by those whose liberty would be restricted. They should be presented for evaluation to an independent jury with powers to reject them on the ground of lack of proof. The idea is to separate evaluation of the arguments for the necessity of a coercive policy from consideration of political opportunity, and to offer protection to the innocent even in the face of hostile public opinion.

The first condition requires proof of some legally relevant harm. The proper criterion for legally relevant harm follows from the principle of the rule of law itself, as interpreted from the natural rights perspective. No one has a right to do anything that deprives another of his faculties (property) without the other's consent.

The second condition requires proof that the potential victims of the activities in question have no practical possibility of getting compensation through the courts, or of avoiding or reducing the risk of harm through contractual arrangements. The mere fact that an activity might be harmful in a legally relevant way does not justify that it be coercively restricted, if those who are harmed by it in a relevant way can easily get compensation in the courts, or if they can easily avoid the harm through negotiation.

The third condition requires proof that the measures proposed do not impose legally relevant harm on innocent third parties. This is a particularly relevant condition in view of the widespread tendencies of governments to impose regulations on a whole class of citizens in response to a few sensational incidents involving only a small number of them. Supposing it were true that alcohol consumption is a source of external costs that cannot be internalized through negotiation or an appeal to the courts, a general tax on alcohol would be rejected as ineffective and inefficient. For there is no reason to suppose that all or even most people who drink cause legally relevant problems. In fact, there is every reason to suppose that in countries where the consumption of alcohol is a generally accepted practice, most drinking will be done by experienced drinkers who can be trusted to know how much they can safely take in various circumstances. In this case, a general tax would fall disproportionately on people who do not cause any problems at all, with little effect on the risks created by alcoholics, who are the least likely to respond to higher prices.

MORALITY AND THE RULE OF LAW

How would the morality campaigns fare if the 'rule of law' test were rigorously applied? The test obviously rules out all forms of direct paternalism. We should consider the claims of the morality campaigns to the extent that they invoke 'harm to others' or 'harm to society' as their ground for coercive regulation.

The 'harm to society' argument is heard most often in connection with claims about the allegedly higher healthcare requirements and the allegedly lower productivity of people with so-called unhealthy lifestyles. Health campaigns have repeatedly urged that people should be refused the benefits of the system on account of their unhealthy lifestyles: 'Why should society bear the costs of those people's sins?'. But is there any indication that the 'sinners' or 'undeserving sick' take more than their fair share out of the system? The question is not an easy one to answer, because one often has no clear idea of how much is paid in, and how much is paid out. For example, alcohol users and smokers pay substantial amounts of taxes for their habit. Even if we grant that the premiums paid by smokers into the healthcare system do not cover the value of the healthcare they receive, these taxes may more than compensate for the extra costs (if any) of treating their diseases. Suppose it is true that heavy alcohol users and smokers are likely to die somewhat sooner than abstainers, then it becomes plausible to argue that, while they pay the same amount of money into the system, they actually takes less out of the healthcare system than the abstainer who goes on to reach that final stage of life when expensive healthcare becomes part of the daily routine.

Turning to the labour market, it should at once be clear that unless a part of the wage being paid to a worker is a charitable donation by his employer, the wage (in a competitive economy) is a reflection of the worker's productivity. Thus, if people with unhealthy lifestyles really are less productive than others, this should manifest itself in lower wages over the whole of their career: their chances of being promoted would be less, their chances of being fired would be higher, etc. Being less productive than one could be is not a crime against society. Under the rule of law, people are owners of their own labour. The fact is that most people work in order to be able to live a life that suits them. Some people may prefer a life of leisure and simple pleasures to one of luxurious but stressful productivity in the market.

The final argument is usually considered with respect to smoking, which allegedly causes harm to others who involuntarily inhale the air polluted by smokers ('passive smoking'). While there are no such things as 'passive drinking' or 'environmental animal fat', various nuisances result from immoderate use of alcohol and the same arguments would apply to them.

The passive smoking argument has a *prima facie* plausibility in that, if smoking creates health risks for the smoker, then perhaps it creates health risks for immediate bystanders. However, from the point of view of the rule of law, the first question is whether smoking creates an unacceptable health risk for others. If it does not, then dealing with the nuisance created by smoking is to be left to private regulations and agreements. Because passive smoking is obviously a problem only in closed rooms where non-smokers are exposed to passive smoking for long periods of time, transaction costs are rarely a significant obstacle to reaching agreements. Very often rooms are marked as 'smoking' or as 'non-smoking' areas, either by explicit signs (notices, presence or absence of ashtrays), or by convention supported by subtle social pressures (just as there are places where people spontaneously whisper rather than talk in a loud voice).

Where there are no clear indications whether the room is of either the one or the other type, conventional good manners and explicit agreement solve most problems. Moreover, since most such places are privately owned (e.g. restaurants, theatres, offices, shops), those in charge have a clear incentive to minimize conflicts of interests, i.e. either an incentive to impose private regulations with respect to smoking, or an incentive to install ventilation devices. If, as at present, smoking is considered a nuisance by many people, the demand for 'smoke free areas' will, in a competitive economy, be met by a matching supply.

SUMMARY AND CONCLUDING REMARKS

The analysis presented in this chapter suggests that the arguments presented by the new morality campaigns are unlikely to pass the 'rule of law' test. They do not pay sufficient heed to the many ways in which people in a free society can use the technical and social skills that have accumulated over time to take the sting out of potentially 'harmful' behaviour.

Moreover, the policies advocated by the morality campaigns usually impose restrictions on people who can in no way be accused of causing legally relevant harm to others, or even of causing an unacceptable risk of such harm. They are therefore themselves incompatible with the rule of law; to implement them is to violate the basic law of society itself.

Whether the people in the morality campaigns are impressed by this analysis and the view of society on which it draws is another question. They are unlikely to understand these points, if they are in fact, as I have suggested, committed to the theory and practice of political paternalism.

For the paternalist, mankind is a self-destructive species that would have disappeared long ago if it had not been saved by wise, benevolent and powerful rulers, the despots. In my view, we should reject despotism, respect choice and strengthen our democratic society.

Part IV

Conclusions

25

Pleasure, Choice and the Quality of Everyday Life

Neil Sherwood

Department of Psychology, University of Reading, Building 3, Earley Gate, Whiteknights Road, Reading RG6 2AL, UK

'Under the pressure of the cares and sorrows of our mortal condition, men have at all times, and in all countries, called in some physical aid to their moral consolations—wine, beer, opium, brandy or tobacco'. (Edmund Burke, *Thoughts and Details on Scarcity*, 1765)

EVERYDAY LIFE

Stressors are an inevitable part of everyday life. Occasional stressors may be motivating or even exciting, but if stressors are encountered continually, changes in body physiology due to repeated release of stress hormones such as cortisol and adrenalin can increase the likelihood of heart attack (Karasek *et al.*, 1981) and reduce the efficiency of the immune system (Schleifer *et al.*, 1983), rendering the individual more susceptible to a range of illnesses, from the common cold (Cohen, Tyrrell and Smith, 1991) to stomach ulcers (Friedman and Booth-Kewley, 1987). Even if physical health is not affected, stressors for many people lead to a series of unpleasant psychological sequelae involving the 'fight or flight' reaction, psychological resistance and, finally, physical exhaustion (Selye, 1976).

Pleasure and Quality of Life. Edited by D.M. Warburton and N. Sherwood
© 1996 John Wiley & Sons Ltd.

Two recent surveys (ARISE/Harris Research, 1994; Institute for Personnel and Development, 1995) have shown that workplace stressors are one of the main problems for Western industrialized societies. It is therefore no surprise that workers have developed a number of strategies to reduce their exposure to stressors. The most extreme of these strategies involves removal from the source through absenteeism. These may be effective methods, but they reduce productivity or impair career prospects (see Warburton and Suiter, this volume).

More effectively, workers can turn to pleasurable products that offer brief but important solace to counteract the stressors at work, and assist the relaxation process later in the day. This, of course, is a restatement of the functional model, which suggests that pleasurable activities provide resources that can improve quality of life (Warburton, this volume).

Another way in which to view substance use is to recognize that the individual is exercising personal control over his or her environment. Experimental work has shown that people are able to cope better with threatening stimuli when they feel that they can exercise some degree of control (Thompson, 1981). Notably, the stress response (as measured by the adrenal hormones, heart rate and mood scales) can be reduced in individuals who know that they can terminate the source of an experimental stressor if it becomes too great compared to a yoked group of subjects who have no such control (Fertig, Peters and Leu, 1995). A major source of stressors in the workplace is the absence of control over job demands (Frankenhaeuser, this volume). In this context, pleasure products provide an accessible and affordable line of defence against the negative affect associated with many jobs.

THE ADVANTAGE OF PLEASURE

Simply stated, pleasure is good for you. In a survey of 100 men, Stone found that while stressors at work weakened the immune system on the day that they occurred, pleasant events enhanced the immune system for up to two days. Notably, a drop in pleasant events predicted susceptibility to the common cold more accurately than an increase in unpleasant events, suggesting that pleasure is a stronger mediator than stressors in everyday life and an essential part of a balanced lifestyle (Stone, Reed and Neale, 1987). Moreover, as Tiger (1992) has argued, pleasure gives evolutionary advantage, from the simple examples of the rewards associated with sex and food through to the relaxation and reflection associated with listening to a favourite piece of music, drinking a fine wine or reading a book.

Pleasure exists within the myriad rewards and punishments that we encounter on a daily basis and our own susceptibility to react to these rewards and punishments. If the contingencies between behaviour and consequence are tuned to our predisposition, pleasure may result. This definition can make sense not only of simple relationships, but also of curious situations such as the punishment perceived if a reward is not forthcoming or the reward felt at the termination of punishment, and may in part explain why there is such a wide divergence of pleasurable activities—bounded by their capacity to deliver rewards and punishment but differing in degree.

THE CONTROL OF PLEASURE

In the character of Emma, Jane Austen wrote that 'One half of the world cannot understand the pleasures of the other'. To paraphrase, it would now appear that one half of the world now seeks to control the pleasure of the other. Few would balk at the restriction of 'pleasures' that involve the non-consensual exploitation of other people and most do not object to the censure of excess behaviours in general, so it is clear that we need certain restrictions to make a civilized society function. But the emergence of a new generation of constraints and the manner by which they are being imposed has become a cause for concern.

In particular, personal responsibility appears to have been eroded and replaced by restrictions on what one may legitimately do to oneself. While this has always been deemed necessary for those who are less able to reach informed decisions (the mentally handicapped, young children and the elderly), it is now the sentient, self-aware public who are being ordered not to smoke, told not to consume excess alcohol, advised to reduce fat consumption and shamed into taking regular exercise.

The many causes for this slide into authoritarianism have been advanced in this volume (see Anderson; Javeau; Botsford). However, one clear result is that the health lobby has stepped into the role of guardian and teacher to the masses, imposing arbitrary standards of correctness enforced through guilt over our 'weaknesses' for chocolate, television, chips and an occasional booze-up. Incredibly, these rules are not solely aimed at those suffering illness (whom one might reasonably presume were the concern of the medical profession), but at healthy individuals simply because it is perceived that they 'could do better'. This is a moral, not a medical, position but it has been advanced under the guise of health promotion.

Unfortunately, the health lobby is increasingly entangled with the state. Governments have always sought to take their share of the pleasure cake, but until recently this was more concerned with filling treasury coffers rather than any health concerns. However, the advent of legislation on how a range of products may be manufactured, distributed, sold and consumed has triggered a debate on the role that public policy should play within a liberal democracy (see Luik, Van Dun, this volume).

The harm may run deeper than simply an affront to democracy. Firstly, the health problems believed to be caused by the restricted items (e.g. butter, watching TV) and the benefits of their recommended replacements (polyunsaturated spreads, jogging) are often unproven and contradictory, reflecting the limits of epidemiological science (Skrabanek, 1995; Taubes, 1995). Secondly, by restricting the opportunities for personal control over our lives, stress levels are likely to rise, leading to more psychological and physical illness. The fact that, 'despite' (and more likely because of) their foibles, the vast majority of people do live rich, happy lives seems to have escaped the attention of many in the medical profession (Skrabanek, 1995)

That some routes to pleasure involve risk and sometimes major risk cannot be denied as long as the risks are factual, made explicit and do not impinge upon the pleasure of others. That many choose to ignore these risks does not mean that they are not recognized (Warburton, this volume), but that under certain (human) analyses the pleasure may outweigh the pain (McKenna, this volume). Furthermore, history has taught us that if people are willing to deny the risks associated with particular pleasures, they will also choose to ignore restrictions placed upon their use (Christie, this volume).

FUTURE DIRECTIONS

Clearly, pleasure is a far broader concept than we have (or could have) dealt with in this volume. For the future, we would do well to establish some themes that deserve our inquiry. As a start, the broad base of pleasure needs to be investigated, including the types, motivations and different techniques for obtaining pleasure. In this vein, Lowe (this volume) has already shown that pleasure, while universal, may be vicarious and need not be life-infirming. Related to this, we must find a common metric(s) of pleasure and establish the psychological and physiological principles by which it operates. This may help us to answer some of the ephemeral, but meaningful questions often put to, but rarely answered by, the social sciences: for example, why a few strokes on a canvas can hold meaning; why certain combinations of notes on a piano can elicit a happy or sad response; why an aged malt can satisfy the connoisseur so much more than a blended supermarket whisky.

Furthermore, we need to understand how we learn about pleasure: not only that we should have access to pleasurable events, but how we are socialized into these pleasures, taught how to use them in a manner that does not affect the enjoyment of others. To this end, a greater appreciation of the importance of personal control will be needed. But, perhaps of greatest importance, we need to develop a nomenclature of pleasure and its related concepts. Most of the current pleasure debate is conducted in medical terminology related to the negative side of the quality of life equation and can hardly be expected to summarize what is a vast, embracing area of human existence on the positive side (see Davies, this volume).

The authors in this volume have established not only that pleasure is a valid and important area for study, but that pleasure is amenable to investigation using a variety of techniques from the social, physical and medical sciences. From these, it is clear that the little pleasures of life do help people relax and increase their happiness, that the vast majority of people have the ability to choose and use their pleasures sensibly even if some are said to be unhealthy, and that the individual should be allowed to enjoy these pleasures without guilt.

References

Alvarez, F.J., Queipo, D., Del Rio, M.C. and Garcia, M.C. (1991) Alcohol consumption in young adults in the rural communities of Spain. *Alcohol and Alcoholism*, **26**:93–101.

American Psychiatric Association (1994) *Diagnostic and Statistical Manual*, 4th revision. Washington, DC: American Psychiatric Association.

Anderson, N. (1942) *Desert Saints*. Chicago, IL: University of Chicago Press.

Anderson, D. (1994) Political interference in pleasurable substances. In: Warburton, D.M. (ed.), *Pleasure: The Politics and the Reality*. Chichester: John Wiley & Sons.

Anonymous (1985) Emotion and immunity (editorial). *Lancet*, **133**:134.

ARISE/Harris Research (1994) *Stress, Relaxation and Pleasure. A Study among Office Workers*. London: ARISE, PO Box 7007, London, WC2N 5BE, UK.

Armitage, A.K., Dollery, C.T., George, C.F., Houseman, T.H., Lewis, P.J. and Turner, D.M. (1975) Absorption and metabolism of nicotine from cigarettes. *British Medical Journal*, **4**:313–316.

Ashton, M.A. and McDonald, R.D. (1985) Effects of hypnosis on verbal and non-verbal creativity. *International Journal of Clinical and Experimental Hypnosis*, **33**:15–26

Bahnson, C.B. (1980) Stress and cancer. The state of the art (Part 1). *Psychosomatics*, **21**:975–981.

Bahnson, C.B. (1981) Stress and cancer: The state of the art (Part 2). *Psychosomatics*, **22**:207–220.

Baker, G.H.B., Irani, M.S., Byrom, N.A., *et al.* (1985) Stress, cortisol concentrations and lymphocyte subpopulations. *British Medical Journal,* 290, 1393.

Balandier, G. (1988) *Le Désordre.* Paris: Fayard.

Barofsky, I. and Sugarbaker, P.H. (1990) Cancer. In: Spilker, B. (ed.), *Quality of Life Assessments in Clinical Trials.* New York: Raven Press.

Baron, R.S., Cutrona, C.E., Hicklin, D., Russell, D.W. and Lubaroff, D.A. (1990) Social support and immune functions among spouses of cancer patients. *Journal of Personality and Social Psychology,* **59**:344–352.

Bartrop, R.W., Luckhurst, E., Lazarus, L., *et al.* (1977) Depressed lymphocyte function after bereavement. *Lancet,* 1:834–836.

Bättig, K. (1985) The physiological effects of coffee consumption. In: Clifford, M.N. and Willson, K.C. (eds), *Coffee: Botany, Biochemistry and Production of Beans and Beverage.* London: Croom Helm.

Bauman, K. and Bryan, E. (1980) Subjective expected utility and children's drinking. *Journal of Studies on Alcohol,* **41**:952–958.

Belfrage, P., Berg, B., Hagerstrand, I., Nilsson-Ehle, P., Tornqvist, H. and Wiebe, T. (1977) Alterations of lipid metabolism in healthy volunteers during long-term ethanol intake. *European Journal of Clinical Investigations,* **7**:127–131.

Bell, N.J. and Bell, R.W. (eds) (1993) *Adolescent Risk Taking.* New York: Sage.

Benton, D. and Sargent, J. (1992) Breakfast, blood glucose and memory. *Biological Psychology,* **33**:207–210.

Berlin, I. (1969) *Four Essays on Liberty.* Oxford: Oxford University Press.

Bindra, D. (1978) How adaptive behavior is produced: a perceptual–motivational alternative to response reinforcement. *Behavioral and Brain Sciences,* **1**:41–91.

Block, W. (1976) *Defending the Undefendable.* New York: Fleet Press.

Board of the Inland Revenue (1974) *Tax Cases Reported under the Board of Inland Revenue,* 49 (I). London: HMSO.

Böhme, M. and Böhme, H.R. (1985) The influence of hormonal contraceptives and caffeine on Farnsworth–Munsell-100-hue-test. *Zentralblatt Gynaekologie,* **107**:1305–1316.

Bonnet, M.H., Webb, W.B. and Barnard, G. (1979) Effect of flurazepam, pentobarbital and caffeine on arousal threshold. *Sleep,* **1**(3):271–279.

Bonnsetter, W., Suiter, J. and Widrick, R. (eds) (1994) *The Universal Language DISC.* Scottsdale, AZ: Target Training International.

Booth, D.A. (1989) Mood- and nutrient-conditioned appetites. Cultural and physiological bases for eating disorders. *Annals of the New York Academy of Sciences,* **575**:122–135, 466–471.

Boulding, K. (1956) *The Image: Knowledge in Life and Society.* Ann Arbor MC: University of Michigan Press.

Boulenger, J.-P. and Uhde, T.W. (1982) Caffeine consumption and anxiety: preliminary results of a survey comparing patients with anxiety disorders and normal controls. *Psychopharmacology Bulletin,* **18**:53–57.

Bozarth, M.A. (1991) The mesolimbic dopamine system as a model reward system. In: Willner, P. and Scheel-Krüger, J. (eds), *The Mesolimbic Dopamine System: From Motivation to Action.* Chichester: John Wiley & Sons, pp.301–330.

Bozarth, M.A. (1994) Pleasure pathways in the brain. In: Warburton, D.M. (ed.), *Pleasure: the Politics and the Reality.* Chichester: John Wiley & Sons, pp.5–14.

Brandon, R. and Davies, C. (1973) *Wrongful Imprisonment: Mistaken Convictions and their Consequences.* London: Allen and Unwin.

Brauer, L.H., Buican, B. and de Wit, H. (1994) Effects of caffeine deprivation on taste and mood. *Behavioural Pharmacology,* **5**:111–118.

Broadbent, D.E. (1971) *Decision and Stress.* London: Academic Press.

Broadbent, D.E., Broadbent, M.H.P. and Jones, J.L. (1989) Time of day as an instrument for the analysis of attention. *European Journal of Cognitive Psychology,* **1**, 69–94.

Brunke, M. and Gilbert, M. (1992) Alcohol and creative writing. *Psychological Reports,* **71**:651–658.

Buchanan, A.E. and Brock, D.W. (1989) *Deciding for Others: The Ethics of Surrogate Decision Making.* Cambridge: Cambridge University Press.

Bull, M. (1990) Secularization and medicalization. *British Journal of Sociology,* **41**:245–261.

Caplan, R. (1983) Person–environment fit: past, present and future. In: Cooper, C.L. (ed.), *Stress Research Issues for the Eighties.* Chichester: John Wiley & Sons.

Cappell, H. (1975) An evaluation of tension models of alcohol consumption. In: Gibbins, R.J., Israel, Y., Kalant, H., Popham, R.E., Schmidt, W. and Smart, R.G. (eds), *Research Advances in Alcohol and Drug Problems*, Vol. 2. New York: John Wiley & Sons.

Carlyon, W.H. (1984) Disease prevention/health promotion – bridging the gap to wellness. *Health Values*, 8:27–30.

Cines, B.M. and Rozin, P. (1982) Some aspects of the liking for hot coffee. *Appetite: Journal for Intake Research*, 3(1):23–24.

Coccaro, E.F. and Siever, J. (1995) The neuropsychopharmacology of personality disorders. In Bloom, F.E. and Kupfer, J. (eds), *Psychopharmacology: The Fourth Generation of Progress*. New York: Raven Press, pp.1567–1579.

Cochrane, A.L. and Holland, W.W. (1971) Validation of screening procedures. *British Medical Bulletin*, 27:3–8.

Cohen, S., Tyrrell, D.A.J. and Smith, A.P. (1991) Psychological stress and susceptibility to the common cold. *New England Journal of Medicine*, 325:606–612.

Cohen, S., Tyrrell, D.A.J. and Smith, A.P. (1993) Negative life events, perceived stress, negative effect and susceptibility to the common cold. *Journal of Personality and Social Psychology*, 64:131–140.

Cools, A.R., Van Den Bos, R., Ploeger, G. and Ellenbroek, B.A. (1991) Gating function of noradrenaline in the ventral striatum: its role in behavioural responses to environmental and pharmacological challenges. In: Willner, P. and Scheel-Krüger, J. (eds), *The Mesolimbic Dopamine System: From Motivation to Action*. Chichester: John Wiley & Sons, pp.141–173.

Craig, A. and Cooper, R.E. (1992) Symptoms of acute and chronic fatigue. In: Smith, A.P. and Jones, D.M. (eds), *Handbook of Human Performance*, Vol. 3: *State and Trait*. Academic Press, London, pp.289–340.

Craig, A., Baer, K. and Diekmann, A. (1981) The effects of lunch on sensory-perceptual functioning in man. *International Archives of Occupational and Environmental Health*, 49:105–114.

Csikszentmihalyi, M. (1975) *Beyond Boredom and Anxiety*. San Francisco, CA: Jossey-Bass.

Csikszentmihalyi, M. (1992) The flow experience and human psychology. In: Csikszentmihalyi, M. and Csikszentmihalyi, I.S. (eds), *Optimal Experience Psychological Studies of Flow in Consciousness*. Cambridge: Cambridge University Press.

Czaikowski, J. (1992) Measurement of quality of life of cancer patients. *Journal of Clinical Oncology*, 2: 472–483.

Davies, C. (1975) *Permissive Britain*. London: Pitman.

Davies, J.C.H. (1982) Sexual taboos and social boundaries. *American Journal of Sociology*, 87:1032–1063.

Davies, J.C.H. (1983) Religious boundaries and sexual morality. *Annual Review of the Social Sciences of Religion*, 6:45–77.

de Wit, H., Metz, J., Wagner, N. and Cooper, M. (1990) Behavioral and subjective effects of ethanol: relationship to cerebral metabolism using PET. *Alcohol: Clinical and Experimental Research*, 14:482–489

Department of Health (1992) New health promotion package. *British Medical Journal*, 305:1369.

Di Chiara, G., Acquas, E. and Carboni, E. (1991) Role of mesolimbic dopamine in the motivational effects of drugs: brain dialysis and place preference studies. In: Willner, P. and Scheel-Krüger, J. (eds), *The Mesolimbic Dopamine System: From Motivation to Action*. Chichester: John Wiley & Sons, pp.367–384 .

Diamond, A.L. and Cole, R.E. (1974) Visual threshold as a function of test area and caffeine administration. *Psychonomic Science*, 20:109–111.

Diamond, A.L. and Smith, E.M. (1979) The effects of caffeine on terminal dark adaptation. In: Moskowitz, H.R., Scharf, B. and Stevens, J.C. (eds), *Sensation and Measurement*. Dordrecht: D. Reidel, pp.339–349.

Doll, R., Peto, R., Hall, E., Wheatley, K. and Gray, R. (1994a) Mortality in relation to consumption of alcohol: 13 years observations on male British doctors. *British Medical Journal*, 309:911–918.

Doll, R., Peto, R., Wheatley, K., Gray, R. and Sutherland, I. (1994b) Mortality in relation to smoking: 40 years observations on male British doctors. *British Medical Journal*, 309:901–911.

Douglas, M. (1966) *Purity and Danger*. London: Routledge and Kegan Paul.

Douglas, M. (1975) *Implicit Meanings*. London: Routledge and Kegan Paul.

Dye, L., Sherwood, N. and Kerr, J.S. (1990) The influence of nicotine on CNS arousal during the menstrual cycle. In: Adlkofer, F. (ed.), *Effects of Nicotine on Biological Systems*. Basel: Birkhauser.

Earl, P. (1983) *The Economic Imagination: Towards a Behavioural Analysis of Choice*. Brighton: Wheatsheaf.

Earl, P. (1986) *Lifestyle Economics: Consumer Behaviour in a Turbulent World*. Brighton: Wheatsheaf.

Eiser, J.R., Morgan, M.J. and Gammage, P. (1987) Belief correlates of perceived addiction in young smokers. *European Journal of Psychology of Education*, 2:375–385.

Elias, N. (1939) *Ueber den Process der Zivilisation*. Basel: Karger.

Elwood, P.C. (1991) Epidemiological studies of cardiovascular diseases. Progress Report VII. MRC Epidemiology Unit, South Wales.

Eurostat (1992) Labour Force Survey, Results 1992. Luxembourg: Statistical Office of the European Communities.

Eysenck, H.J. (1991a) Cancer and personality. In: Cooper, L.C. and Watson, M. (eds), *Stress and Cancer*. Chichester: John Wiley & Sons, pp.3–25.

Eysenck, H.J. (1991b) *Smoking, Personality and Stress: Psychosocial Factors in the Prevention of Cancer and Coronary Heart Disease*. New York: Springer-Verlag.

Eysenck, H.J. and Eysenck, M.W. (1985) *Personality and Individual Differences*. New York: Plenum Press, Chapter 9.

Eysenck, M.W. (1982) *Attention and Arousal: Cognition and Performance*. Berlin: Springer-Verlag.

Family Heart Study Group (1994) Randomised controlled trial evaluating cardiovascular screening and intervention in general practice: principal results of British Family Heart Study. *British Medical Journal*, 308:313–320.

Feinberg, J. (1986) *Harm to Self*. New York: Oxford University Press.

Fertig, J., Peters, R. and Leu, J. (1995) Human response to uncontrollable stress and high dose naloxone. *Abstracts of the Society for Neuroscience*, 21:1687.

Fine, B. (1990) *Consumer Behaviour and the Social Sciences: A Critical Review*. London: Queen Mary College.

Fine, B.J. and McCord, L. (1991) Oral contraceptive use, caffeine consumption, field-dependence and the discrimination of colors. *Perceptual and Motor Skills*, 73:931–941.

Fisher, S. (1988) Life stress, control strategies and the risk of disease: a psychobiological model. In: Fisher, S. and Reason, J. (eds), *Handbook of Life Stress, Cognition and Health*. Chichester: John Wiley & Sons, pp.581–602.

Fitzgerald, F. (1994) The tyranny of health. *New England Journal of Medicine*, **331**:196–198.

Fitzmaurice, M.A. (1988) Physiological relationships among stress, viruses and cancer, in experimental animals. *International Journal of Neuroscience*, **39**:307–324.

Folkow, B. (1975) Vascular changes in hypertension. Review and recent animal studies. In: Berglund, C., Hansson, L. and Werkö, L. (eds), *Pathophysiology and Management of Arterial Hypertension*. Stockholm: Lindgren & Söner.

Follenius, M., Brandenberger, G. and Hietter, B. (1982) Diurnal cortisol peaks and their relationship to meals. *Journal of Clinical Endocrinology*, **55**:757–761.

Forbes, J.A., Jones, K.F., Kehm, C.J., Smith, W.K., Gongloff, C.M., Zeleznock, J.R., Smith, J.W. and Beaver, W.T. (1990) Evaluation of aspirin, caffeine and their combination in postoperative oral surgery pain. *Pharmacotherapy*, **10**:387–393.

Forni, G., Bindoni, M., Santoni, A., *et al.* (1983) Radio-frequency destruction of the tubero-infundibular region of hypothalamus permanently abrogates NK cell activity in mice. *Nature*, **300**:181–184.

Fox, T. (1965) Purposes of medicine. *Lancet*, **ii**:801–805.

Foxcroft, D.R. and Lowe, G. (1993) Self-attributions for alcohol use in older teenagers. *Addiction Research*, **1**:1–9.

Frankenhaeuser, M. (1971) Behavior and circulating catecholamines. *Brain Research*, **31**:241–262.

Frankenhaeuser, M. (1975) Experimental approaches to the study of catecholamines and emotion. In: Levi, L. (ed.), *Emotions – Their Parameters and Measurement*. New York: Raven Press, pp.209–234.

Frankenhaeuser, M. (1980) Psychobiological aspects of life stress. In: Levine, S. and Ursin, H. (eds), *Coping and Health*. New York: Plenum Press, pp.203–223.

Frankenhaeuser, M. (1986) A psychobiological framework for research on human stress and coping. In: Appley, M.H. and Trumbell, R. (eds), *Dynamics of Stress*. New York: Plenum Press, pp.101–116.

Frankenhaeuser, M. (1991a) The psychophysiology of workload, stress and health: comparison between the sexes. *Annals of Behavioral Medicine*, 4:197–204.

Frankenhaeuser, M. (1991b) The psychophysiology of sex differences as related to occupational status. In: Frankenhaeuser, M., Lundberg, U. and Chesney, M.A. (eds), *Women, Work and Health. Stress and Opportunities*. New York: Plenum Press, pp.39–61.

Frankenhaeuser, M. (1993) A biopsychosocial approach to stress in women and men. In: Adesso, V.J., Reddy, D.M. and Fleming, R. (eds), *Psychological Perspectives on Women's Health*. Washington, DC: Taylor & Francis, pp.39–56.

Frankenhaeuser, M. and Johansson, G. (1986) Stress at work: psychological and psychosocial aspects. *International Review of Applied Psychology*, 35:287–299.

Frankenhaeuser, M., Parr, D. and Ekvall, G. (1994) A psychophysiological study of female and male clinical managers: comparison between work and off-work conditions. Report no. 4. FA Institute for Research on Business and Work Life Issues.

Frankenhaeuser, M., Lundberg, U., Fredrikson, M., Melin, B., Tuomisto, M., Myrsten, A.-L., Hedman, M., Bergman-Losman, B. and Wallin, L. (1989) Stress on and off the job as related to sex and occupational status in white-collar workers. *Journal of Organizational Behavior*, 10:321–346.

Freeman, R. and Bell, L. (1994) Why do Americans and Germans work different hours? National Bureau of Economic Research Working Paper 4808, Cambridge MA.

Friedman, M. and Booth-Kewley, S. (1987) *The Disease-Prone Personality*. New York: Knopf.

Friedmann, L.A. and Kimball, A.W. (1986) Coronary heart disease mortality and alcohol consumption in Framingham. *American Journal of Epidemiology*, 124:481–489.

Furnham, A. (1992) *Personality at Work*. London: Routledge.

Galbraith, N.G. (1986) Alcohol: its effect on handwriting. *Journal of Forensic Science*, 31:580–588.

Goldman, P.R. and Vogel, W.H. (1984) Striatal dopamine-stimulated adenylate induced mammary tumour development. *Carcinogenesis*, 5:971–973.

Goodin, R.E. (1989) The ethics of smoking. *Ethics*, **99**:574–624.

Goodwin, D. (1973) The muse and the martini. *Journal of the American Medical Association*, **24**:25–38.

Goodwin, D.W. (1991) *Alcohol and the Writer*. New York: Viking/Penguin.

Goodwin, D.W. (1992) Alcohol as muse. *American Journal of Psychotherapy*, **46**:422–433.

Grant, M. (1981) Drinking and creativity: a review of the alcoholism literature. *British Journal of Alcohol and Alcoholism*, **16**:88–93.

Greer, S. (1983) Cancer and the mind. *British Journal of Psychiatry*, **143**:535–543.

Greer, S. and Morris, T. (1975) Psychological attributes of women who develop breast cancer. A controlled study. *Journal of Psychosomatic Research*, **19**:147–153.

Gross, J. (1989) Emotional suppression in cancer onset and progression. *Social Science and Medicine*, **12**:1239–1248.

Grossarth-Maticek, R. and Eysenck, H.J. (1990) Coffee-drinking and personality as factors in the genesis of cancer and coronary heart disease. *Neuropsychobiology*, **23**:153–159.

Grossarth-Maticek, R., Eysenck, H.J. and Vetter, H. (1988) Personality type, smoking habit and their interaction as predictors of cancer and coronary heart disease. *Personality and Individual Differences*, **9**:479–495.

Gupta, U. and Gupta, B.S. (1990) Caffeine differentially affects kinesthetic after-effect in high and low impulsives. *Psychopharmacology*, **102**:102–105.

Gupta, U., Dubey, G.P. and Gupta, B.S. (1994) Effects of caffeine on perceptual judgment. *Neuropsychobiology*, **30**:185–188.

Gustafson, R. and Norlander, T. (1994) Effects of alcohol on persistent effort and deductive thinking during the preparation phase of the creative process. *Journal of Creative Behavior*, **28**:124–132.

Haier, R.J., Reynolds, C., Prager, E., Cox, S. and Buchsbaum, M.S. (1991) Fluribiprofen, caffeine and analgesia: interaction with introversion/extroversion. *Personality and Individual Differences*, **12**(12):1349–1354.

Hajcak, F.J. (1976) The effects of alcohol on creativity. Doctoral dissertation, Temple University.

Hancock, P.A. and Caird, J.K. (1993) Experimental evaluation of a model of mental workload. *Human Factors*, **35**:413–429.

Hansard (1972) Parliamentary Debates, House of Commons, Standing Committee E, Finance Bill, 9th sitting. London: HMSO.

Helman, C. (1984) *Culture, Health and Illness*. Bristol: Wright.

Henningfield, J.E. (1984) Behavioral pharmacology of cigarette smoking. In: Thompson, T., Dews, P.B. and Barrett, J.E. (eds), *Advances in Behavioral Pharmacology*, Vol. 4. New York: Academic Press, pp.131–210.

Herbert, M., Johns, M.W. and Dore, C. (1976) Factor analysis of analogue scales measuring subjective feelings before sleep and after sleep. *British Journal of Medicine and Psychology*, **49**:373–379.

Herbert, T.B. and Cohen, S. (1993) Depression and immunity: a meta-analytic review. *Psychological Bulletin*, **113**:472–486.

Hindmarch, I., Sherwood, N. and Kerr, J.S. (1994). The psychoactive effects of nicotine, caffeine and alcohol. In: Warburton D.M. (ed.), *Pleasure: The Politics and the Reality*. Chichester: John Wiley & Sons.

Horne, R.L. and Picard, R.S. (1979) Psychosocial risk factors for lung cancer. *Psychosomatic Medicine*, **41**:503–514.

Hosseini, H. (1990) The archaic, the obsolete and the mythical in neoclassical economics. *American Journal of Economics and Sociology*, **49** (1): 81–92.

Imperial Cancer Research Fund OXCHECK Study Group (1994) Effectiveness of health checks conducted by nurses in primary care: results of OXCHECK study after one year. *British Medical Journal*, **308**:308–312.

Institute for Personnel and Development (1995) *All Work and No Play*. London: Institute for Personnel and Development, IPD House, Camp Road, London, SW19 4UX, UK.

Ireland, M.A., Vandongen, R., Davidson, L., Beilin, L.J. and Rouse, I.L. (1984) Acute effects of moderate alcohol consumption on blood pressure and plasma catecholamines. *Clinical Science*, **66**:643–648.

James, J.E. (1991) *Caffeine and Health*. London: Academic Press.

Janz, N.K. and Becker, M.H. (1984) The health belief model: a decade later. *Health Education Quarterly*, **11**:1–46.

Jeffrey, R.W. (1989) Risk behaviours and health: contrasting individual and population perspectives. *American Psychologist*, **44**:1194–1202.

Jemmott, J.B. and Magloire, K. (1988) Academic stress, social support, and secretory immunoglobin A. *Journal of Personality and Social Psychology*, **55**:803–810.

Jemmott, J.B., Borysenko, M., McClelland, D.C., *et al.* (1983) Academic stress, power motivation and decrease in secretion rate of salivary secretory immunoglobulin A. *Lancet*, **1**:1400–1402.

Johnston, D.W. (1991) Behavioral medicine: the application of behavior therapy to physical health. *Behavioral Psychotherapy*, **19**:100–108.

Johnston, L.D. and O'Malley, P.M. (1986) Why do the nation's students use drugs and alcohol? Self-reported reasons from nine national surveys. *Journal of Drug Issues*, **16**:29–66.

Joshi, V. (1995) *Unable to Curb Cigarette Smuggling, Singapore now Targets Smokers*. A.P.Worldstream, 24th January.

Jung, K. (1995) *Wein – Genuß und Gesundheit*. Mainz: Waschek-Verlag.

Justice, A. (1985) Review of the effects of stress on cancer in laboratory animals. Importance of time of stress application and type of the tumour. *Psychological Bulletin*, **98**:108–138.

Kahn, R.L. (1981) *Work and Health*. New York: John Wiley & Sons.

Karasek, R.A. (1979) Job demands, job decision, latitude and mental strain: implications for job redesign. *Administrative Science Quarterly*, **24**:285–308.

Karasek, R.A. and Theorell, T. (1990) *Healthy Work*. New York: Basic Books.

Karasek, R.A., Baker, D., Marxer, F., Ahlbom, A. and Theorell, T. (1981) Job decision latitude, job demands, and cardiovascular disease: a prospective study of Swedish men. *American Journal of Public Health*, **71**:694–705.

Karlan, S.C. and Cohn, C. (1946) Hypoglycemic fatigue. *Journal of the American Medical Association*, **130**:553–555.

Kastenbaum, R. (1988) How some older people find pleasure and meaning in alcoholic beverages. *Generations*, **12**:68–73.

Katz, J. (1988) *Seductions of Crime: Moral and Sexual Attractions in Doing Evil*. New York: Basic Books.

Kelleher, C. (1995) Health promotion: shades of Lewis Carroll. *Journal of Epidemiology and Community Health*, **49**:1–4.

Kenny, A. (1963) *Action, Emotion and Will*. London: Routledge and Kegan Paul.

Kerr, B., Shaffer, J., Chambers, C. and Hallowell, K. (1991) Substance use of creatively talented adults. *Journal of Creative Behavior*, **25**:145–153.

Kiecolt-Glaser, J.K. and Glaser, R. (1991) Stress and immune function in humans. In: Ader, R., Felten, D.L. and Cohen, N. (eds), *Psychoneuroimmunology*, 2nd edn. San Diego, CA: Academic Press, pp.849–867.

Kiecolt-Glaser, J.K., Stephens, R.E., Lipetz, P.D., *et al.* (1985) Distress and DNA repair in human lymphocytes. *Journal of Behavioral Medicine*, **8**:311–320.

Kind, P. and Sorenson, J. (1993) The costs of depression. *International Clinical Psychopharmacology*, **7**:191–195.

Klatsky, A.L., Armstrong, M.A. and Friedmann, G.D. (1992) Alcohol and mortality. *Annals of Internal Medicine*, **117**:646–654.

Kohen, L., Zrenner, E. and Schneider, T. (1986) The influence of theophylline and caffeine on the sensory function of the human retina. *Fortschritte der Ophtalmologie*, **83**:338–344.

Kole, A., Snel, J. and Lorist, M.M. (1996) Effects of background odour on visual ERPs (in preparation).

Koski-Jannes, A. (1985) Alcohol and literary creativity – the Finnish experience. *Journal of Creative Behavior*, **19**:120–136.

Krantz, D.S., Lundberg, U. and Frankenhaeuser, M. (1976) Stress and type A behavior. In: Baum, A. and Singer, J.E. (eds), *Handbook of Psychology and Health (Volume 5): Stress and Coping*. Hillsdale, NJ: Erlbaum.

Kunreuther, H., Ginsberg, R., Miller, L., Sagi, P., Slovic, P., Borkan, B. and Katz, N. (1978) *Disaster Insurance Protection: Public Policy Lessons*. New York: John Wiley & Sons.

Laing, D.G. and Clark, P.J. (1983) Puberty and olfactory preferences of males. *Physiology and Behavior*, **30**:591–597.

Lang, A.R., Verret, L.D. and Watt, C. (1984) Drinking and creativity: objective and subjective effects. *Addiction and Behavior*, **9**:395–399.

Langer, E.J. (1975) The illusion of control. *Journal of Personality and Social Psychology*, **32**:311–328.

Lapp, W.M., Collins, R.L. and Izzo, C.V. (1994) On the enhancement of creativity by alcohol: pharmacology or expectation? *American Journal of Psychology*, **107**:173–206.

Laska, E.M., Sunshine, A., Mueller, F., Elvers, W.B., Siegel, C. and Rubin, A. (1984) Caffeine as an analgesic adjuvant. *Journal of the American Medical Association,* **251:** 1711–1718.

Lazarus, R.S. (1966) *Psychological Stress and the Coping Process.* New York: McGraw-Hill.

Leichter, H.M. (1991) *Free to be Foolish.* Princeton, NJ: Princeton University Press.

Levine, A.S. and Levine, A.E. (1990) Creativity in scientists: do we know it when we see it? *New Biology,* **2:**207–209.

Levine, S. and Ursin, H. (eds) (1980) *Coping and Health.* New York: Plenum Press.

Lieberman, H.R. (1992) Caffeine. In: Smith, A.P. and Jones, D. (eds), *Handbook of Human Performance,* Vol. 2. London: Academic Press, pp.49–72.

Lindén, I. (1978) *The Last Trump, an Historico-Genetical Study of Some Important Chapters in the Making and Development of the Seventh Day Adventist Church.* Band 17 of the Studien zur Interkulturellen Geschichte des Christentums. Frankfurt am Main: Peter Lang.

Lopes, L.L. (1993) Reasons and resources: the human side of risk taking. In: Bell, N.J. and Bell, R.W. (eds), *Adolescent Risk Taking.* London: Sage.

Lorist, M.M., Snel, J. and Kok, A. (1994) Influence of caffeine on information processing stages in well rested and fatigued subjects. *Psychopharmacology,* **113:**411–421.

Lorist, M.M., Snel, J., Kok, A. and Mulder, G. (1994) Effects of caffeine on selected attention in well rested and fatigued subjects. *Psychophysiology,* **31:**525–534.

Lowe, G. (1994) Pleasures of social relaxants and stimulants – the ordinary persons attitudes and involvement. In: Warburton, D.M. (ed.), *Pleasure: The Politics and the Reality.* Chichester: John Wiley & Sons, pp.95–108.

Lowe, G., Foxcroft, D.R. and Sibley, D. (1993) *Adolescent Drinking and Family Life.* Chur, Switzerland: Harwood Academic.

Ludwig, A.M. (1990) Alcohol input and creative output. *British Journal of Addiction,* **85:**953–963.

Luik, J.C. (1993) Pandora's box: the dangers of politically corrupted science for democratic public policy. *Bostonia Magazine,* winter 1993/94.

Lundberg, U., Mårdberg, B. and Frankenhaeuser, M. (1994) The total workload of male and female white collar workers as related to age, occupational level, and number of children. *Scandinavian Journal of Psychology*, **35**:315–327.

Lyle, W.M. (1974) Drugs and conditions which may affect color vision. Part one. *Journal of the American Optometric Association*, **45**:47–60.

Lyng, S. (1993) Dysfunctional risk-taking: criminal behaviour as edgework. In: Bell, N.J. and Bell, R.W. (eds), *Adolescent Risk Taking*. London: Sage.

Maddux, J.E. and Rogers, R.W. (1983) Protection motivation and efficacy: a revised theory of fear appeals and attitude. *Journal of Experimental Social Psychology*, **19**:469–479.

Maimonides, M. (1963) *The Guide of the Perplexed*. Chicago, IL: University of Chicago Press.

Maisto, S.A., Connors, G.J., Tucker, J.A., McCollam, J.B. and Adesso, V.J. (1980) Validation of the sensation scale: a measure of subjective physiological response to alcohol. *Behavior Research and Therapy*, **18**:37–43.

Mann, G.V. (1994) Metabolic consequences of dietary trans-fatty acids. *Lancet*, **343**:1268–1271.

Mant, D. (1994) Health checks – time to check out? *British Journal of General Practice*, **44**:51–52.

Marlatt, G. and Rohsenow, D. (1980) Cognitive processes in alcohol use: expectancy and the balanced placebo design. In: Mello, N. (ed.), *Advances in Substance Abuse: Behavioural and Biological Research*, Vol. 1. Greenwich, CT: JAI Press, pp.159–199.

Marston, W.M. (1928) *The Emotions of Normal People*. Minneapolis, MN: Persona Press (reprinted 1979).

Matthews, G., Davies, D.R. and Holley, P.J. (1993) Cognitive predictors of vigilance. *Human Factors*, **35**:3–24.

May, R. (1975) *The Courage to Create*. Toronto: Bantam Books.

McBride, R.L. (1990) *The Bliss Point Factor*. Melbourne: Macmillan.

McBride, R.L. (1994) The bliss point as a measure of pleasure. In Warburton, D.M. (ed.), *Pleasure, the Politics and the Reality*. Chichester: John Wiley & Sons, pp.67–76.

McCarthy, R.G. (1959) *Drinking and Intoxication*. Glencoe, IL: Free Press.

McCormick, J.S. (1988) The multifactorial aetiology of coronary heart disease: a dangerous delusion. *Perspectives in Biology and Medicine*, 32:103–108.

McCormick, J.S. (1990) The abominable no-men: a cautionary tale. *Perspectives in Biology and Medicine*, 33:187–189.

McCormick, J.S. and Anderson, D. (1992) *Risk, Health and the Consumer*. London: Social Affairs Unit.

McKechnie, R. (1993) Drinking as a skilled behaviour. Paper presented at the British Psychology Society Annual Conference, April 1993, Blackpool.

McKenna, F.P. (1993) It won't happen to me: unrealistic optimism or the illusion of control? *British Journal of Psychology*, 84:39–50.

McKenna, F.P., Warburton, D.M. and Winwood, M. (1993) Exploring the limits of optimism: the case of smokers' decision making. *British Journal of Psychology*, 84:389–394.

McNeil, B.J., Weichselbaum, R. and Pauker, S.G. (1978) Fallacy of the five year survival in lung cancer. *New England Journal of Medicine*, 299:1397–1401.

McNeil, B.J., Weichselbaum, R. and Pauker, S.G. (1981) Speech and survival: tradeoffs between quality and quantity of life in laryngeal cancer. *New England Journal of Medicine*, 30:982–987.

Mela, D.J. (1989) Caffeine ingested under natural conditions does not alter taste intensity. *Pharmacology, Biochemistry and Behavior*, 34:483–485.

Mela, D.J., Mattes, R.D., Tanimura, S. and Garcia-Medinas, M.R. (1992) Relationship between ingestion and gustatory perception of caffeine. *Pharmacology, Biochemistry and Behavior*, 43:513–521.

Mencken, H.L. (1923) *Prejudices*, 3rd Series. London: Jonathan Cape.

Mettler, C.C. and Mettler, F.A. (1947) *History of Medicine*. Philadelphia, PA: Blakiston.

Mill, J.S. (1983) *On Liberty*. London: Everyman.

Netter, P. and Vogel, W.H. (1990) The effect of drinking habits on catecholamine and behavioral responses to stress and ethanol. *Neuropsychobiology*, 24:149–158.

Newcomb, M.D., Chou, C., Bentler, P.M. and Huba, G.J. (1988) Cognitive motivations for drug use among adolescents: longitudinal tests of gender differences and predictors of change in drug use. *Journal of Counselling and Psychology*, 35:426–438.

Nicholson, M. (1994) *Smugglers Charter: A Study of How High Tobacco Taxation Around the World Increases Crime*. London: FOREST.

Niemi, T. and Jaakelainen, J. (1980) Cancer morbidity in depressive persons. *Journal of Psychosomatic Research*, **22**:117–120.

Noble, E.P., Runco, M.A. and Ozkaragoz, T.Z. (1993) Creativity in alcoholic and nonalcoholic families. *Alcohol*, **10**:317–322.

Observer (1994) *Re-Writing the Rules*. Study conducted by Gallop, June 5th.

O'Dea, T.F. (1957) *The Mormons*. Chicago, IL: University of Chicago Press.

Oldenburg, R. (1989) *The Great Good Place*. New York: Paragon House.

Orwell, G. (1949) *Nineteen Eighty-Four*. London: Gollancz.

Paget, J. (1870) *Surgical Pathology*, 2nd Edn. London: Longmans Green.

Parke, B. (1984) Toward objectifying the measurement of creativity. *Roeper-Review*, **6**: 216–218.

Perloff, L.S. and Fetzer, B.K. (1986) Self-other judgments and perceived vulnerability to victimization. *Journal of Personality and Social Psychology*, **50**:502–510.

Peters, R.S. (1958) *The Concept of Motivation*. London: Routledge and Kegan Paul.

Phillips, A.G., Pfaus, J.G. and Blaha, C.D. (1991) Dopamine and motivated behavior: insights provided by in vivo analyses. In: Willner, P. and Scheel-Krüger J. (eds), *The Mesolimbic Dopamine System: From Motivation to Action*. Chichester: John Wiley & Sons, pp.199–224.

Pohler, G. (1989) *Krebs und Seelischer Konflikt*. Frankfurt: Nexus.

Porter, J.R. (1976) *The Cambridge Bible Commentary: The New English Bible – Leviticus*. Cambridge: Cambridge University Press.

Post, F. (1994) Creativity and psychopathology. *British Journal of Psychiatry*, **165**:22–34.

Pribram, K.H. and McGuinness, D. (1975) Arousal, activation and effort in the control of attention. *Psychological Review*, **82**:116–149.

Pritchard, R., Dunnette, M. and Jorgensen, D. (1992) Effects of perceptions of equity and inequity on worker performance and satisfaction. *Journal of Applied Psychology*, **57**:75–94.

Rae, J. (1993) The case for dialogue and collaboration between the health community and the alcohol industry. Paper presented at the 9th International Conference on Alcohol, September 1993, University of Liverpool.

Ravnskov, U. (1992) Cholesterol lowering trials in coronary heart disease: frequency of citation and outcome. *British Medical Journal*, **305**:15–19.

Renaud, S. and de Lorgeril, M. (1992) Wine, alcohol, platelets and the French paradox for coronary heart disease. *Lancet*, **339**:1523–1526.

Rice, D.P. (1994) The economic burden of anxiety disorders. Abstracts of the XIXth Congress of the Collegium Internationale Neuropsychopharmacologium (CINP), 1994.

Riley, V. (1981) Psychoneuroendocrine influences on immunocompetence and neoplasia. *Science*, **212**:1100–1102.

Rissanen, A., Heliovaara, M., Knekt, P., Aromaa, A., Reunanen, A. and Maatela, J. (1989) Weight and mortality in Finnish men. *Journal of Clinical Epidemiology*, **42**:743–750.

Robertson, L.S. (1977) Car crashes: perceived vulnerability and willingness to pay for crash protection. *Journal of Community Health*, **3**:136–141.

Roe, A. (1946) Alcohol and creative work. *Quarterly Journal of Studies in Alcohol*, **6**:415–467.

Rogers, P.J. (1994) Mechanisms of moreishness and food craving. In Warburton, D.M. (ed.), *Pleasure: The Politics and the Reality*. Chichester: John Wiley & Sons.

Rogers, R.W. (1983) Cognitive and physiological processes in attitude change: a revised theory of protection motivation. In: Cacioppo, J. and Petty, R. (eds), *Social Psychophysiology*. New York: Guilford Press, pp.153–176.

Rosch, P. J. (1979) Stress and cancer: a disease of adaptation. In: Tache, J., Selye, H. and Day, S.B. (eds), *Cancer, Stress and Death*. New York: Plenum Press.

Rose, R.M. and Fogg, L.F. (1993) Definition of a responder. Analysis of behavioral, cardiovascular and endocrine responses to varied workload in air traffic controllers. *Psychosomatic Medicine*, **55**:325–338.

Rothenberg, A. (1990) Creativity, mental health and alcoholism. *Creative Research Journal*, **3**:179–201.

Royal College of General Practitioners (1992) Guidelines for the management of hyperlipidaemia in general practice. Occasional Paper no.55. London: Royal College of General Practitioners.

Russell, M.A.H., Peto, J. and Patel, U.A. (1974) The classification of smoking by a factorial structure of motives. *Journal of the Royal Statistical Society*, **137**:313–346.

Sanders, A.F. (1983) Towards a model of stress and human performance. *Acta Psychologica*, **51**:61–97.

Saunders, J.B., Beevers, D.G. and Paton, A. (1981) Alcohol induced hypertension. *Lancet*, **2**:653–656.

Sawynok, J. and Yaksh, T.L. (1993) Caffeine as an analgesic adjuvant: a review of pharmacology and mechanisms of action. *Pharmacological Reviews*, **45**(1):43–85.

Scheier, M.F. and Carver, C.S. (1987) Dispositional optimism and physical well-being: the influence of generalized outcome expectancies on health. *Journal of Personality*, **55**:169–210.

Schiffman, S.S., Diaz, C. and Beeker, T.G. (1986) Caffeine intensifies the taste of certain sweeteners: role of adenosine receptor. *Pharmacology, Biochemistry and Behavior*, **24**:429–432.

Schiffman, S.S., Gill, J.M. and Diaz, C. (1985) Methylxanthines enhance taste: evidence for modulation of taste by adenosine receptor. *Pharmacology, Biochemistry and Behavior*, **24**:429–432.

Schleifer, S.J., Keller, S.E., Camerino, M., Thornton, J.C. and Stein, M. (1983) Suppression of lymphocyte stimulation following bereavement. *Journal of the American Medical Association*, **15**:374–377.

Schonfield, J. (1975) Psychological and life experience differences between Israeli women with benign and cancerous breast lesions. *Journal of Psychosomatic Research*, **19**:229– 234.

Schor, J.B. (1991) *The Overworked American; The Unexpected Decline of Leisure*. New York: Basic Books.

Scitovsky, T. (1976) *The Joyless Economy*. Oxford: Oxford University Press.

Scitovsky, T. (1981) *The Desire for Excitement in Modern Society*. Chicago IL: Kyklos.

Scitovsky, T. (1986) *Human Desire and Economic Satisfaction*. Brighton: Wheatsheaf.

Seltzer, C.C. (1989) Framingham Study data and 'Established wisdom: about cigarette smoking and coronary heart disease'. *Journal of Clinical Epidemiology*, **42**:743–750.

Selye, H. (1974) *Stress without Distress*. Philadelphia, PA: Lippincott.

Selye, H. (1976) *The Stress of Life*. New York: McGraw-Hill.

Sherwood, N. (1995) Effects of cigarette smoking on performance in a simulated driving task. *Neuropsychobiology*, **32**:161–165.

Shin, D.C. and Johnson, D.M. (1978) Avowed happiness as an overall assessment of the quality of life. *Social Indicators Research*, **5**:475–492.

Shipps, J. (1985) *Mormonism, the Story of a New Religious Tradition*. Urbana, IL: University of Illinois Press.

Siegel, R.K. (1989) *Intoxication: Life in Pursuit of Artificial Paradise*. New York: Dutton.

Sinnett, E.R. and Morris, J.B. (1977) Temporal patterns of the use of non-prescribed drugs. *Perceptual and Motor Skills*, **45**:1239–1245.

Skinner, B.F. (1938) The Behavior of Organisms. New York: Appleton–Century–Crofts.

Skrabanek, P. (1992) Politics and ideology of health promotion. *Medical Audit News*, **2**:82–83.

Skrabanek, P. (1994) Coffee, tea , alcohol—at your doctors displeasure. In: Warburton, D.M. (ed.), *Pleasure: The Politics and the Reality*. Chichester: John Wiley & Sons, pp.84–94.

Skrabanek, P. (1995) *The Death of Humane Medicine*. London: Social Affairs Unit.

Slama, A.-G. (1993) *L'angélisme exterminateur*. Paris: Grasset.

Slovic, P., Fischhoff, B. and Lichtenstein, S. (1978) Accident probabilities in seat belt usage: a psychological perspective. *Accident Analysis and Prevention*, **10**:281–285.

Slovic, P., Fischhoff, B. and Lichtenstein, S. (1982) Why study risk perception? *Risk Analysis*, **2**:83–93.

Smith, A. (1902) *An Enquiry into the Nature and Causes of the Wealth of Nations*. London: Routledge.

Smith, A.P. and Kendrick, A.M. (1992) Meals and performance. In: Smith, A.P. and Jones, D.M. (eds), *Handbook of Human Performance*, Vol. 2. London: Academic Press, pp.1–23.

Smith, A.P. and Miles, C. (1986a) Effects of lunch on cognitive vigilance tasks. *Ergonomics*, **29**:1251–1261.

Smith, A.P. and Miles, C. (1986b) Acute effects of meals, noise and night work. *British Journal of Psychology*, **77**:377–387.

Smith, A.P. and Miles, C. (1987) Effects of lunch on selective and sustained attention. *Neuropsychobiology*, **16**:117–120.

Smith, A.P., Kendrick, A. and Maben, A. (1992) Effects of caffeine, lunch and alcohol on human performance, mood and cardiovascular function. *Proceedings of the Nutrition Society*, **51**:325–333.

Smith, A.P., Rusted, J.M., Eaton-Williams, P., Savory, M. and Leathwood, P. (1990) Effects of caffeine given before and after lunch on sustained attention. *Neuropsychobiology*, **23**:160–163.

Smith, A.P., Kendrick, A.M., Maben, A.L. and Salmon, J. (1994) Effects of breakfast and caffeine on performance, mood and cardiovascular functioning. *Appetite*, **22**:39–55.

Smith, J. (1845) *Book of Doctrines and Covenants of the Church of Jesus Christ of Latter-Day Saints: Selected from the Revelations of God*. Liverpool: Wilfred Woodruff.

Snow, H.L. (1893) *Cancer and the Cancer Process*. London: Churchill.

Soler, J. (1973) Semiotique de la nourriture, dans la Bible. *Annales, Economies, Societies, Civilizations*, **28-11**(4):943–955.

Solomon, G. (1987) Psychoneuroimmunology: interaction between central nervous system and immune system. *Journal of Neuroscience Research*, **18**:1–9.

Solvasan, H., Ghauta, V. and Hiramoto, R. (1988) Conditioned augmentation of natural killer cell activity. Independence on interferon-delta. *Journal of Immunology*, **140**:661–665.

Spring, B., Maller, O., Wurtman, J., Digman, L. and Gozolino, L. (1983) Effects of protein and carbohydrate meals on mood and performance: interactions with sex and age. *Journal of Psychiatric Research*, **17**:155–167.

Steptoe, A. (1981) *Psychological Factors in Cardiovascular Disorders*. London: Academic Press.

Sternberg, S. (1969) The discovery of processing stages: extensions of Donders method. *Acta Psychologica*, **30**:276–315.

Stone, A.A., Reed, B.R. and Neale, J.M. (1987) Changes in daily event frequency precede episodes of physical symptoms. *Journal of Human Stress*, **13**:70–74.

Strandberg, T.E., Salomaa, V.V., Naukkarinene, E., Vanhanen, H.T., Sarno, S.J. and Miettinen, T.A. (1991) Long-term mortality after 5-year multifactorial primary prevention of cardiovascular disease in middle-aged men. *Journal of the American Medical Association*, **266**:1225–1229.

Swift, C.G. and Tiplady, B. (1988) The effects of age on the response to caffeine. *Psychopharmacology*, **94**:29–31.

Taubes, G. (1995) Epidemiology faces its limits. *Science*, **269**:164–169.

Temoshok, L. (1985) Biopsychosocial studies on cutaneous malignant melanoma. Psychosocial factors associated with prognostic indicators, progression, psychophysiology and tumour host response. *Social Science and Medicine*, **20**:833–840.

Tesch, R. (1990) *Qualitative Research: Analysis Types and Software Tools*. London: Falmer Press.

Tharion, W.J., Kobrick, J.L., Lieberman, H.R. and Fine, B.J. (1993) Effects of caffeine and diphenhydramine on auditory evoked cortical potentials. *Perception and Motor Skills*, **70**:707–715.

Thomas, P.D., Goodwin, J.M. and Goodwin, J.S. (1985) Effect of social support on stress-related changes in cholesterol level, uric acid level, and immune function in an elderly sample. *American Journal of Psychiatry*, **142**:735–737.

Thompson, J.C. (1981) Will it hurt less if I control it? A complex answer to a simple question. *Psychological Bulletin*, **90**:89–101.

Tiger, L. (1992) *The Pursuit of Pleasure*. Boston, MA: Little, Brown.

Tiplady, B. (1991) Alcohol as a comparator. In: Keppler, I.D., Sanders, L.D. and Rosen, M. (eds), *Ambulatory Anaesthesia and Sedation: Impairment and Recovery*. Oxford: Blackwell, pp.26–37.

Tocqueville, A. de (1981) *De la démocratie en Amérique*, Vol. II. Paris: Garnier- Flammarion, p.385.

Torrance, E.P. (1974) *Torrance Tests of Creative Thinking*. Lexington, MA: Personnel Press.

Tversky, A. and Kahneman, D. (1973) Availability: a heuristic for judging frequency and probability. *Cognitive Psychology*, **4**:207–232.

Tyler, T.R. and Cook, F.L. (1984) The mass media and judgments of risk: distinguishing impact on personal and societal level judgments. *Journal of Personality and Social Psychology*, **47**:693–708.

USDHHS (1993) *Depression in Primary Care*, Vol. 1. AHCPR publication no. 93-0550. Washington, DC: US Department of Health and Human Services.

Van der Stelt, O. and Snel, J. (1993) Effects of caffeine on human information processing – a cognitive–energetic approach. In: Garattini, S. (ed.), *Caffeine, Coffee and Health*. New York: Raven Press, pp.291–316.

Wagenaar, W.A. (1988) *Paradoxes of Gambling Behaviour*. Chichester: John Wiley & Sons.

Warburton, D.M. (1975) *Brain, Behaviour and Drugs*. Chichester: John Wiley & Sons.

Warburton, D.M. (1979) Stress and the processing of information. In: Hamilton, V.H. and Warburton, D.M. (eds), *Human Stress and Cognition*. Chichester: John Wiley & Sons, pp.469–475.

Warburton, D.M. (1987a) The functions of smoking. In: Martin, W.R., Van Loon, G.R., Iwamoto, E.T., Davis, D.L. (eds), *Tobacco Smoking and Nicotine: a Neurobiological Approach*. New York: Plenum Press, pp. 51–61.

Warburton, D.M. (1987b) Drugs and the processing of information. In: Stahl, S.M., Iverson, S.D. and Goodman, E.C. (eds), *Cognitive Neurochemistry*. Oxford: Oxford University Press, pp.111–134.

Warburton, D.M. (1990) All substance use pleasures are not the same. In: Warburton, D.M. (ed.), *Addiction Controversies*. London: Harwood Academic, pp.45–52.

Warburton, D.M. (1991) Stress and distress in response to change. In: Box, H. (ed.), *Primate Responses to Environmental Change*. London: Chapman & Hall, pp.337–356.

Warburton, D.M. (1995) The effects of caffeine on cognition and mood without caffeine abstinence. *Psychopharmacology*, **119**:66–70.

Warburton, D.M. and Suiter, J. (1994) Discovering the person at work. In: Bonnsetter, W., Suiter, J. and Widrick, R. (eds), *The Universal Language DISC*. Scottsdale, AZ: Target Training International.

Ward, N., Whitney, C., Avery, D. and Dunner, D. (1991) The analgesic effects of caffeine in headache. *Pain*, **44**:151–155.

Watson, G. (1992) Hours of work in Great Britain and Europe: evidence from the UK and European labour force surveys. *Employment Gazette*, November, pp. 539–557.

Watson, G. (1993) Working time and holidays in the EC: how the UK compares. *Employment Gazette*, September, pp. 395–403.

Watson, M. and Ramirez, A. (1991) Psychological factors in cancer prognosis. In: Cooper, L.C. and Watson, M. (eds), *Cancer and Stress*. Chichester: John Wiley & Sons, pp.47–71.

Weinstein, N.D. (1980) Unrealistic optimism about future life events. *Journal of Personality and Social Psychology*, **39**:506–820.

Weisman, A.D. and Wordem, J.W. (1977) *Coping and Vulnerability in Cancer Patients*. Boston, MA: privately printed.

White, E.G. (1864) *Spiritual Gifts*, Vol. 4: *Spiritual Gifts, Important Facts of Faith, Laws of Health and Testimonies*. Battle Creek, MI: Seventh Day Adventist Publishing Association.

Whitlock, F.A. and Siskind, M. (1979) Depression and cancer: a follow-up study. *Psychological Medicine*, **9**:747–752.

WHO (1958) *The First Ten Years. The Health Organization*. Geneva: World Health Organization.

Wodehouse, P.G. (1934) *Right Ho, Jeeves*. London: Herbert Jenkins.

Woodman, R.W. and Schoenfeldt, L.F. (1990) An interactionist model of creative behaviour. *Journal of Creative Behavior*, **24**:279–290.

Woods, S.C. and Porte, D. (1974) Neural control of the endocrine process. *Physiological Review*, **54**:596–619.

Wurtman, J.J. and Wurtman, R.J. (1979) Drugs that enhance central serotonergic transmission diminish selective carbohydrate consumption by rats. *Life Sciences*, **24**:895–903.

Yano, K., Rhoads, G.G. and Kagan, A. (1977) Coffee, alcohol and risk of coronary heart disease amongst Japanese men living in Hawaii. *New England Journal of Medicine*, **297**:405.

Yates, J.F. (ed.) (1992) *Risk-Taking Behaviour*. Chichester: John Wiley & Sons.

Yingling, C.D. and Skinner, J.E. (1977) Gating of thalamic input to cerebral cortex by nucleus reticularis thalami. In: Desmedt, J. (ed.), *Attention, Voluntary Contraction and Event-Related Brain Potentials*, Progress in Clinical Neurophysiology no. 1. Basel: Karger, pp.70–96.

Young, P.T. (1966) *Motivation and Emotion*. New York: John Wiley & Sons.

Zahn, T.P. and Rapaport, J.L. (1987) Acute autonomic nervous system effects of caffeine on prepubertal boys. *Psychopharmacology*, **91**:40–44.

Index

Index compiled by C. Purton